4 *After* each note write a higher note to form the named *melodic* interval, as first answer. The key is D major.

3rd

8th/8ve

2nd

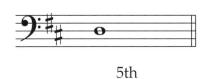

5th

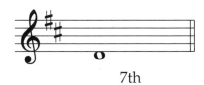

7th

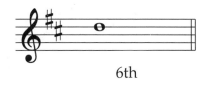

6th

5 Add the correct rest(s) at the places marked ✳ in these two melodies to make each bar complete.

6 (a) Name the degree of the scale (e.g. 2nd, 3rd) of each of the notes marked ✳, as shown in the first answer. The key is B♭ major.

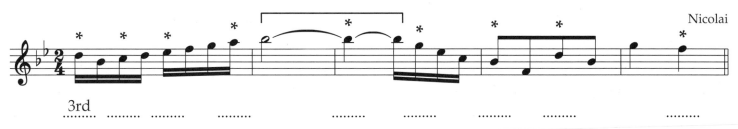

3rd
....

(b) How many semiquavers (16th notes) are the tied notes marked with a bracket (⌐————————¬) worth in total? ....

7 Rewrite the following in notes of *half* the value, beginning as shown.

8 Look at this folksong melody and then answer the questions below.

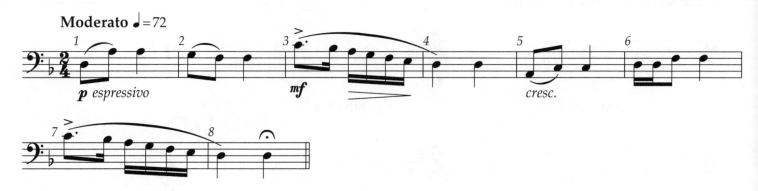

Write your answer to question (c) on the stave below.

(a) Give the meaning of each of these:

Moderato ....

♩=72 ....

espressivo ....

cresc. (bar 5) ....

> (e.g. bar 7) ....

(b) (i) Give the letter name of the *lowest* note in the melody. .... | 10 |

(ii) Draw a circle around two notes next to each other that are a 3rd apart.

(iii) How many times does the rhythm ♪. ♪ occur? ....

(iv) In which bar is the performer told to pause or hold on to the note? Bar ....

(v) Underline one of the following words that best describes how you think bars 1–4 of this melody should be played:

                 legato (smoothly)   or   *staccato* (detached)

(c) Copy out the music from the start of the melody to the end of bar 4, exactly as it is | 10 | written above. Don't forget the clef, key signature, time signature, tempo marking, dynamics and all other details. Write the music on the blank stave above question (a). (Marks will be given for neatness and accuracy.)

Theory Paper Grade 2   2010   B

TOTAL MARKS
100

Duration 1½ hours

Candidates should answer ALL questions.
Write your answers on this paper – no others will be accepted.
Answers must be written clearly and neatly – otherwise marks may be lost.

1 Add the time signature to each of these five melodies.

10

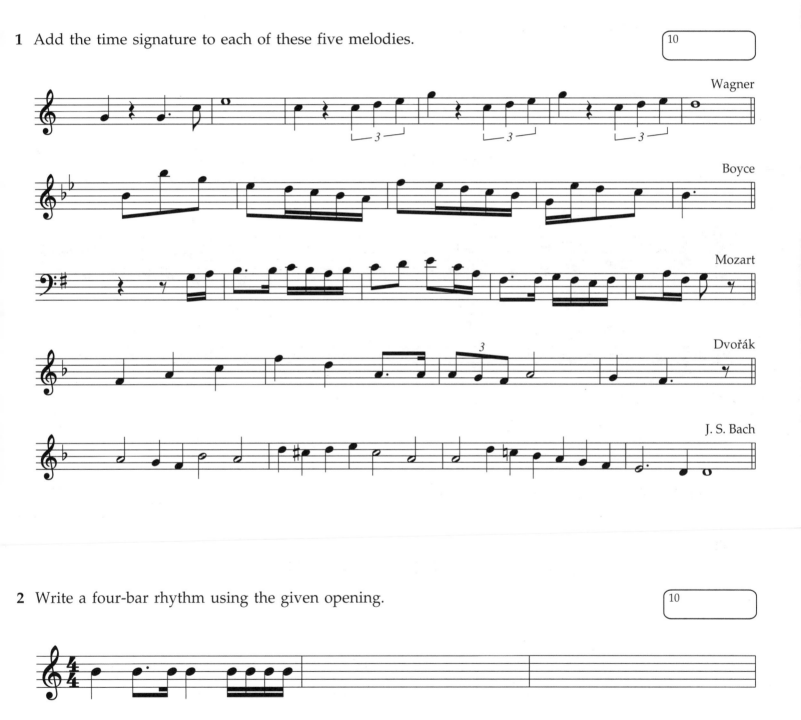

2 Write a four-bar rhythm using the given opening.

10

3 (a) Give the letter name of each of the notes marked **∗**, including the sharp or flat sign  where necessary. The first answer is given.

Boyce

E
....

(b) How many bars contain semiquavers (16th notes)? ....

4 Rewrite this melody in the bass clef, keeping the pitch the same. The first two notes are  given.

Fauré

5 Write as semibreves (whole notes) the scales named below.

E minor, descending, with key signature

Which form of the minor scale have you used? ....

D major, ascending, without key signature but adding any necessary sharp or flat signs

6 Add the correct clef and key signature to each of these tonic triads.

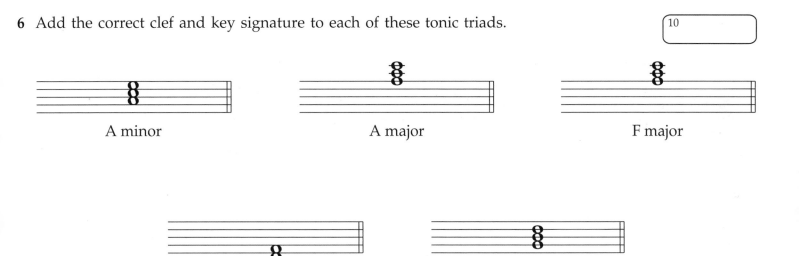

A minor   A major   F major

D minor   B♭ major

7 Give the number (e.g. 2nd, 3rd) of each of these harmonic intervals, as shown in the first answer. The key is G major.

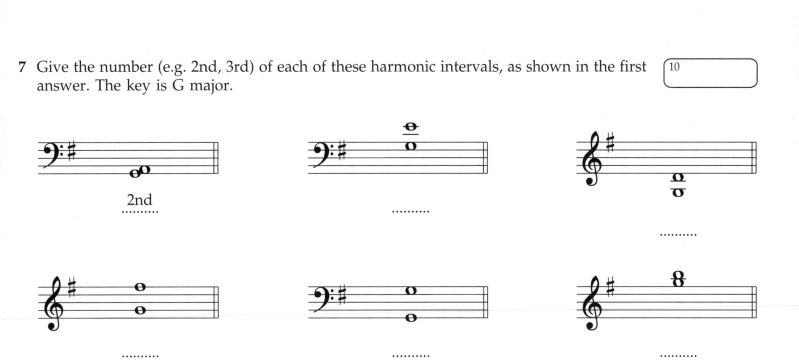

2nd

....

....

8 Look at this melody by Mozart and then answer the questions below.

Write your answer to question (c) on the stave below.

(a) Give the meaning of each of these: [10]

   Andante ....

   p ....

   ⌢. (bar 2) ....

   fp (e.g. bar 3) ....

   ⌣ (e.g. bar 7) ....

(b) (i)   Draw a bracket (⌐‾‾¬) over two notes next to   [10]
       each other that are tied together.

    (ii) Name the degree of the scale (e.g. 3rd, 4th)
       of the *last* note in the melody. The key is E♭ major. ....

    (iii) Draw a circle around a note in this melody that is *not* in the key of E♭ major.

    (iv) Complete this sentence: The **8** in $\frac{3}{8}$ means ....

    (v) Give the letter name of the first note in bar 2 (marked ✳). ....

(c) Copy out the music from the start of bar 3 to the end of the melody, exactly as it is   [10]
   written above. Don't forget the clef, key signature, dynamics and all other details.
   Write the music on the blank stave above question (a). (Marks will be given for
   neatness and accuracy.)

Theory Paper Grade 2   2010   C

Duration 1½ hours

TOTAL MARKS
100

Candidates should answer ALL questions.
Write your answers on this paper – no others will be accepted.
Answers must be written clearly and neatly – otherwise marks may be lost.

1   Add the time signature to each of these five melodies.

10

2   Write a four-bar rhythm using the given opening.

10

3 (a) Rewrite these bass clef notes in the treble clef, keeping the pitch the same.
  The first answer is given.

(b) In which major key are all these notes found? ....

4 Rewrite this melody using the key signature of B♭ major. Leave out any unnecessary
accidentals, but remember to include any that are needed. The first three notes are given.

J. C. F. Bach

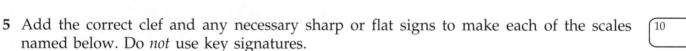

5 Add the correct clef and any necessary sharp or flat signs to make each of the scales
named below. Do *not* use key signatures.

D minor

Which form of the minor scale have you used? ....

A major

6 Add the correct clef to make each of these named notes, as shown in the first answer.

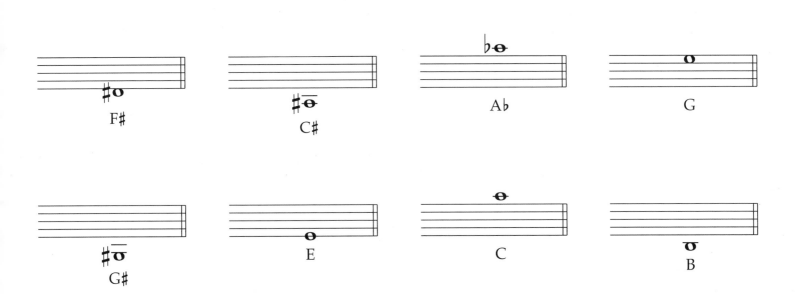

7 Name each key as shown by its key signature. The first answer is given.

11

8 Look at this melody, adapted from a piece by Fauré, and then answer the questions below.

Write your answer to question (c) on the stave below.

(a) Give the meaning of each of these: 10

   Allegro ....

   molto ....

   f ....

   pp (bar 4) ....

   dolce (bar 4) ....

(b) (i)   Give the letter name of the first note in the melody.   10

   (ii) Complete this sentence:
         The lower **4** in **4/4** means ....

   (iii) How many semiquavers (16th notes) are the
         tied notes in bar 5 (marked ⌐‾‾⌐) worth in total? ....

   (iv) How many bars contain a minim (half note)? ....

   (v)   Answer TRUE or FALSE to this sentence:
         All of the notes in this melody should be played *staccato* (detached). ....

(c) Copy out the music from the start of bar 5 to the end of the melody, exactly as   10
   it is written above. Don't forget the clef, key signature and all other details.
   Write the music on the blank stave above question (a). (Marks will be given for
   neatness and accuracy.)

12

Theory Paper Grade 2   2010   S

Duration 1½ hours

TOTAL MARKS
100

Candidates should answer ALL questions.
Write your answers on this paper – no others will be accepted.
Answers must be written clearly and neatly – otherwise marks may be lost.

1   Add the missing bar-lines to these two melodies. The first bar-line is given in each.   10

Wagner

Albicastro

2   Write a four-bar rhythm using the given opening.   10

3   *Above* each note write another note to form the named *harmonic* interval, as shown in the first answer. The key is G major.   10

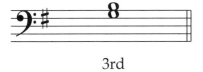

3rd

8th/8ve

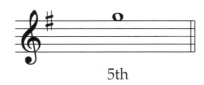

5th

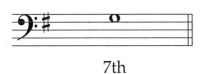

7th

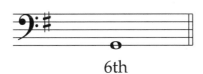

6th

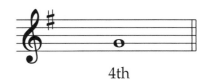

4th

4 Rewrite the following in notes of *twice* the value, beginning as shown.

Clementi

5 Add the correct clef and any necessary sharp or flat signs to make each of the scales named below. Do *not* use key signatures.

A minor

Which form of the minor scale have you used? ....

Bb major

6 (a) Give the letter name of each of the notes marked ∗, including the sharp or flat sign ‎ where necessary. The first answer is given.

G ....

(b) Give the time name (e.g. crotchet or quarter note) of the *shortest* note in the melody.

....

7 Rewrite the following melody, grouping (beaming) the notes correctly. ‎

8 Look at this melody by Reinecke and then answer the questions below.

Write your answer to question (c) on the stave below.

(a) Give the meaning of each of these: [10]

Più   ....

lento   ....

mf   ....

espressivo   ....

 (bar 4)   ....

(b) (i)   Name the degree of the scale (e.g. 2nd, 3rd)   [10]
            of the *first* note in the melody. The key is D minor. ....

     (ii) Which other key has the same key signature as D minor? ....

     (iii) Give the letter name of the *lowest* note in the melody. ....

     (iv) How many pairs of tied notes are there in the melody? ....

     (v)   Underline one of the following words that best describes how you think bars 1–4
            of this melody should be played:
                        legato (smoothly)   or   *staccato* (detached)

(c) Copy out the music from the start of the melody to the first note of bar 5, exactly   [10]
     as it is written above. Don't forget the clef, key signature, time signature, tempo
     marking, dynamics and all other details. Write the music on the blank stave above
     question (a). (Marks will be given for neatness and accuracy.)

ABRSM
24 Portland Place
London W1B 1LU
United Kingdom

www.abrsm.org

Theory of Music Exams Model Answers
are also available.

Published by ABRSM (Publishing) Ltd,
a wholly owned subsidiary of ABRSM

Printed in England by Page Bros (Norwich) Ltd
10/10

ISBN 978-1-84849-287-5

9 781848 492875

WILD
THAILAND

WILD THAILAND

Photographs *by* **GERALD CUBITT**
Text by **BELINDA STEWART-COX**

Produced in association with the Seub Nakhasathien Foundation

SEUB NAKHASATHIEN FOUNDATION

KASETSART UNIVERSITY ALUMNI ASSOCIATION BUILDING, 50 PHAHOLYOTHIN ROAD, BANGKOK 10900

We are extraordinarily lucky with the natural character of our country. It is a land of great beauty, richly endowed with resources, blessed with a cornucopia of wildlife and, away from the hurly-burly of modern life, it is still surprisingly serene. Such has been the bounty and splendour of this land that we have tended to take it for granted. This has now changed. For the first time in the history of our country, because of overuse and abuse of natural resources, we are threatened with environmental poverty in place of the wealth we inherited. The time has come to take our role as guardians of this land and all its native inhabitants more seriously, for our own sake as well as for theirs.

This is why *Wild Thailand* is so welcome, reminding us how very beautiful Thailand is, even now, and how much there still is to conserve. Happily, we do already have an extensive network of national parks and wildlife sanctuaries, though outside the conservation areas (and even inside some of them) nature is not as well respected as it should be. However, we are hopeful that as more people learn to appreciate our wildlife and natural environment, they will want to protect it. Certainly the last ten years have seen great advances in conservation awareness in Thailand and this book will make another important contribution to that.

RATAYA CHANTIAN
CHAIRWOMAN
SEUB NAKHASATHIEN FOUNDATION

First published in 1995 by
New Holland (Publishers) Ltd
London • Cape Town • Sydney • Singapore

24 Nutford Place	PO Box 1144	3/2 Aquatic Drive
London W1H 6DQ	Cape Town 8000	Frenchs Forest, NSW 2086
UK	South Africa	Australia

ISBN 1 85368 517 8

Publishing Director: Charlotte Parry-Crooke
Editors: Ann Baggaley, James Harrison
Additional text: David Stone
Assistant Editor: Nancy Webber
Editorial Assistants: Lisa Guthrie, Sophie Bessemer Clark
Designer: Behram Kapadia
Page make-up: Sally Kapadia
Cartography: Julian Baker
Index: Alexandra Corrin

Reproduction by Typongraph s.r.l., Verona, Italy
Printed and bound in Hong Kong by South China Printing Co Ltd

CONTENTS

FOCUS ON SOUTH THAILAND *page 154*

Photographic Acknowledgements

The publishers and photographer extend their thanks to the following people who kindly loaned their photographs for inclusion in this book. All the photographs in the book, with the exception of those listed below, were taken by Gerald Cubitt.

Asia Images (Allen W. Hopkins): page 92; page 96 (top); *(Matthew Burns)*: page 170 (top right); page 195 (top).

Hans Bänziger: page 59; page 60 (bottom left and centre).

Ashley J. Boyd: page 121 (top left); page 171 (bottom three subjects); page 199 (both subjects); page 200 (all subjects); page 201.

Jim Comber: page 31 (top right; centre, all three subjects; bottom, all three subjects).

Suraphon Duangkhae: page 124 (right).

John Everingham: page 40 (right); page 191 (all three subjects); page 192 (top right; bottom); page 194; page 198.

Feature Magazine (Wiwat Panthawuthiyanon): page 17 (bottom right); *(Mongkonsawat Luengvorapant)*: page 75; *(Sakol Kasemphant)*: page 83; *(Mongkonsawat Luengvorapant)*: page 187 (centre).

Footprints (Mark Graham): page 170 (top left) .

Thomas Kunz: page 124 (left).

Oceanic Impressions (Mark Strickland): page 7; page 121 (right, top, centre and bottom); page 171 (top).

Pilai Poonswad: page 144 (bottom left).

Scope Features (Brian Moody): page 60 (top right).

G. Seidenfaden: page 85 (bottom right).

Belinda Stewart-Cox: page 16 (bottom right); page 23 (bottom three subjects); page 25 (bottom left); page 27 (bottom left); page 43 (bottom left); page 44 (bottom); page 61; page 63 (bottom left and right); page 65 (bottom left); page 108 (top); page 133 (bottom left); page 135 (top left); page 140 (top right); page 162 (top left); page 187 (top, left and right; bottom); page 195 (bottom).

Still Pictures: *(Mark Edwards)*: page 173.

Uthai Treesucon: page 172 (bottom right).

Merlin D. Tuttle, Bat Conservation International: page 161 (bottom, centre).

Adisak Vidhidharm: page 144 (bottom right); page 185 (all three subjects).

FURTHER THANKS

The photographer also gratefully acknowledges the generous support of the following during his travels in Thailand:

Shangri-la Hotel, Bangkok

Dusit Rayavadee Resort Hotel, Krabi • Eastern and Oriental Express, Orient Express Hotels • Imperial Tongsai Bay Hotel, Koh Samui • Le Meridien Baan Boran Hotel • Le Meridien Hotel, Phuket • Royal Cliff Beach Hotel, Pattaya • Sea Tours Co Ltd

Baan Taling Ngam Resort, Koh Samui • Central Maesod Hill Hotel • Clarion M. P. Resort Hotel, Trang • Chumphon Cabana Resort • Dhevaraj Hotel, Nan • Holiday Inn, Mae Hong Son • Koh Chang Resort • Krabi Meritime Hotel • Long Beach Cha-Am Hotel • Mae Nam Kong Grand View Hotel, Nakhon Phanom • Melia Hotel, Hua Hin • Pailyn Hotel, Phitsanulok• Phang Nga Bay Resort Hotel • Phi Phi Palm Beach Hotel • Pimarn Hotel, Nakhon Sawan• River View Lodge, Chiang Mai • Royal Crown Hotel, Songkhla • Royal Princess Hotel, Khorat • Tanyong Hotel, Narathiwat • Wang Tai Hotel, Suratthani

Illustrations appearing in the preliminary pages are as follows:

HALF TITLE: Lotus (*Nelumbo nucifera*), Thale Noi.
FRONTISPIECE: Coastal view, Koh Samui.
PAGE 5: Red-breasted Parakeet (*Psittacula alexandri*).
PAGE 6: Tiger (*Panthera tigris*).
PAGE 7: Reef garden with fan coral.
PAGE 10: Sunset over the reservoir, Kaeng Krachan National Park.

Acknowledgements

The author, photographer and publishers wish to express their thanks to the following for providing much generous and valuable assistance during the preparation of this book:

Tourism Authority of Thailand
Thai Airways International
Think Earth/Siam Motors Co Ltd
Lever Brothers (Thailand) Ltd
Lennart Roth, Thai-Scand Environment Company

THAILAND

Royal Forest Department

Dr Thawatchai Santisuk • Pong Leng-Ee • Sawai Wanghongsa • Wattana Kaeokamnerd • Seri Vejaboosakorn • Wicharn Wittayasak • Dr Chawalit Niyomdhamma • Dr Wirachai Nanakorn • Dr Schwann Tunhikorn • Preecha Ratanaporn • Thanardj Photisaro • Chachawan Pisdamkhan • Mattana Srikrajang • Siriporn Thongaree • Kalyanee Boonkird • Theerapat Prayurasiddhi • Saksit Simcharoen • Manaet Bunyanan • Songtan Jaikwang • Pinit Suwanno • Pongboon Pongtong

Thanks and appreciation are also extended to:

Jarujin Nabhitabhata, Ecological Research Department, TISTR • Dr Sangad Bunyopas, Mineral Resources Department • Dr Prinya Nutalaya, Asian Institute of Technology • Chulalongkorn University: Dr Kumthorn Thirakupt and Peter-Paul van Dijk • Mahidol University: Dr Pilai Poonswad; Adisak Vidhidharm; Dr Warren Brockelman; Dr Sompoad Srikosamatara; Uthai Treesucon • Chiang Mai University: Dr Stephen Elliott and Dr Hans Bänziger • Kasetsart University: Dr Uthis Kutintara and Naris Bhumpakkapan • Dr Somsak Boromthanarat, Prince of Songkhla University • Seub Nakhasathien Foundation: Rataya Chantian; Wanchai Tan; Nitaya Wongsawat • Dr Oy Kanchanavanit • Suraphon Duangkhae, Wildlife Fund Thailand • Kim DeRidder, Asia Foundation • Dr Ian Baird, Earth Island Institute • Dr Tyson Roberts • Terrance Morin, Gibbon Rehabilitation Project, Phuket • Junnaree Atchaneeyasakun • Phornthep Phornprapha, President, Think Earth/Siam Motors Co Ltd • Wilai Wongongworawadee, Thai Airways International • Rose Forbes • Sarah Hogg • Nicholas Cumming-Bruce • Sumonta Nakornthab (Director of Public Relations) and Chalermlap Ganachara na Ayudhaya, Tourism Authority of Thailand • Alan Guignon (Director of Marketing) Shangri-la Hotel, Bangkok • Ayutthaya Princess Co Ltd • Celia Pleshakov, Safari World • Kitti Kreetiyutanont, Phu Khieo Wildlife Sanctuary

GREAT BRITAIN

Royal Botanic Gardens, Kew

Dr John Dransfield • Dr Phillip Cribb • Dr David Du Puy • Dr Soejatmi Dransfield • Dr David Simpson • Jeffrey Wood • Jim Comber • Peter Boyce

Natural History Museum, London

Martin Brendell • Dr Ian Kitching • Stuart Hine • Dr Colin McCarthy • Dr Paul Hillyard • Mick Webb • Oliver Crimmen • Steve Brooks • Dr David Jones • Pat Wolseley • Paul Clark

Thanks and appreciation are also extended to:

Dr Michael Cox, Institute of Entomology, London • Dr Andrew Turton, School of Oriental and African Studies • Dr Roy Watling, Royal Botanic Garden, Edinburgh • Dr Tim Whitmore, Cambridge University • Dr Adrian Marshall, Aberdeen University • Dr Kath MacKinnon • Dr Thomas Kunz • Richard Grimmett, Birdlife International • Derek Scott • Rosalind Coles, WWF-UK • Keith Howman, World Pheasant Association • Richard Howard, British Trust for Ornithology • Royal Geographical Society: Dr John Hemming; Nigel and Shane Winser; Helen Lawrenson; Janet Turner • Phithak Phrombubpha, Royal Thai Embassy, London • Jeff Bacall, The Imperial Family of Hotels • Joanne Watkins and Fiona Ferrier, Shangri-la Hotels and Resorts • Jack Jackson • Dr Peter Ng

Janet Cubitt

SPECIAL ACKNOWLEDGEMENT

Philip D. Round, Mahidol University, Bangkok, for his interest and support

INTRODUCTION

A LAND OF CONTRAST AND CHARM

Set at the heart of South-east Asia, Thailand is a land of great natural beauty and cultural charm. It is also a land of contrasts, with wild places that vary from rugged mountain ranges in the north and west to broad, cultivated plains in the centre and north-east, and towering, humid forests in the south. The southern regions also have an enchanting coastline which is lapped by warm translucent seas and overlooked by hundreds of offshore islands with fringing coral reefs and richly coloured marine life.

Exploring wild Thailand can be like playing a game of chance; sometimes you gain a bonus, at other times incur a forfeit, but either way, the game itself is a pleasure. Trekking around the north – with its picturesque mix of valleys and mountain forests, montane flora and colourful peoples – is very different from tramping through hot deciduous forests looking for tiger spoor, mineral licks or streams that still have water. The big vistas and small vignettes always vary. Visitors who venture up the flat-topped mountains of the north-east are rewarded with wonderful views across rhododendron shrublands while those who penetrate the forests of the south and west will hear, but may not see, gibbons duetting from the tree-tops at dawn. Others eschew the land to dive beneath the sea and explore the multi-coloured treasures of the coral reefs.

There are surprises everywhere, but only alert and careful people will experience the full rewards of this beautiful land. Watching wildlife in its natural home is not as easy as many think. It is certainly much harder to watch, or even see, animals in dense or dark Asian forests than it is in open African savannas. Most of Thailand's forest species, including tigers, bears, wild oxen, pheasants, monkeys and hornbills, are wary and shy while other species, such as the Sun Bear, Slow Loris and Binturong (or Bear Cat) are nocturnal. However, with time and patience, wildlife enthusiasts do begin to appreciate the sophisticated interaction of plants, animals and habitats.

Thailand is blessed with a remarkably diverse flora and fauna, even by Asian standards, though much of it has yet to be studied. Its wilderness areas harbour thousands of different plants and animals, some of which are found nowhere else. Over 10 per cent of the world's known animals are found there, including at least 280 mammal species ranging from the smallest, Kitti's Hog-nosed Bat, to one of the largest, the Asian Elephant. Thailand also gives refuge to some 925 species of birds – compare that to the 600 birds known from the entire European continent – as well as thousands of flowering plants, many of which are orchids.

The diversity of Thailand's wildlife is matched by that of the people who inhabit the country, for they belong to various Oriental races who have settled there at different times over the last 1,000 years. Some are more indigenous than others, but all now contribute to the rich culture for which Thailand is justly famous. This richness is reflected in the dazzling temples and palaces which ornament the country and bear witness to the major role played by royalty and religion. That role is increasingly important to natural life, for as more and more of nature is lost, Thai people are beginning to realize how much it means, not just economically, but culturally and spiritually as well. Their traditional ways and their quality of life are threatened and the threat has brought about a revived awareness of the beauty and value of nature, long taken for granted.

The cause of this new awareness is modernization, for Thailand

The modern city of Bangkok was founded only 200 years ago by the first king of the present Chakri dynasty, Rama I. It straddles the mouth of the Chao Phraya river, and already accommodates some 10 million people, many of whom are unrecorded migrants from the poorer rural areas. It is by far the largest city in Thailand, and is very much the focus of commercial, political and social life. Roads have supplanted the city's network of canals and high-rise developments have erased many lovely buildings and overwhelmed the rest. This 'city of angels'– as its Thai name, Krungthep, translates – is now known for its floods, its fumes and its legendary traffic jams. The river, too, is much busier (and noisier) as more and more people resort to motor-boat taxis, but its age-old function is still apparent, most notably when a string of rice-barges glides by.

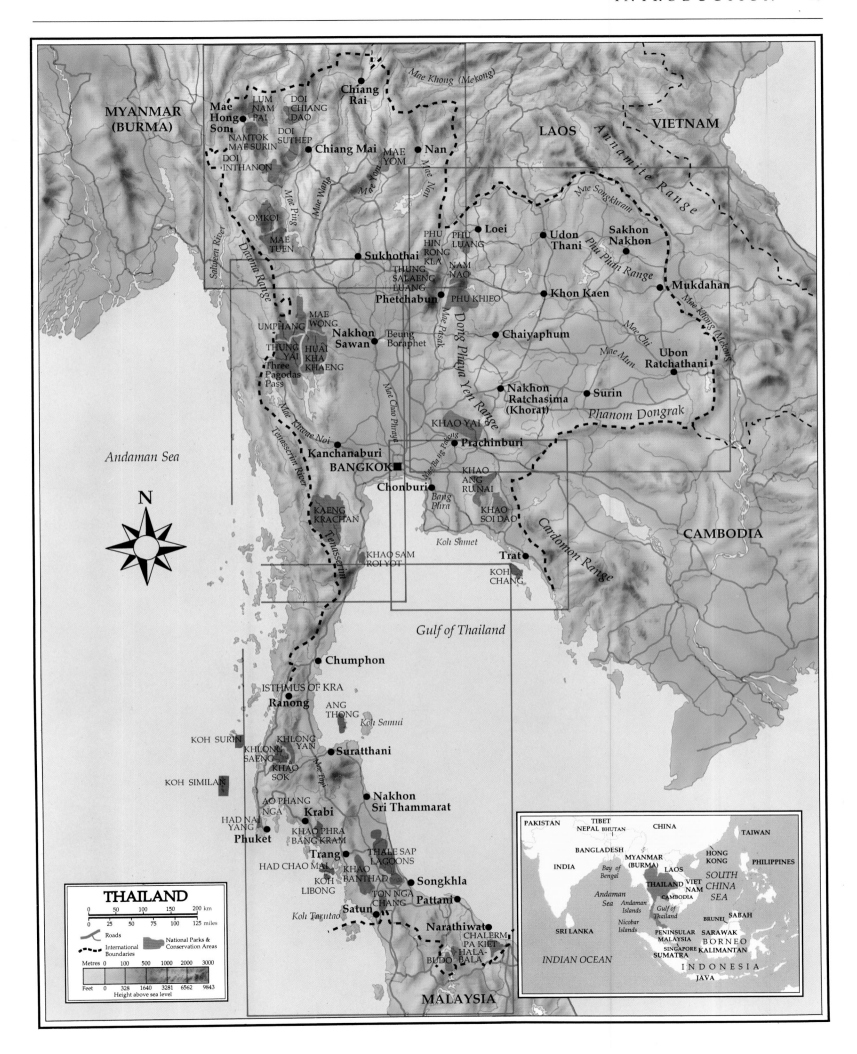

MYANMAR
(BURMA)

LAOS

VIETNAM

Mae Khong (Mekong)

Chiang
Rai

Mae
Hong
Son

LUM
NAM
PAI

DOI
CHIANG
DAO

DOI
SUTHEP

NAMTOK
MAE SURIN

DOI
INTHANON

Chiang Mai

MAE
YOM

Nan

Annamite Range

Mae Wang

Mae Ping

Mae Yom

Mae Nan

Mae Songkhram

OMKOI

MAE
TUEN

Sukhothai

Salween River

Dawna Range

THUNG
SALAENG
LUANG

Phetchabun

PHU
HIN
RONG
KLA

PHU
LUANG

Loei

NAM
NAO

PHU KHIEO

Udon
Thani

Sakhon
Nakhon

Khon Kaen

Pha Phan Range

Mukdahan

Mae Khong (Mekong)

UMPHANG

MAE
WONG

Nakhon
Sawan

Beung
Boraphet

THUNG
YAI

HUAI
KHA
KHAENG

Three
Pagodas
Pass

Mae Khwang Noi

Tenasserim River

Mae Pasak

Dong Phaya Yen Range

Chaiyaphum

Mae Chi

Mae Mun

Ubon
Ratchathani

Nakhon
Ratchasima
(Khorat)

Surin

Phanom Dongrak

Andaman Sea

Mae Chao Phraya

KHAO YAI

Prachinburi

N

Kanchanaburi

BANGKOK

Chonburi

Mae Bang Pakong

KHAO
ANG
RU NAI

CAMBODIA

Koh Samet

Bang
Phra

KHAO
SOI DAO

Cardomon Range

KAENG
KRACHAN

Tenasserim

Trat

KHAO SAM
ROI YOT

KOH
CHANG

Gulf of Thailand

Chumphon

ISTHMUS OF KRA

Ranong

ANG
THONG

Koh Samui

KOH SURIN

KHLONG
SAENG

KHLONG
YAN

Suratthani

KHAO
SOK

KOH SIMILAN

Mae Pmp

AO PHANG
NGA

Krabi

Nakhon
Sri Thammarat

HAD NAI
YANG

Phuket

KHAO PHRA
BANG KRAM

Trang

THALE SAP
LAGOONS

HAD CHAO MAI

KHAO
BANTHAD

KOH
LIBONG

TON NGA
CHANG

Songkhla

Pattani

Satun

Koh Tarutao

Narathiwat

CHALERM
PA KIET
HALA-
BALA

BUDO

MALAYSIA

THAILAND

Metres 0	100	500	1000	2000	3000
Feet 0	328	1640	3281	6562	9843

Height above sea level

Roads

International
Boundaries

National Parks &
Conservation Areas

0 50 100 150 200 km
0 25 50 75 100 125 miles

PAKISTAN

TIBET

CHINA

NEPAL BHUTAN

TAIWAN

BANGLADESH

MYANMAR
(BURMA)

HONG
KONG

PHILIPPINES

INDIA

Bay of
Bengal

LAOS

VIET
NAM

SOUTH
CHINA
SEA

THAILAND

Andaman
Sea

Andaman
Islands

CAMBODIA

Gulf of
Thailand

Nicobar
Islands

BRUNEI

SABAH

SRI LANKA

PENINSULAR
MALAYSIA

SARAWAK

SINGAPORE

BORNEO

KALIMANTAN

INDIAN OCEAN

SUMATRA

INDONESIA

JAVA

ABOVE Young urban Thais enjoying the modern mode of transport. The rapid growth of Thailand's economy has brought equally rapid changes in people's way of life. Tractors are replacing buffaloes in the fields and people who used to cycle or walk are now using motor vehicles. Motorbikes are especially popular because they are cheap and can be negotiated swiftly through congested traffic.

BELOW Villagers harvesting paddy rice by hand in the central plains of Thailand, the 'rice bowl of Asia'. According to the season, the colour of these fields changes from the vivid emerald of young rice shoots to the golden-brown of a ripening crop or the sun-burnt sienna of stubble. Seventy per cent of the population lives in rural areas, and most of those are farmers. Rice was Thailand's main export commodity for many years, until tourism escalated, barely ten years ago. As rural life becomes more mechanized, traditional scenes such as this will disappear.

is becoming an economically developed country that is widely seen as one of the most stable and progressive in Asia. However, development has been achieved by exploiting natural resources: a highly fertile central plain, timber, minerals and fish. For many years, Thailand was a leading rice and timber exporter but has more recently been exporting fish and prawns as well as rice (timber now being exhausted). These exports have helped the country maintain a 7-9 per cent growth for over a decade.

With such heavy reliance on natural resources, it is not surprising that development has taken place to the detriment of the environment. The latest indication of this is the dramatic increase in seaside hotels and beach-huts all along the country's glistening coasts, prompted by the tourist deluge that resulted from several 'Visit Thailand' promotions. The country is no longer an exotic backwater for intrepid backpackers but a mainstream international tourist destination. Such has been the impact of this influx on the natural and cultural environment of Thailand that many analysts now question whether it is, in fact, beneficial to the country, even in economic terms, for the long-term costs are considerable. But the greatest impact of development on natural resources has been the rapid depletion of the country's forests. Just fifty years ago, forest still dominated the Thai landscape. Then commercial logging of hardwoods began on a grand scale and huge volumes of timber were exported at a rate that was unsustainable. This continued, unquestioned and unchecked, until the late 1980s when the effects of deforestation became apparent. But by then the hydrology of the country was transformed, and every ecosystem was affected detrimentally, from the mountains to the sea.

That is not to say that man's imprints have not been evident in the past – they have – but, by and large, they were benign because no more was taken than nature could give. In some areas, Neolithic hunter-gatherers left simple stone tools in the caves they occupied while elsewhere, notably the north-east, there is evidence that agriculturalists formed settlements over 5,000 years ago, leaving behind beautiful clay pots, ancient bronzeware and elaborate cave paintings. Many paintings depict everyday scenes with wild

animals, indicating that early inhabitants of this land lived close to nature, a relationship that is symbolized in many of the murals and carvings of latter-day temples. Some of this reverence can still be seen today in rural areas where people have long been dependent on nature's bounty and have developed a way of life that is in keeping with their environment.

However, there can be no dispute that modern man is responsible for endangering Thailand's ecological wellbeing, through forest degradation, road and dam construction, urban expansion, uncontrolled tourism and pollution. All these impacts derive from a rapid growth in human numbers. Most of the population is based in rural areas, though the proportion of farmers has dropped from 80 per cent to nearer 60 per cent in recent years. Thus a relatively small proportion of urban residents has placed the greatest demand on the country's natural resources, a demand that is increasing as the urban way of life becomes ever more dependent on conveniences such as perpetual air-conditioning and limitless tapped water.

Long before the arrival of man, Thailand was the crossroads through which Asia's plants and animals dispersed from north to south, west to east, and vice versa. That is why it harbours such a wealth of wildlife species but, once again, this magical land is at a crossroads, this time of man's own making. Drastic new controls are needed if Thailand is to preserve the natural heritage and beauty for which it was so well known. Any further loss of forest cover or wetland drainage would not only spell the extinction of many animals and plants but would also compromise the Thai quality of life. One traditional security is already undermined. The famous old inscription – 'there are fish in the water, there is rice in the fields' – was undoubtedly true, but no one can be sure of that anymore. Thai people have come to understand that nature cannot be taken for granted and that caring for the natural environment is essential for their own and their country's future.

GEOGRAPHY

Thailand is the third largest country in South-east Asia, after Indonesia and Myanmar (Burma), with a land area of 513,115 square kilometres (198,115 square miles). As the crow flies it is roughly 1,650 kilometres (1,000 miles) from north to south and 800 kilometres (500 miles) from east to west at its widest part from Three Pagodas Pass to the Mekong river, but only 11 kilometres (7 miles) wide at its narrowest part in the peninsula. It is bordered by Myanmar to the west, Laos to the north and east, Cambodia to the south-east and Malaysia in the south. Most of Thailand's 5,326-kilometre (3,310-mile) land boundary is marked by natural features, usually rivers or mountain ridges. However, its 2,815-kilometre (1,750-mile) coastline is also important, for it touches two major seas, the Gulf of Thailand (part of the South China Sea) and the Andaman Sea, and includes a mass of offshore islands, most of them idyllic, many encircled by dazzling coral reefs with a wealth of marine life.

Thailand's topographical character and biological inheritance derive largely from its geographic position at the centre of South-east Asia, for it is located between three of the region's super-highways: the Dawna-Tenasserim mountain range, the Salween and the Mekong river valleys. The Dawna-Tenasserim is the middle one of three cordilleras which extend south-east from the great Himalayan Ranges in Tibet. The other two are the Arakam Yoma due west of Thailand and the Annamitic Chain due east. The former runs from the China Hills in Myanmar through the Andaman Islands to Sumatra and Java while the latter runs from southern China to Laos and Vietnam. Of the three, the Dawna-

Tenasserim Range has the longest overland connection, from eastern Tibet to Singapore, a connection that has not been broken in time, during the ice ages, or space, by sea.

All four major rivers of South-east Asia – the Brahmaputra, the Salween, the Mekong and the Yangtze – originate in Tibet's eastern mountain ranges. Continental Thailand extends between the middle two and contains important tributaries of both while also enclosing a river all its own (the Chao Phraya) as well as all its drainage. Because it is so central and because it is linked to three of the region's natural thoroughfares, Thailand has long been a conduit to every part of South-east Asia. As a result, it has accommodated many colonizing tribes and cultures as well as animals and plants which dispersed from one area to another.

Thailand's Principal Regions

Maps of Thailand are often likened to the profiled head of an elephant: its towering crown is the north, its ears the north-east, its jaw the south-east, its face the central plains, its long forehead the west and its attenuated trunk the southern peninsula. The most conspicuous features of Thailand's mapped landscape are its striated mountains and valleys and the broad plains in between, but there are many contrasts among the regions. Five regions are highlighted in this book, the delineation of each being based on geographic location, landforms and river drainage.

The **north** of Thailand is mainly mountainous and extends along the borders of Myanmar and Laos reaching south to about 18°N. These highlands mostly drain into the Chao Phraya Basin, though some slopes supply the Salween and Mekong rivers, and all provide a range of dramatic sceneries and habitats. Every ridge reaches over 2,000 metres (6,500 feet) and runs in a roughly north-south direction with fertile valleys in between lying at around 300 metres (1,000 feet) above sea level. Although the valleys have long been settled and cultivated there was, until recently, extensive forest cover on most mountain slopes above 800 metres (2,600 feet) but this has been greatly reduced by the spread of hill-rice cultivation and cash-crop opium. As wild montane habitats have disappeared, so too has montane wildlife, but the north is still home to many stunning species, some exclusive to the region.

The **north-east** comprises the Khorat Plateau, a broad, shallow basin which lies only 100–200 metres (300–650 feet) above sea level. The floodplains of the Mun, Chi and Songkram rivers cover most of the region but a low line of hills rises to almost 700 metres (over 2,000 feet) between Udon Thani and Mukdahan and mountains ring the south and west sides of the plateau in the Phetchabun and Phanom Dongrak Ranges respectively. The northern and eastern border is delineated by the Mekong, recipient of most of the region's drainage. Overall, this is a region of poor soils, low rainfall and many people. The plateau is largely devoid of forest cover except in the hills and land that is not cultivated supports only grasses and scrub. But the peripheral mountains and their species are spectacular and the three river plains contain many lakes, ponds and marshlands which sustain a winter-season influx of waterfowl. This region is also home to Khao Yai, Thailand's first and most famous national park.

The **south-east** encompasses the northern extension of the Cardomom Range which crosses the border from neighbouring Cambodia. It is the smallest region and is typically hilly, though the northern part contains the Prachinburi floodplain. Ecologically, it has two points of particular interest. First, it is unusually wet for an area of continental Thailand and supports a special kind of semi-evergreen forest with Indo-Chinese affinities. Although this is now much reduced, notable tracts do survive in the Khao Ang Ru Nai and Khao Soi Dao Wildlife Sanctuaries and adjoining national parks. Second, the region has a surprising number of

The people of Thailand are by no means homogenous for although most are Thai, they are regionally distinct and others are not Thai at all but members of tribal minorities. TOP ROW, LEFT TO RIGHT Northern Thai farmers wearing traditional working clothes – wrap-over pantaloons with matching indigo shirts and bamboo sun-hats; northern Thai maidens in ceremonial dress – tubular *pa-sin* and shoulder sashes, silver belts and ornamented hair; urban Chinese Thais, whose families immigrated from three to seven generations ago. BOTTOM ROW, LEFT TO RIGHT Veiled Muslim woman of southern Thailand; a Thai-Malay man wearing a *pakkamar* (an all-purpose long piece of cloth) as a turban; Karen elder in full traditional dress.

endemics including four attractive birds and one enchanting mammal.

The **west** consists largely of two long mountain chains, the Dawna and Tenasserim, and runs along the Myanmar border from Umphang (around 18°N) to the Isthmus of Kra (around 10°N). This upland region is segmented by two main rivers and their tributaries, the Khwae Yai and Khwae Noi, which both feed into the Mae Khlong. The Kwae Noi divides the Dawna and Tenasserim Ranges. Most waterways drain into the Gulf of Thailand but a few drain west into Myanmar. The western half of the region receives a good deal of rain from the south-west monsoon, precipitated by its high mountain ridges, but the eastern side is in a rainshadow and is therefore very much drier. Because this is Thailand's least developed and least populated region, it retains the most forest and has the greatest concentration of protected areas in the country. The Thung Yai and Huai Kha Khaeng Wildlife Sanctuaries became World Heritage Sites in 1991.

The **south** has the highest rainfall and humidity and is therefore evergreen. It extends south from the Isthmus of Kra to the Malay border. Covering less than 14 per cent of the country, the region is divided by three mountain chains which decrease in height from north to south. All three are extensions of the Tenasserim. One runs along the neck of the peninsula from Kra to Phuket and rises to 1,395 metres (4,577 feet) at Khao Lang Kha Tuk. Another runs north-south from Suratthani to Satun and contains Khao Luang, the region's highest mountain at 1,835 metres (6,020 feet) while the third curves along the Malay border and merges with mountains further south. The coastal lowlands on either side of the ridges retain little forest cover, having been cleared for cultivation and, more recently, rubber and palm oil plantations. Large tracts of forest survive only on the hills. The large rivers of the region drain into the Gulf of Thailand but the rest also drain into the Andaman Sea. Most islands lie off the Andaman coast, including the well-known marine parks of Surin, Similan, Phi Phi and Tarutao while the Gulf coast boasts Koh Samui, Koh Phangan, Koh Tao and Koh Ang Thong, the last of which is a marine park.

The **central plains** must feature in this overview, although they do not have a chapter of their own because they retain so little wild habitat. They are known as the 'rice bowl of Asia' because they are so fertile. In 1857, this region was described by an English diplomat, John Bowring, as 'a vast, fertile and ferocious jungle' which, if cultivated, would 'no doubt, be magnificently productive'. Bowring was not alone in assuming that tropical forest grows on highly fertile soils and it took another 120 years for scientists to realize that the underlying soils are, in fact, extremely fragile and do not retain their fertility without healthy forest cover.

TOP ROW, LEFT TO RIGHT The Karen hilltribe are known for their strong sense of identity, but the younger generation are beginning to abandon traditional dress; a young woman belonging to a Karen sub-tribe known as the long-necks or Paduang; small boy of the Hmong people, many of whom moved to the mountains of northern Thailand from Laos a few decades ago. BOTTOM ROW, LEFT TO RIGHT Akha woman in a heavy silver head-dress which includes colonial coins from Myanmar; Yao woman traditionally adorned with elaborately embroidered pantaloons and a woolly red collar; members of the Spirits of the Yellow Leaves, or Mlabri tribe, one of only two small surviving groups of hunter-gatherers in Thailand, the other being the aboriginal Sakai of the south.

As an alluvial floodplain, the Chao Phraya Basin would retain more natural fertility if the river were allowed to flood, as it should, during the rains to deposit new layers of silt, but flooding is now regulated by dams and little silt reaches the land. However, these plains do have several small but vital conservation areas, including the semi-natural lake of Beung Boraphet, the stork colony of Wat Phai Lom and the private ponds of Lung Tua ('Uncle Tua'), all of which support large numbers of over-wintering birds. Paddy fields, canals and residual patches of swamp also support small animals (mainly waterbirds, snakes and amphibians) but not as many as they did a few years ago, before farmers started using agrochemicals.

ORIGINS AND EVOLUTION

There is still debate about the geohistory of Thailand but the evidence suggests that back in the mists of time, some 200 million years ago, Thailand was part of the landmass known as Laurasia – the circumpolar continent of the northern hemisphere – and that its position has changed relatively little since then, although its topography has changed considerably.

About 150 million years ago, during the Age of the Dinosaurs, the circumpolar continent of the southern hemisphere, Gondwanaland, split into separate parts and India began floating north-easterly towards Asia. Some 100 million years later, after dinosaurs were extinct, India finally collided with Tibet – then an underwater shelf at the southern edge of Asia – and slid under the larger, more stable continental plate, thereby pushing Tibet out of the sea. As this enormous region rose, it was subject to several million years of weathering and erosion which carved out the valleys and created the ranges we now know as the Himalayas. At the same time, an enhanced monsoon (prompted by the rise in rainfall induced by higher elevations) is thought to have dissolved carbon dioxide from the atmosphere which caused the Earth to radiate more solar heat. As a result, temperatures cooled and the first of four ice ages began about three million years ago. By the time the last one ended, some 10,000 years ago, the species composition of Asia, and more especially of Thailand, had altered radically and modern man – Homo sapiens – had evolved from his ape-like predecessors, Homo habilis and Homo erectus.

Long before ice bound up the world, however, Thailand was remoulded by the subsidiary effects of India's tectonic collision with Asia. As the Tibetan ranges rose, the impact rebounded at right-angles and caused mainland South-east Asia to buckle and fold along three near-parallel lines. Thus were the main mountain

ABOVE Mushroom-like formations such as these are characteristic landmarks of Esarn. They evolve when one block of rock is more resistant to weathering than others around it and becomes a protective cap to the softer stone below. In many cases these sandstone sculptures have assumed a recognizable shape by which they are named – for instance, Turtle Rock, Cow Rock.

LEFT Sandstone occurs in various forms throughout Thailand but is most apparent in the north-east region (known as Esarn) where it has become a notable feature in many places as a result of weathering. Here erosion has created what looks like a shelf of stacked loaves in the Phu Hin Rong Kla National Park of north-west Esarn.

BELOW LEFT Most Thai mountain ranges (except those in Esarn) are largely composed of limestone with granite intrusions and limestone outcrops also protrude from adjacent plains. It is not uncommon to see a Buddha positioned at the foot of such an outcrop.

BELOW RIGHT Many of the crumpled mountain ridges of north, west and south Thailand have a core of granite rock. Here, the magnificent Vachirathan waterfall, in the Doi Inthanon National Park, plunges in a sheer drop down a granite escarpment.

ranges of the region – Arakam Yoma, Dawna-Tenasserim and Annam – created, with a series of secondary ranges in between. This explains the densely folded uplands of the north, the minor ranges of the east and south-east and the presence of limestone in the Dawna-Tenasserim for, like Tibet, this land was once under the sea. However, most ranges also include intrusions of igneous rock (mostly granitic) which were forced to the surface when the Earth's crust crumpled.

These crustal movements also created block faulting, as a result of which a large tectonic basin formed at the centre of what is now Thailand, extending across the central plains and into the Gulf. Over millions of years, this basin filled with fluvial sediment and the shoreline moved steadily south. This advance still continues. A thousand years ago, Suphanburi and Saraburi would have been coastal settlements with Bangkok well out to sea but another thousand years from now, Bangkok will be well inland if global warming does not drown it first.

As India continued shunting north-north-easterly, pushing up the Dawna-Tenasserim (as well as the ranges east and west) and sinking the central plain, the north-east plateau warped upwards and steep escarpments formed along its south and west boundaries with gentle slopes facing in. The plateau consists of two basins squeezed into a triangle of mountain ranges (the largest being the Annamitic Chain in Laos) and is divided by a low line of hills, the Phu Phan Range. It is underlain by sedimentary rocks of the Jurassic and Cretaceous periods (100–150 million years old) comprising sandstone, conglomerate and layers of salt, for before this upheaval, the region was an intermittent inland sea.

The steepest escarpment of the north-east runs along the Phanom Dongrak Range, overlooking Cambodia, and follows the line of a fault which cracked in opposition to the rising Phetchabun Range. It is one of many faults in Thailand, but the only one of any significance in the north-east. The rest occur on the western side of Thailand, from Mae Hong Son to Krabi. The longest two almost exactly follow the Dawna-Tenasserim mountain range along what is now the border with Myanmar. This more or less parallels the deep-sea Sunda Trench which curves round Sumatra and Java from Bangladesh to Timor and marks the point of impact between the Indian and Asian plates. Most earthquakes occur along these trenches, the Philippine Trench (from Japan to New Guinea) being the most active in Asia. But faults trigger earthquakes and volcanic activity as well, and Thailand has been subject to both.

The extinct volcanoes of the north (such as Mae Mo) and north-east (such as Khao Phanom Rung) bear witness to old eruptions, as do the flat-topped mountains of basalt which characterize the Phetchabun Range. Thailand's famous rubies and sapphires, mined in the south-east and west, are both products of violent underground forces, being subjected to intense heat and pressure, as are the marble, slate and gneiss found in various areas of the west. For all that, Thailand today is much more stable than other

The western side of the country from north to south is dotted with hot springs wherever there is a geological fault. Tremors and minor earthquakes are a frequent occurrence, but most take place deep underground and go unnoticed by the general population. In some areas hot (RIGHT) and cold (ABOVE RIGHT) springs occur in close proximity; both these springs are in the Khao Pra Bang Kram Wildlife Sanctuary in Krabi. Thailand's geological history is a tale of tectonic collision, volcanic eruption, magmatic intrusion, orogenic upheaval and the relocation of rock strata in which sea beds have become mountains, basins have become plateaux and summits have been washed to the plains. Ironically, this evolutionary drama is evidenced by quiet springs such as this, where underground water has encountered an impervious substrate and is channelled to the surface through porous rock, in this case limestone, hence the greenish tinge to the water.

parts of Asia and is unlikely to relive the geological violence of the past, though its landforms are constantly changing.

Changes that took place over the last 30 million years were also caused by fluctuations in climate – themselves the result of orogenic upheavals. For most of that period, Asia was warm and wet, forest proliferated and most modern genera evolved, but then came the ice ages. These had as great an impact on South-east Asia as they had on Europe, though the region did not freeze. But with so much of the world's water held as ice, sea levels dropped some 80 metres (260 feet) and the South China and Andaman Seas shrank to deeper levels, thereby exposing the shallow sea-bed that links Thailand with Sumatra, Java and Borneo. At the same time, the climate was drier and cooler so that forest receded and grassland took its place in the plains. Sylvan species retreated to the evergreen refuges (mostly in the hills) while herbivores and other adaptable species took advantage of the modified vegetation to colonize new lands. However, between each ice age, the pattern reversed and the region reverted to forest. These prolonged periods of climatic change prompted so much speciation and extinction that, when the last ice age was over, South-east Asia had a new flora and fauna, much of which had colonized Thailand.

LANDFORMS

A lively geological past has endowed Thailand with an intriguing variety of landforms. In general, the country can be divided into three physiographic regions based on geological structure and the underlying rock.

The north, west and south consist of a series of linear folded mountain ranges lying roughly north-south. The core of many ridges consists of granitic rock that solidified from magma 40–400 million years ago, but granite in the Dawna-Tenasserim Range formed about 50 million years ago when the Indian Plate cracked and crumpled the continent of Laurasia. Between the mountain ranges there are rich alluvial valleys and plains with many major rivers. In the north, the Ping, Wang, Yom and Nan flow south to combine as the Chao Phraya while smaller rivers flow west to join the Salween or east to join the Mekong. In the west, the two biggest rivers are the Khwae Yai and Khwae Noi which then become the Mae Khlong, while the south has only one large river, the Tapi, which empties into the Bay of Bandon at Suratthani. The peninsula of southern Thailand and Malaysia rests upon the Sunda Shelf. This landmass links the South-east Asian mainland to the islands of the Andaman Sea, Indonesia and Borneo. Most of the Sunda Shelf is under the South China Sea, but during the ice ages, it was above water.

The central region consists of two plains which are divided by a low line of hills lying east-west across Nakhon Sawan, just below the point where the rivers Ping and Nan converge to become the great Chao Phraya. Both basins are bounded to the north, east and west by hills and to the south by sea. The central plains, and the Gulf, supply most of Thailand's petroleum, lignite and gas – products of alluvial sediment deposited over 50 million years.

The north-east is the most ancient part of Thailand because it rests on the part of Indosinia that was least disrupted by the mountain orogeny of the region. The core of the Khorat Plateau has been stable since the Jurassic period (120–150 million years ago) but was over-run by sea several times during the Upper Mesozoic (70–120 million years ago). The whole region slopes gently south-east and is drained by the Mekong river. To the west it is rimmed by the Phetchabhun and Dong Phaya Yen Ranges, to the south by the Phanom Dongrak. All three ranges have sandstone mountains which are characterized by their flat tops.

The soils of Thailand reflect the nature of the underlying rock, the rate of erosion and the pattern of river drainage. Those of upland areas are different from those of foothills and plains. However, most Thai soils are poor in plant nutrients and minerals except in the Chao Phraya floodplain where alluvial clays have built up over millennia. The sandy loams of the north-east are among the most infertile in the country because they are derived from weathered sandstone and do not retain much moisture. In some areas, they are also becoming saline where rock salt is shallow and the surface is being left to dry out.

The limestone ridges of the north, west and south, contribute little to the surrounding soils because they are mostly calcium carbonate which weathers only by dissolving in water with carbon dioxide and acid absorbed from air and soil. Pure limestone is more resistant to weathering than other rocks, hence the characteristic crags and outcrops that surmount the relief of adjacent sedimentary and igneous rocks. Their most important contribution to agriculture is to accommodate millions of cave-dwelling bats which, if left alone, produce tonnes of phosphatic guano which farmers can use to fertilize impoverished fields.

Soils derived from granite and metamorphic rock prevail in the folded mountains and valleys of the north, west and south. They are shallow, well-drained, clayey soils of reddish-brown or yellow but, according to one soil expert, 'are useful chiefly for wild forest' because they erode so readily. Forest cover protects fragile soils from the weathering elements of wind and rain. When this cover is removed or disturbed, these soils are exposed and vulnerable. This is a growing problem in Thailand as agriculture reaches higher up the hillsides and large upland areas are cleared for cash crops.

CLIMATE

Thailand is a tropical monsoon country with a pronounced dry season which lasts from November to April in most areas, though it is shorter in the south. Most rain falls from May to October, during the south-west monsoon, but the eastern side of the peninsula and the south-east region also receive rain in the north-east monsoon when typhoons blow in from the South China Sea. In these regions, the average annual rainfall often exceeds 3,000 millimetres (120 inches) but most of the country receives between 1,000–2,000 millimetres (40–80 inches). Mean annual temperatures of 25°–28°C (77°–82°F) do not vary very much, but significant fluctuations occur in the north, north-east and northern parts of the west because they are furthest from the sea and occupy higher elevations. Day-time temperatures can exceed 44°C (111°F) in parts of continental Thailand while night-time temperatures sink below 10°C (50°F) in December and January.

THE WILDLIFE HABITATS OF THAILAND

Thailand has witnessed major changes to its natural environment over the last century. In the late 1930s, forest covered some 70 per cent of the country. By the early 1960s this had been reduced to around 50 per cent. Today, undisturbed forest covers barely 15 per cent of the country's land area, although this figure is subject to much debate as different organizations produce different figures. Government figures are more optimistic, but they usually include areas of plantation and scrub. Thailand's rate of forest loss, and the scale of it, is higher than that of any other South-east Asian country with the exception of Singapore.

The immense variety of Thailand's topography, soils and climate has given rise to a diverse pattern of vegetation, the dominant

ABOVE There are two main types of deciduous forest in Thailand: mixed deciduous and dry deciduous dipterocarp. Teak forest is a mixed deciduous formation of northern Thailand. The dry deciduous forest shown here is typified by its puny stature and open canopy, and this is a formation which once occurred throughout continental Thailand, where water is scarce and soils poor. The four dipterocarp species which dominate these formations can withstand long periods of drought and are fire-resistant. BELOW Dipterocarp fruits are highly distinctive and many bear two or more characteristic wings.

ABOVE Thailand's seasonal evergreen and rainforests also have a predominance of dipterocarp species, but in these formations the trees are often very large, closing in a dense upper canopy over a crowded variety of palms, bamboos and smaller trees.

BELOW Fifty years ago, 70 per cent of Thailand was still forested. Today that figure has dropped to less than 20 per cent. Some denuded areas are not cultivated either, because the land is too poor. These areas have been reduced to scrub which is usually subject to over-grazing and fire. The landscape here is typical of north-east Thailand.

type being tropical forest. There are, however, many different types of forest represented, from the rich evergreen forests of the south (mangrove and broadleaved) to the seasonal and montane formations of continental regions, and interspersed between them there are other types of habitat, both natural and unnatural. In any given area, there may be a mosaic of different habitats, with a graded eco-tone in between.

Terrestrial Forests

There are two main types of terrestrial forest in Thailand: evergreen and deciduous. The presence of each is determined by the availability of water and that in turn is influenced by rainfall, soil type (porous or retentive) and humidity. Areas with a high rainfall and few dry months, as in the peninsula and parts of the south-east, support evergreen forest in upland and lowland areas, whereas in continental Thailand (north of the Isthmus of Kra), deciduous forest is found in most lowland areas with evergreen taking over with increasing elevation. However, some evergreen forest occurs in lowland areas as well – in gulleys and along waterways, for example – and this is sometimes referred to as 'gallery' or 'ribbon' forest. The origin of this description is obvious from an aerial view of the lowlands in the dry season, when threads of evergreen stand out against the parched yellowing browns of deciduous forest and the land shimmers through the heat haze. Evergreen forests must once have been more extensive in the lowlands of continental Thailand but, over the years, logging has exposed them to the drying effects of the sun.

Tropical Evergreen Rainforest
In the peninsula there are two types of evergreen rainforest, a Thai-type and a Malay-type. The latter, being more or less aseasonal, is found between the Malaysian border and the Satun-Pattani line, in the toe of Thailand or the tip of its elephant trunk, whereas the Thai-type rainforest stretches north from Satun to the Isthmus of Kra. The difference between these two formations and forest types further north is created by higher rainfall and a shorter, less severe dry season the further south you go. Humidity is also higher and there is less evaporation.

To the untrained eye, both formations look the same but are, in fact, distinguished by slight variations in floral composition. In general, however, they are both characterized by a predominance of trees from the family Dipterocarpaceae, as are the seasonal evergreen forests of continental Thailand. Dipterocarps belong to a family of Old World tropical hardwoods which are highly prized for their timber and, in some species, their resin. The name comes from the Greek word meaning 'two-winged fruit' – a slight misnomer, for although many dipterocarps do have two-winged fruits, some have more wings while others have none. However, all are distinctive.

Like all tropical evergreen forests, these show a distinct stratification in the arrangement of trees and other plants, with four storeys being evident. The top storey consists of well-spaced emergent trees which tower above the canopy at heights of around 50 metres (165 feet) and are usually supported by a ribbed pedestal of buttresses which help hold the tree upright. Beneath these forest giants, a dense canopy is formed by trees 25–35 metres tall (80–115 feet) which are festooned with climbing plants and epiphytes such as ferns, lianas, mosses and orchids. Epiphytes are plants which grow on trees but do not feed off them, drawing nutrients instead from the atmosphere, the rain or from animal debris. Between the canopy and the undergrowth there is an uneven layer of bamboos, palms, tall shrubs and small trees which subsist in the dim half-light that filters through the upper canopy. When a gap occurs after a tall tree has fallen, saplings grow at a rapid rate to fill the canopy space before their rivals do so. Below them, there is a rich ground flora of seedlings, herbs, ferns and shrubs, many of which are cultivated as house-plants because they do well in so little light. There are also weird and wonderful fungi which, along with various insects and micro-organisms, are the great recyclers of the forest floor. Together they make dead matter the matrix of new life and growth, turning debris into the humus that softens unburned forest floors.

A walk in evergreen forest is a different sensory experience from one in deciduous forest. For a start it is cooler but more humid, and obscurity prevails. In low light you can be inconspicuous, not only because the shadows are concealing but because the soft, moistened floor and sparse ground cover make movement relatively noiseless. The same, of course, is true for native creatures and, as their senses are better adapted than ours to life in the gloom,

it is harder for us to notice them than vice versa. Animal sightings are therefore rare in evergreen forest, but sounds abound – from the crashing of monkeys in bamboo to the croaking of frogs, the chirrup of small birds or the screech of an eagle overhead – and now and then a wafting smell, sometimes sweet, sometimes foul, may catch your nose. But most of the time, it is the forest itself which diverts you; its immense buttresses, its lichen-embossed barks, its twisting, tangled lianas as thick as nautical ropes, the textures and shapes of its ground cover where splashes of yellow, red and white occasionally relieve the greens and browns of its basic colour character. Unless you sit on a seam of ants or stumble into the spiny stems of rattan, evergreen forest is a soothing place to be – quiet but not silent, muted but not colourless, still but not lifeless.

The evergreen forests of southern Thailand safeguard myriad plant and animal species because they are the most diverse of all Thailand's terrestrial habitats. Over 200 species of tree can occur in a hundred square metres of rainforest, while 187 resident bird species have been recorded in one small patch of lowland forest in Krabi. Many species, such as the Flat-headed Cat, Glossy Horseshoe Bat, Crested Fireback Pheasant, Blue-rumped Parrot, Red-naped Trogon, Rhinoceros Hornbill and Maroon Woodpecker, occur in both southern forest types but others are more particular, sticking to one type alone. For example, Black-handed Gibbons, and birds such as Blue-crowned Hanging Parrots and Garnet Pittas inhabit the Malay-type rainforest only, whereas Fea's Barking Deer and Gurney's Pitta are exclusive residents of semi-evergreen rainforest in Thailand and Myanmar.

Seasonal Evergreen Forest
This is also known as semi-evergreen and dry evergreen forest because it is drier than rainforest and has a deciduous component. It occurs all over continental Thailand, north of Kra, wherever conditions allow – 1,000–2,000 millimetres (40–80 inches) of rain a year, and good soil – but it is now most abundant in the highlands of the north and west and in hill areas of the north-east. It represents over half the surviving forest cover of Thailand, a figure that can be accounted for by the fact that most conservation areas are in upland areas where evergreen forest prevails. Seasonal evergreen forest is similar in structure to southern rainforest, though not as tall, and is also dominated by dipterocarps, albeit different species. It is also similar in character and feel, but is a lot less humid than rainforest. As a result, it is the favourite forest type of many field researchers. These forests support some 70 per cent of vertebrate land species in continental Thailand, although many of those also occur in moist deciduous forests.

Hill Evergreen Forest
This occupies higher parts of the country, where rainfall normally exceeds 2,000 millimetres (80 inches) a year, altitudes rise above 1,000 metres (3,240 feet) and temperatures can be quite cool at night, often dropping below 10°C (50°F) in December and January. Mist and cloud mantle the forest most mornings, creating a mysterious atmosphere which lifts as soon as the sun is up. Here, the dominant trees are oaks and chestnuts and other plants include magnolias, rhododendrons and laurels. This forest differs considerably from other evergreen formations, not only in its floral composition but also in its structure. The trees are mostly shorter and more widely spread and the canopy is lower and more open, with more light reaching the ground. Mosses, lichens, lianas and epiphytes swathe the trunks and branches. Epiphytes are more abundant in the moist atmosphere of higher elevations even though the trees themselves are smaller. On dry ridges, trees may not grow taller than 10 metres (30 feet). In the north, this habitat is home to

LEFT Bamboo is a tall, fast-growing grass which can be found in most habitat types, both natural and cultivated. In Thailand there are 60 species of bamboo from 14 genera, each known by the structure and colour of its shafts, and at least 10 species are cultivated for a specific economic end. Highly adaptable, bamboo can be used as a water carrier (BELOW LEFT), as scaffolding or building material (BELOW CENTRE), as a kettle or cooking pot (BELOW RIGHT) or as bowls and cups. Local markets sell bamboo utensils. ABOVE This stall has bamboo tables, sticky rice carriers of varying sizes, a large all-purpose basket, back-scratchers, waste-paper baskets, paint brushes, brooms, hats and several musical instruments.

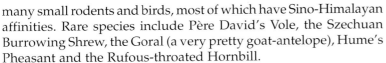

many small rodents and birds, most of which have Sino-Himalayan affinities. Rare species include Père David's Vole, the Szechuan Burrowing Shrew, the Goral (a very pretty goat-antelope), Hume's Pheasant and the Rufous-throated Hornbill.

Tropical Mixed Deciduous Forest

Mixed, or moist, deciduous forest is also known as monsoon forest because it is so seasonal. It is one of two main types of deciduous forest in Thailand, the other being dry deciduous dipterocarp forest. Of the two, this is the more luxuriant because it grows on richer, more absorbent soils where the total annual rainfall is under 2,000 millimetres (80 inches). Where rainfall or moisture levels are higher (as in gulleys, streambeds and shaded slopes) it gives way to seasonal evergreen forest. The two are quite different, in

structure and in species composition, and are usually quite easy to distinguish. Mixed deciduous forest has only three storeys and an airy canopy which fosters a vigorous growth of grasses (including pygmy bamboo) at ground level. Now and then there are groves of tall bamboo with different species – such as thorny bamboo (*pai nam*), powder bamboo (*pai nuan*) or elephant tail bamboo (*pai hang chang*) – associated with different micro-conditions, but whatever the species the ground is virtually clear, except for a carpet of yellowing leaves, because bamboo takes all the moisture.

Other areas of mixed (and dry) deciduous forest are rather taxing to walk through because the undergrowth is so scratchy and thick and the unshaded sun so intense. In the early dry season, it is also hard to walk quietly for the ground is covered in crisp discarded leaves which crunch and crackle underfoot, advertising your presence to every animal around. As a result, you see them for just a few seconds before they flee. The only ones which welcome your arrival are the ticks that lurk on blades of grass, waiting for hot-blooded bodies to come by. They can be a nuisance for although they do not hurt (unless they bite into sensitive areas like eyelids), they do irritate because they inject a toxin which can itch for weeks. They also transmit diseases (unlike leeches) such as tick fever and scrub typhus.

But, for all these physical discomforts, deciduous forests are also beautiful in the dry season. Before the trees discard their leaves, they turn to various shades of yellow and red and glow like embers in the slanting sun of ebbing afternoons. Then, after weeks of apparent inactivity, they burst into flower, cheering the sad, seared forest with brilliant explosions of colour like fireworks in a monotone sky. *Lagerstroemias* adorn themselves in lovely purples and pinks, *Cassias* are draped in clusters of startling yellow while *Erythrina* , *Bombax* and *Butea* are a blaze of oranges and reds. By the time the rains arrive, these trees have flowered, fruited and grown new shoots in readiness for the season of growth.

The upper canopy of mixed deciduous forest may reach 30 metres (100 feet) or more but, unlike most evergreen formations, it is not dominated by dipterocarps although one, *Dipterocarpus alatus*, is found there. Known in Thai as *ton yang*, this tree is widely tapped for its sticky resin which is used as a sealing glue in boats and as fire-lighter fuel. Unfortunately this custom, in which burning rags are put inside a hole that is dug in the trunk to stimulate the flow of sap, not only threatens the tree if it is repeated too often but also threatens the forest as the flames invariably spread to the flammable undergrowth alongside, thereby weakening other trees as well. As a result, the canopy in some areas is more open than it should be and the undergrowth is drier – conditions which favour the spread of the species-poor dry dipterocarp formation that includes fire-resistant species. This, in turn, poses a threat to numerous plants and animals which thrive in mixed deciduous forest, including most large herbivores (such as elephants, wild cattle and deer) and carnivores (such as tiger, Red Dog and Golden Cat) and a fabulous community of birds.

Other trees of this formation are as valued for their timber as those of evergreen forest. For over 50 years the timber industry of Thailand focused exclusively on the mixed deciduous forests of the north where teak (*Tectona grandis*) occurs. This handsome tree, with its large leaves and fluffy inflorescences, was especially favoured because its wood is robust and weather-proof, its high tannin content makes it disease-resistant and its fine grain is easy to shape. For this reason, old Thai buildings, elaborate carvings, furniture (indoor and outdoor), ox-carts and elephant howdahs were mostly made of teak. But, because its range is limited and because it was so heavily logged, teak forest and large teak trees are now extemely rare. Other valuable trees of this forest type include *Xylia xylocarpa* and *Afzelia kerrii*, both providing the red wood that is used to make expensive Oriental furniture, often with inlaid mother-of-pearl, while *Diospyros mollis* provides ebony.

Mixed deciduous forest used to be more widespread than it is today. In north, west and central Thailand, it was more abundant than evergreen forest but because it grew on good soils in valleys, peneplains and foothills below 800 metres (2,600 feet), it ceded to settlements and cultivated land. Worldwide, it is the most threatened tropical forest type.

Dry Deciduous Dipterocarp Forest

Also known as savanna forest, this replaces mixed deciduous forest in areas with less than 1,200 millimetres (50 inches) of rain a year, a long dry season and soils that are porous and poor. It is the predominant forest type in the north-east and is interspersed with mixed deciduous forest in the north and west, its presence in some parts being encouraged by repeated burning. It is easily identified because its structure is simple and its trees are markedly puny in comparison to the forests described above.

Dry dipterocarp forest is dominated by four xeric, or dryland, dipterocarps (hence its common epithet): *Dipterocarpus obtusifolius*, *D. tuberculatus*, *Shorea obtusa* and *S. siamensis*. These tend to grow to a uniform height of under 15 metres (50 feet) and do not form a canopy, so the ground is thick with grasses. This forest type supports far fewer animal species than most other formations because its simple structure and hot, dry conditions do not provide as many foraging niches as wetter, more stratified forests do. Some birds (such as the Lineated Barbet and Rufous Treepie) and mammals (such as rodents, small carnivores and deer) make use of it, but most species need more water and shade.

Every year, this forest burns. The fires are man-made, both deliberate and accidental. Until recently no one worried about them, believing them to be natural, or at any rate long-established by man, and knowing that dry dipterocarp trees and seeds are fire-resistant. But ecologists now realize that they are, in fact, doing a great deal of harm because they have become so widespread and so regular. Besides killing saplings in dry dipterocarp forest, fires are decimating mature trees in mixed deciduous formations and are creeping into dry evergreen forest as well. If this persists, the vicious cycle of drying that fires induce will impoverish every seasonal forest type in Thailand as well as the native flora and fauna, thereby undermining the country's biological diversity.

There are few sights so depressing as a newly burned strip of deciduous forest. It is so still, so silent, so forlorn. But then few sights are as thrilling as a sunset over deciduous forest in the dry season, when its leaves are turning to yellow and red.

Limestone Forest

As its name suggests, this forest occurs on the limestone ridges and outcrops which dominate western Thailand, from north to south. Many are islands, surrounded either by sea or by lower-lying plain, as in the Chao Phraya and Tapi Basins. Limestone forests are dry and stunted because their substrate is porous, and they have shallow soils. Their plants are therefore sparse and deciduous, and many are endemic because they have been separated so long from related populations. Fig trees, seeded by birds and bats, are common here, as are calcicolous shrubs. These inaccessible areas provide refuge for animals in a number of ways. Some species such as the Limestone Wren Babbler and Neill's Rat, are found nowhere else but others, such as Edible-nest Swiftlets, Dusky Crag Martins and the Blue Whistling Thrush use them as safe nesting sites. Bats use their quiet caves to roost at night, feeding in nearby fields and forests during the day, while Serow, nimble-footed goat-antelopes, descend only to mate or drink. Good examples of limestone forest are found in Ao Phang Nga, Koh Ang Thong and Khao Sam Roi Yot National Parks. Caves in Kanchanaburi and Mae Hong Son are of anthropological interest as many were inhabited by Neolithic Man who left behind various bones and artefacts.

Pine Forest

This still occurs naturally in small tracts in some upland areas of Thailand between 800–1,800 metres (2,625–5,900 feet) where soils are sandy and ridges exposed. The two native pines are *Pinus merkusii* and *P. kesiya*, a two-needled and three-needled species respectively. These lofty trees sometimes occur as pure stands but are more often mixed with dry dipterocarps at lower elevations and hill evergreen oaks at higher elevations. Where fires are

ABOVE Beung Boraphet is the most important site for wintering ducks in Thailand. Over a dozen species congregate here along with many other waterbirds. The large Comb Duck (*Sarkidiornis melanotos*) is now a rare Thai resident and winter visitor and may no longer breed, but Beung Boraphet is one of the few sites where it is still seen. The drake in this picture sports the extraordinary protuberance that gives the species its name.

RIGHT No stream or river can rival Beung Boraphet's annual spectacle of thousands of over-wintering ducks. This semi-natural lake lies at the very centre of the Chao Phraya floodplain, near the confluence of the Nan and Ping rivers, and is the largest freshwater lake in Thailand. In 1930 the natural swamp was dammed in order to develop a lacustrine fishery. Similar lakes, meant for fish and irrigation, occur all over Thailand and can help conserve indigenous aquatic life because they are shallow and seasonal. Deep hydro-electric reservoirs do not provide such habitats because they draw down unnaturally and hold a lot of dead water.

BELOW The Apple Snail, *Pila ampullacea*, is the largest freshwater snail in Thailand, measuring some 10 centimetres (4 inches), and is seen here ovipositing on the floating vegetation of Beung Boraphet. Its egg-mass is white when laid but then turns a dark yellowish-brown. This snail, along with other molluscs and bivalves, is food for the Open-billed Stork (*Anastomus oscitans*) (RIGHT) and the bird's bill, shaped like a pair of nutcrackers, is well suited for carrying its enormous shell.

frequent, pines often replace broadleaved trees. Coniferous forests support very few animal species because pine needles are acidic but some birds, including the Giant Nuthatch, the Great Tit and several woodpeckers, inhabit them and they support some stunning grassland flowers. The best examples of pine forest are in Thung Salaeng Luang and Phu Kradeung National Parks.

Freshwater Swamp Forest

Such forest once existed beside many rivers and in peaty depressions that were subject to permanent flooding, but most of it has been cleared for irrigated rice cultivation. The largest surviving tract is now protected by the Chalerm Pa Kiet Wildlife Sanctuary in Narathiwat, better known as *Pa Phru* (Thai for 'swamp forest'). This extraordinary formation, with its tangled roots and dark, silent waters, is home to many plants and animals not now found elsewhere in Thailand, among them a lovely red-stemmed palm, *Eliodoxa conferta*, and the Peat Swamp Frog. Small patches of swamp forest survive along the Tapi river, at Nong Tung Tong, and north of Thale Noi, but most of the latter has now been drained and only *Melaleuca* trees remain among the reeds and other marshland plants.

Freshwater Wetlands

Thailand has many freshwater wetlands besides swamp forest, ranging from streams and rivers to lakes, seasonal ponds and marshes. These are as important as any other natural habitat to the economic and cultural life of Thailand as well as to its ecological health and nature conservation. Like forests, all have suffered from degradation with different, but equally serious, results.

River Systems

Thailand's rivers and their tributaries support an exceptionally diverse fish fauna as well as other vertebrate and invertebrate species, many of which have not yet been studied. There are six river systems nationwide: the largest are the Salween and Mekong, but the Chao Phraya, Mae Khlong and Tapi are big rivers too, while those of the south-east are mostly rather short, as are those in the south apart from the Tapi. Through these river systems, Thailand has acquired fish from three zoogeographic zones: Indo-Burmese ones from the Salween and Mae Khlong, Indo-Chinese ones from the Mekong and Sundaic ones from the south. Chao Phraya fish are predominantly Indo-Chinese but the other affinities are represented. Many species appear to be endemic to the Salween and Mekong rivers (including the Giant Mekong Catfish), but far fewer fish are found exclusively in the other river systems. There has been too much exchange too recently.

These river basins, and therefore their aquatic floras and faunas, have all been disrupted and degraded to a greater or lesser extent. The least affected so far is probably the Salween, though its two main tributaries in Thailand, the Mae Pai and Mae Moei, are much altered. The Moei river valley has been hardest hit because it is so densely settled by Karen. Most river damage has been done by agriculture, deforestation and dams. Besides channelling and diverting waterways, agriculture has drained and cleared the land around rivers and their feeder streams. Dams have blocked the lateral (tributaries) and linear (main river) flow of fish and nutrients within river systems, thereby disrupting spawning and feeding patterns. Forest clearance has so seriously reduced water levels during the long, dry season that many streams now dry up, while others (especially those with dams) are filling with silt that erodes from deforested slopes.

As a result of these various impacts, species diversity and fish numbers are now much reduced, often by as much as 50 per cent or more. Add to that over-fishing by a desperate rural population,

pollution by domestic, industrial and agricultural effluents and the release of non-native fish and it becomes clear why Thailand's river systems are in trouble: their ecological balance has been so badly disrupted.

Lakes, Ponds and Marshes

There are not many large natural lakes in Thailand – two of the most notable being Thale Noi in the south and Nong Han Kumphawi in the north-east – but there are a number of semi-natural ones which are as important for wildlife. These were once marshlands, but the streams were dammed to create shallow lakes for fisheries. The best known are Beung Boraphet, in the central plains, Kwan Payao in the north, Nong Han in the north-east and Bang Phra in the south-east. All these lakes, both natural and semi-natural, give refuge to thousands of resident and over-wintering waterfowl while also providing fish for local communities.

The lower Chao Phraya Basin was once an enormous wetland as well, being a mix of river, marsh and swamp forest. Crocodiles used to slide between its tall *Phragmites* grasses while elephants, Javan Rhinoceroses and Schomburgk's Deer roamed wherever they pleased. None of these animals survives there today. It has been the rice bowl of Asia for many years but is targeted as a development site for industrial parks, to many people's alarm and astonishment.

Coastal Habitats

These are not divorced, ecologically, from the terrestrial habitats inland. In fact, from sea to land, each interacts with and, in some ways, is dependent upon the habitat next door. Unfortunately, coastal habitats have generally been regarded as rather separate from those inland and there is no conservation area on the Thai mainland which incorporates the whole ecological continuum from coral reef to rainforest. This could have been achieved in Phang Nga and Ranong where mountain forests sit close to the sea, but a road now cuts along the narrow coastal plain from Takua Pa to Chumphon, and that opportunity has been lost.

Coral Reefs

One of Thailand's greatest wildlife treasures, coral reefs may well shelter as many species as the lush evergreen forests, for just as geophysical variation on land fosters biological diversity, so it does under the sea. Compared to the terrestrial habitats, Thai reefs are badly under-studied but they are known to support over 400 species of fish and 250 species of hard coral as well as myriad soft corals and other marine organisms. The reef environment is as colourful as any child's painting, with brilliant reds, blues, greens and yellows dominating its psychedelic landscape in a fever of shapes and patterns.

As well as being home to underwater creatures, coral reefs provide a livelihood for local fishing communities. All Thailand's reefs are chronically threatened by overfishing (for fish and shellfish) and by the use of dynamite and bottom trawls. Pollution from coastal cities, industrial centres and intensive agriculture, sediment from tin mining and waterfront construction, anchoring and scuba-diver damage take their toll, not to mention periodic attacks by Crown-of-Thorns Starfish. In many areas, reefs have already been completely destroyed by man and the rich assemblage of corals, crustacea and fish has gone forever. Those that do survive more or less intact are those which are furthest away from human interference, for even designated national parks cannot always be protected from fishermen, tourists and pollution. In the Gulf, there are good reefs around Koh Chang and Koh Tao, but the best ones are off the Andaman Coast, around the islands of Surin and Similan, where the sea is never turbid.

ABOVE Beung Boraphet now has semi-conservation status, being a non-hunting area where fish, molluscs and lotuses can be harvested but birds and aquatic mammals are meant to be left alone. This dual role is, in theory, a happy compromise but in practice can be problematic. Every 15 years or so the Fisheries Department drains and dredges the lake, causing massive disruption to thousands of resident and over-wintering waterfowl, but most populations appear to recover. However, one rare bird is evidently more sensitive. The White-eyed River Martin (*Pseudochelidon sirintarae*) was discovered there in 1968, and reported infrequently thereafter, but has now not been seen for 20 years. No one knows where it breeds or whether it survives. The Siamese Crocodile used to inhabit the lake but it was hunted out by fishermen. Some 5,000 fishermen derive their livelihood from the lake today, but a million more people depend upon its resources. Its water is used to irrigate rice and cattle fodder; lotus leaves are used as wrapping material and the seeds and stems of the plant provide food; water hyacinth and other aquatic plants are fed to pigs; and the lake is a popular tourist destination.

BELOW LEFT This is the commonest landscape of central Thailand's Chao Phraya Basin (although you may not often see an old woman carrying her fishing rod home, along with a home-made basket). Paddy fields have become a significant man-made habitat in Thailand as rice is the single largest export crop and the staple food. Until recently, paddy fields provided other food apart from rice, such as frogs, small fish, crabs, grasshoppers and beetles, all of which were a valuable source of protein for poorer rural Thais. Since the aggressive marketing of agro-chemicals nationwide, these edible inhabitants have been reduced along with paddy field pests, adding to the problems of Thailand's cash-strapped farmers who must now buy more of their food while also trying to repay the agro-chemical loan.

BELOW Mangrove forests are important wildlife habitats, providing shelter for a huge variety of plants and animals, and rich feeding grounds for many marine creatures.

Seagrass Beds

Away from the outflow of river mouths, where sandy substrates replace the oozing silt of mangrove forests and mudflats, shallow coastal waters were once enriched by seagrass beds. These underwater meadows are the habitat of young open-sea fish and Thailand's most famous marine mammal, the Dugong or Sea Cow. This huge gentle creature is a herbivore, feeding exclusively on seagrasses. Herds of many hundreds were once encountered in shallow waters of the western coast. Weighing almost 400 kilograms (880 pounds) and reaching lengths of 3 metres (10 feet), these harmless creatures have been all but extirpated by deliberate and accidental persecution – they often get caught, and drown, in trawler nets – and by losing their grazing grounds to pollution and drag netting. However, local fisherman are slowly coming to their rescue, for in defending their traditional fishing grounds from the commercial trawler fleet, they also protect the seagrass beds and the Dugong itself. The most important Dugong site at present is the Had Chao Mai–Koh Libong conservation area in Trang.

Intertidal Mudflats

Thailand's 2,815 kilometres (1,752 miles) of coastline provides two intertidal habitats for wildlife: mudflats and mangrove forests. Mudflats are part of the mangrove system, being areas that have not yet been colonized by the salt-tolerant mangrove trees. They are major feeding grounds for molluscs and marine invertebrates that crawl into their thick, shifting sediments, emerging from their burrows to feed when the tide is in. This they do by taking tiny marine organisms from the water by means of specialized claws and tentacles, or by sucking copious amounts of water across mucous-covered glands to extract nutrient particles.

Mudflats are immensely important for millions of shore-birds, including migrating and over-wintering waders. Over 40 coastal species use the mudflats of Thailand. Key protected sites are Koh Libong Wildlife Sanctuary (where 4,340 waders were recorded in one month), Khao Sam Roi Yot National Park, Pak Phanang Estuary and Tarutao National Park. Major unprotected sites include the Bay of Bandon, the mouth of the Mae Khlong and Tha Chin rivers and inlets between Ranong and the Lam Son National Park.

Mangrove Forest

Where sea meets the land in sheltered bays that are filled with nutrient-rich sediment brought there by rivers, mangrove species stake their claim. These plants can withstand severe environmental stress including alternating mixes of fresh and salty water, prolonged submersion or exposure with every tide and mud that has no oxygen and a high sulphur content.

Mangrove trees survive in this environment because they have evolved specialized features. For example, tree roots do not grow deep into the mud but spread wide and intertwine, forming a dense mat above and below the mud, securing themselves against the forceful tides. Some mangrove trees have also developed breathing roots (pneutomatophores) which, unlike most roots, grow upwards out of the mud. These have pores which take in the oxygen necessary for making food and for eliminating salt from the water absorbed by other roots. Other trees, such as *Sonneratia* , expel salt through their leaves. Mangrove forests have many plants from the Rhizophoraceae family as well as *Sonneratia* cork trees, the Nipa Palm and the Sea Holly. Left alone, the tallest of these can reach 25–30 metres (80–100 feet), supported by their stilt-like roots.

To most people, mangrove forests are uninviting but in fact they are amazing places to visit. For one thing they support an astonishing variety of plants and animals because they provide stable and sheltered cover in rich marine feeding grounds. Indeed, they are often referred to as the nurseries of marine life because they nurture so many of the sea's fish, crabs and crustacea as well as coastal aquatic animals. Consequently, they are very important wildlife refuges. Of the 36 mammal species recorded from Thailand's mangroves, those seen most often are Dusky Leaf-monkeys, Crab-eating Macaques, Small-clawed Otters, Fishing Cats, mongooses and fruit-eating bats. One fruit bat, *Cynopterus sphinx*, is solely responsible for pollinating the *Sonneratia* trees that are a key feature of healthy mangrove forests.

Some 204 bird species, both resident and migratory, have also been recorded in Thailand's mangrove forests, along with 32 reptiles, 6 amphibians, 72 species of fish and 54 kinds of crab, all of which provide rich pickings for the great flocks of waders and waterfowl which migrate to these key coastal sites. Two bird species are exclusive residents of mangrove forest: the Brown-winged Kingfisher and the Mangrove Pitta, both of which have been lost to all but the better mangrove forests of the Andaman coast. Another endangered bird of this habitat is the Masked Finfoot.

The economic and ecological value of mangroves has long been underestimated. Widely regarded as a wasteland habitat, large areas of mangrove have been cleared throughout South-east Asia, either to create additional building land (often adjacent to port facilities) or to convert into shrimp and coastal fish farms. Local people have long relied on mangrove forests as a generous source of protein, construction timber and fuelwood (for conversion to charcoal) and, as a result, they appreciate the hidden benefits of a fully functioning mangrove ecosystem. Mangrove forests act as an essential breakwater, their barrier of roots protecting the land from sea storms and strong tidal currents as well as entrapping the soft silt and sediment which rivers carry out to sea. Moreover, their leaves add organic matter to the food chain below, augmenting the nutrients provided by the river-borne silt. And because they are so sheltered and so well provided with food, they are the breeding grounds for hundreds of marine fish species, many of which are of considerable economic importance to fishermen. Undue interference in this finely tuned ecosystem disrupts its vital natural balance.

Mangrove forests have long been worked commercially for their timber. These concessionary forests are managed on 30-year cycles during which strips are clear-cut and either left to replant themselves from adjoining strips or they are replanted with pure stands of *Rhizophora apiculata* in place of the 70-plus plant species they would normally contain. Very few areas of mangrove forest survive undisturbed in Thailand today and those that remain are mostly waiting to be cut, for mangrove forest was not included in the national logging ban of 1989. The current estimate of mangrove cover in Thailand is less than 1,500 square kilometres (600 square miles), most of it along the west peninsular coast, from Ranong to Satun. Just 99 square kilometres (38 square miles), or 3 per cent, of the original mangrove area is currently protected. Omission of this habitat from an otherwise extensive system of national parks and wildlife sanctuaries is a major oversight.

One of the most important protected areas for mangrove forest is the Ao Phang Nga National Park which has 53 square kilometres (20 square miles) of terrestrial habitat, the rest being open sea. Even here, however, logging has been carried out in the past and some areas have been encroached upon by shrimp farmers. The richest mangrove in the area lies outside the park. Other areas of protected mangrove forest are found in the Tarutao National Park and Koh Libong Wildlife Sanctuary – both key conservation areas – but perhaps the best tracts of all are found off Takua Pa on the north coast of Phang Nga. Here small fishing communities manage the area to their own advantage, but as more and more boats use the local ports to exploit Surin and Similan, the integrity of these mangroves, and the way of life they have so long supported, is threatened.

The best mangrove forest on the Gulf side of Thailand fringes the bay of Nakhon Sri Thammarat. This bay, formed by the Talumpak spit, is the outlet of the Mae Pak Panang, the river that services the highly productive marshland north of the Thale Sap lagoons. The geography of this bay is changing all the time as the sea deposits sand which extends the spit northwards while the river deposits silt which steadily fills the bay. Thus the mangrove niche is expanding but so too are the shrimp farms which usurp its natural place.

Beach Forest
While mangrove species occupy intertidal mudflats, a thin band of beach forest lines the high-water mark, fringing sandy stretches of the mainland and offshore islands. The trees of this forest type include the wispy coastal pine *Casuarina equisetifolia* , the Indian almond tree *Terminalia catappa*, *Pandanus* screw pines (with fruits looking like pineapples), a yellow-flowered hibiscus and a very conspicuous cycad, *Cycas rumphii*. Because the seeds of these species tend to disperse by sea, they occur all over South-east Asia. Other notable plants which adorn Thailand's coastal fringe include the Gloriosa Lily, a climbing herb which produces a delicate flower with corkscrew petals of yellow and red, Beach Morning Glory with its pretty pink trumpets, Spinifex Grass and the Crab's Eye or Rosary Bead Vine whose attractive black and red seeds are used to make necklaces even though they are deadly poisonous.

The coastal strands that support this forest type have been much affected by tourism and coastal development, for these are the areas that attract holiday visitors. Some stretches of beach forest do survive but mostly on islands either side of the peninsula. One mainland park in Phuket (Had Nai Yang) protects this habitat and the beaches that go with it, not only for its own sake but also for the turtles which return there each year to lay their eggs. Unfortunately, the best beaches for turtles – those with gentle slopes of soft sand – are also those which appeal to tourists.

Man-made Habitats
As so little of Thailand's natural vegetation survives intact, it follows that there are huge areas of unnatural habitat. Four such habitats are worth mentioning.

Grasslands
These occur in many conservation areas and are usually known as *thungs* ('fields' in Thai), for example, Thung Yai and Thung Salaeng Luang. Few of them are natural. Most were once cultivated fields and are now maintained by fire. They are popular areas in national parks because they attract large herbivores, such as elephant, wild cattle and deer, during the early rains when young shoots appear. In Thailand, grasses grow naturally in deciduous forest and in open river valleys.

Farmlands
With so much of Thailand given over to cultivation, these have become significant habitats for species that can adapt. Paddy fields support a remarkable array of fish, crabs, insects, snakes, turtles, frogs, birds and small mammals (including insect-eating bats) but since agrochemicals were introduced, wildlife numbers have dropped dramatically. Few other cultivated fields provide much of a niche, though sugarcane harbours reedbed birds, rodents and snakes. Fields in marginal areas often have lone 'lollipop' trees, tall trees with tight round crowns. These reveal that the field was recently forest, for they got their form from filling a canopy gap.

Tree Plantations
Many Thai foresters still regard tree plantations as equivalent to forest though a plantation has one or two tree species while a natural formation has 100 or more, but if forest is valued for timber alone, this view is understandable. Large areas of continental Thailand are planted with teak and eucalyptus, the latter an Australian import. Pine is often planted on deforested land in the north, even in conservation areas. In the south, rubber and oil palm trees cover huge tracts of what was the richest evergreen forest of all, lowland rainforest, and coconut plantations cover sandy coastal soils. Plantations support very little wildlife compared to natural forest, though they do attract some species such as bats, rodents and snakes.

Hydro-electric Reservoirs
Big dam builders like to maintain that they are doing wild animals a favour by providing much more water than they would have had access to otherwise. Unfortunately, this is wishful thinking. Large reservoirs do not compensate for the loss of riverine habitats. Their characters are totally different. Rivers are like arteries carrying lifeblood to an area. Reservoirs are like haemorrhages: the larger ones can kill.

THE FLORA AND FAUNA OF THAILAND

The flora and fauna of Thailand are uncommonly diverse, partly because the country has so many varied habitats – lying as it does across the seasonal divide with a range of altitudes in between – and also because it is linked to the region's two biogeographic realms, the Oriental and the Indo-Malayan. More than that, it is the junction between the four sub-regions of those realms: the Sino-Himalayan, Sundaic, Indo-Chinese and Indo-Burmese which extend due north, south, east and west of the country respectively.

Thailand shares many species with each of its neighbouring countries, but not all of them with any one. Overall, its floral and faunal communities are exclusively its own. Within the country, however, there are clear delineations in distribution. The flora and fauna of Peninsular Thailand, for example, have close affiliations to those of Peninsular Malaysia, while a majority of species in continental Thailand share affinities with Indo-China and Myanmar. This exchange means that Thailand has fewer endemic species than more isolated countries (although it does have some remarkable ones) but, for its size, it has one of the richest floras and faunas in South-east Asia.

Flora
Thailand's flora is not yet fully documented although ten volumes of the great 22-part project, *The Flora of Thailand*, have been published, but a shortage of money and expertise delays its completion. It is a massive undertaking, for at present there are thought to be some 25,000 vascular plant species in Thailand, around 12,000 of which are flowering plants.

Although the written records of Thailand's native flora are not yet complete, there have long been unwritten records of ways in which plants can be used, or not used, by man. Caves in western Thailand that were occupied by primitive hunter-gatherers 10,000 years ago contain the debris of plant parts that were eaten, while 5,000 years ago, early settlers in the north-east were evidently cultivating wild rice. No doubt they were also harvesting bamboo, for that is another wild grass that is widely used today to make every kind of 'mod-con'.

Bamboo was (and for many people still is) the main construction material for houses and farm shelters, but as villages became more

Habenaria mandersii. North and north-east regions.

Dendrobium unicum. Upland forests of the north-east.

Vanda coerulea. High altitudes in the north-west.

Dendrobium heterocarpum. Moist evergreen forest.

Phalaenopsis cornu-cervi. Widespread in South-east Asia.

Bulbophyllum picturatum. Found in northern Thailand.

Rhynchostylis coelestis. Forests of west and north-west Thailand.

Calanthe cardiogossa. Evergreen forests of west and north-west Thailand.

Dendrobium secundum (Toothbrush Orchid). Epiphyte of the Sunda region.

Vanda liouvillei. Higher mountains of northern and north-eastern Thailand.

Dendrobium gibsonii. Mountains of northern Thailand.

Paphiopedilum sukhakulii. Endemic to north-east Thailand.

Ascocentrum curvifolium. Occurs in north and west regions.

Schoenorchis fragrans. Known only from far north-east Thailand.

Brachycorythis helferi. Grasslands, commonest in the north.

Ascocentrum ampullaceum. Known only from northern Thailand.

Mischobulbum wrayanum. Recorded in Thailand only at the Khao Yai National Park.

Eulophia spectabilis. Grasslands throughout Thailand.

Dendrobium linguella. Species of aseasonal South-east Asia.

Dendrobium thyrsiflorum. High altitudes, Nepal to northern Indo-China.

Dendrobium trigonopus. Mid- to high-altitude species.

Dendrobium lindleyi. Mid-altitude forests of mainland Asia.

Staurochilus fasciatus. Southern evergreen forests and moist areas of south-east Thailand.

Dendrobium aphyllum. Epiphytic species, mid-altitudes in mainland Asia.

Dendrobium nobile. North and north-east Thailand.

Dendrobium chrysotoxum. Northern deciduous forests from 600–800 metres (2,000–2,600 feet).

Dendrobium fimbriatum. Mainland Asia.

settled and more affluent, timber took its place. Many of Thailand's native forest trees are good timber species including teak, rosewood and ironwood (one of numerous dipterocarps). Another group of forest trees of equal ecological importance are the figs, members of the mulberry family Moraceae. These are no good for timber, but they are vital to wildlife because they are perennial larders.

Over 300 fig species are found in Thailand. Most are native, but two well-known ones are not, *Ficus religiosa* (the Buddha Tree) and *F. bengalensis* (the Banyan). Native fig trees grow in moist forest (mixed deciduous and evergreen) at low to mid-altitudes and they fruit asynchronously so there are always some fruiting somewhere in the forest. This is hugely important for fruit-eating animals such as gibbons, monkeys, hornbills and bats which would otherwise go hungry at lean times of year. In fact figs are flowers before they ripen into fruits. Male and female flowers line the inside of a fig but they cannot self-fertilize. They need a female fig-wasp to bring pollen from another fig. The wasps are equally dependent, for they hatch, mate, lay their eggs and die inside a fig. Male fig-wasps never leave the fig they were born in.

Another oddity of the figs is the fact that some species strangle their host. Strangler figs start life as an epiphyte on the branch of a tall forest tree. A seed is randomly dropped there by a fig-eating animal and the seedling then grows long, adventitious roots which tap into the ground. These roots then thicken while others interlock sideways until the host tree is encircled by a constricting lattice-work of limbs which eventually deprives it of life. This description may sound savage, but it all takes so long that the host tree will have seeded many times before its eventual demise. The fig does not deny it a genetic future.

Other famous forest plants of Thailand are the orchids. Thailand has over 1,300 species, some terrestrial, but the majority are epiphytic – either growing near the ground or high up in the trees. A few species are found in open woodland and grasslands, but most are dependent on forest. All wild orchids are threatened, not just by habitat destruction but more especially by illegal collection. The pillage of these exquisite flowers is particularly sad because most orchids can now be propagated in nurseries anyway.

The orchids of Thailand reflect the country's physical and biological geography. Species which occur in the north at the higher elevations where temperatures are cool and conditions moist are more typical of southern China and the Himalayas, while those in other parts of continental Thailand are adapted to a marked dry season. Indeed, some species will not flower unless they are subject to a periodic drought and many Thai orchids flower during the dry season. Others survive long periods of no rain by shedding their leaves, as does *Dendrobium aphyllum*, while others have large pseudobulbs which help avoid desiccation, and many ground orchids, including several *Habenaria* species, die back completely, leaving only underground stem tubers. Some of the most beautiful and therefore most coveted orchids from the seasonal part of Thailand are those in the genera *Dendrobium* and, because they are adapted to climate changes, they are often seen in orchid collections in Europe. Orchids that are found in south Thailand are less well suited to temperate collections because they are adapted to the warm, season-less climate typical of areas around the equator such as Malaysia, Indonesia and Borneo. However, many of these species have been used to produce hybrids which are widely marketed by the cut flower trade. There are many commercial orchid nurseries in Thailand, some of them using highly sophisticated techniques to grow plants from seed and culture.

Orchids are not the only non-timber forest plants to be exploited commercially in Thailand. Others provide spices and medicines and many, of course, are foods. In fact some spices which characterize Thai cuisine – such as ginger, galangal and lemon grass – are wild plants with medicinal properties. So extensive is Thailand's traditional pharmacopoeia that several research units have been set up to document the knowledge before it, and its wild ingredients, disappear. To date, well over 1,000 herbal cures have been recorded but that is likely to be a fraction of what there is to learn. Medicinal plants not yet known to man may well be known to native forest mammals. Naturalists have noticed that elephants and primates eat particular plants when they are feeling unwell, apparently treating themselves with illness-specific medicines.

The health of forest itself can be monitored by studying lichens and this is being done in a pioneering project involving the British Museum of Natural History, Chiang Mai University and the Royal Forest Department. Lichens are micro-organisms consisting of symbiotic fungi and algae. They occur all over the tropics on tree trunks, branches, bamboos, rocks and stones, creating a mosaic of colours, textures and patterns. Their differential sensitivity to atmospheric pollution, temperatures and fire makes them very good indicators of environmental health and change. The history of an area is recorded in its lichens: whether a forest has been logged or otherwise degraded, for example, or whether it has long been subject to fire. Thai forests have hundreds of lichen species, many of them exclusive to certain forest types. Thus it may be possible, one day, to map changes in Thai forest cover using lichens instead of satellites.

Fauna

Thailand's fauna is as diverse as its flora and for all the same reasons: its evolutionary history, its central location and its variety of habitats. Over 10 per cent of the world's known animal species (4,253 out of 41,600) occur there including at least 280 mammals and some 925 birds. About 140 species appear to be endemic, which is 3 per cent of the country's total fauna. These include 70 freshwater fish, 50 saltwater fish, 31 reptiles, 13 amphibians, 8 mammals and 2 birds. There is, as yet, no estimate of the number of insects found in Thailand but over 10,000 beetles have been recorded, along with 1,200 butterflies and 200 hawk-moths. Entomologists are finding as much diversity among insects as botanists have found among plants, suggesting that there may be as many species in the seasonal forests of Thailand as there are in the supposedly far richer rainforests of Indonesia and Malaysia.

Mammals

Thailand harbours around 12 per cent of the world's mammal species, but larger ones survive only in big undisturbed conservation areas and, because of heavy persecution over the years, all of them are secretive and shy. Consequently, they are not often seen except in areas they know to be safe, as around the headquarters of the Khao Yai National Park.

The Asian Elephant is the largest terrestrial mammal in Thailand and has for many centuries played a major part in Thai life, both as a beast of burden and as a symbol of sovereignty and prestige. So highly was it once valued that an elephant protection act was introduced in 1921, forty years before any other wildlife laws were passed. The flag of Siam carried a white elephant until 1932 when the name, and the emblem, of the country changed but, even now, a white elephant (actually albino or pale grey) must be given to the King as soon as it is weaned.

One might expect this special status to have protected elephants in Thailand but, sadly, it has not. They are perilously close to extinction in the wild with just a few thousand surviving in large conservation areas. Their decline is caused by habitat loss (elephants need huge areas to survive in viable numbers) and their usefulness, as most domestic elephants are captured from the wild. A hundred years ago, there were 100,000 trained elephants in Thailand, many used by loggers. Today there are barely 5,000. They have been displaced by machinery, yet they are vastly superior to vehicles for hauling logs from forest because they are more versatile, they can extract a tree without damaging others and they do not need access roads. They are also quieter, more attractive and more intelligent. Since the 1989 logging ban, many trained elephants have had no work and some owners, in desperation, bring them to Bangkok to earn their keep, though how they find 200 kilograms of fodder a day in that cemented city is anybody's guess. There is something truly pathetic and sad about an elephant in Bangkok, as it walks along a crowded street with awe-inspiring dignity. The sight of a lone baby elephant being paraded round a luxury hotel for the entertainment of tourists is equally distressing to those who know what its natural way of life, in a herd, would be.

Thailand once boasted 18 ungulate species: 3 odd-toed ungulates (a tapir and 2 rhinoceros species) and 15 even-toed ungulates (one wild boar, 8 deer species, 4 bovids and 2 goat-antelopes). Today, one is extinct (Schomburgk's Deer), another (Kouprey) is probably extinct as it only ever occurred in north-east Thailand (where it has disappeared), southern Laos and northern Cambodia (where years of strife have undoubtedly taken their toll), four others (Javan and Sumatran Rhinoceroses, Hog and Brow-antlered Deer) vanished from the wild in Thailand but the deer are being bred for reintroduction, and seven species (Greater Mouse Deer, Fea's Barking Deer, Wild Water Buffalo, Gaur, Banteng, Serow and Goral) are endangered. The only ungulates not in any immediate danger of extinction are Tapir, Lesser Mouse Deer, Common Barking Deer, Sambar Deer and Wild Boar but even they are threatened.

As for most large mammals and birds, hunting and habitat loss have been the primary causes of ungulate decline. Schomburgk's Deer was restricted to the Chao Phraya swamplands which gave way to rice production many years ago. The last one, a tame male, was killed in 1938 at its temple home near Bangkok by a drunk. Brow-antlered Deer and Hog Deer were ungulates of open lowlands and also lost their habitat to man, while Kouprey have not been reliably reported since mid-1970. Their fate was sealed when loggers opened up the Phanom Dongrak Range and let settlers in. Since then, Cambodia's civil war has kept people in that area hungry and well armed. All even-toed ungulates are killed for food but Gaur, Banteng and Serow are also killed for their heads; the cattle for trophies, Serow for medicine. The prices paid for rhinoceros parts doomed them in Thailand long ago, though unconfirmed reports of Sumatran Rhinoceros signs have come from Kaeng Krachan and Phu Khieo in recent years, but as both areas are frequented by hunters, rhino survival would be a miracle.

In spite of losing the Kouprey, Thailand still accommodates more wild cattle species than any other country in Asia. The Gaur, or Asian Bison, is the most numerous because it inhabits upland evergreen forest (a lot of which survives in conservation areas) whereas the Banteng is a deciduous forest animal and survives in safe numbers only in Mae Wong and Huai Kha Khaeng. Huai Kha Khaeng is also the last refuge of Wild Water Buffalo, fearsome beasts with huge, handle-bar horns and enormous feet. Goral and Fea's Barking Deer are threatened because their ranges are so limited; the former inhabits high rugged mountains in the north while the latter roams upland evergreen forests in the south.

Thailand has 13 primates – 3 apes (all gibbons), 9 monkeys (5 langurs, 5 macaques) and a loris. Gibbons are much the most vocal, their bold melodious calls informing the forest each morning. They

are broadly allopatric, that is they occupy different areas, but the relict population of Black-handed Gibbons that is found in the very far south appears to be surrounded by White-handed Gibbons which range from the mountains of Malaysia to those of west, north and north-east Thailand where they meet the Pileated Gibbon. In one small area of Khao Yai National Park, these two species interbreed, producing hybrids which sing a hybrid song, for the call of the gibbon is inherited, not learned. Khao Yai is as far west as Pileated Gibbons go. Due east, they occupy the mountain forests of the Cardomom and Phanom Dongrak Ranges but are most numerous in Khao Soi Dao and Khao Ang Ru Nai.

The similarity of gibbons and their restricted range (they are exclusive to South-east Asia) suggests they evolved quite recently, perhaps only 500,000 years ago, from a common arboreal ancestor and then diverged into species during the Pleistocene glaciations when evergreen forest receded to the hills and was discontinuous. Gibbon populations would then have been isolated for thousands of years as gibbons do not descend to the ground to get from place to place, they swing from tree to tree. Open ground is a barrier, as are big rivers.

Today, trade in babies is as much a threat to gibbon survival as the loss of evergreen forest. Naive animal lovers buy them at their most enchanting age, as tiny frightened balls of fur, little knowing that for every baby that reaches the street alive, 8 to 10 gibbons have died from injury or trauma. The only way to get a baby gibbon from the wild (and those on sale are mostly from the wild) is to shoot a nursing mother from the tree. When she falls her baby falls with her and usually dies as well, then or later, and the sad irony in this is that gibbons are not good pets. They are too needy and strong and too difficult to discipline. Pet gibbons are usually caged or abandoned as soon as they become troublesome, but still the trade continues because buyers do not know the harm they do and dealers do not enlighten them.

Monkeys are also traded as pets but less so than gibbons. Macaques used to be exported by the hundred to medical research establishments in Europe and America and Pig-tailed Macaques are trained to harvest coconuts, but more monkeys are killed for food and as agricultural pests. Phayre's Leaf-monkey (or Langur) is especially prized for its gall-stones which grow like golf-balls from drinking at limestone springs. These stones are made into health-enhancing tonics by traditional Chinese pharmacists. Thai leaf-monkeys are hard to distinguish. Their colour, shape and sizes are alike and three have white eye-rings but, like macaques, they occupy different areas and habitats. Macaques are less endearing than other primates, perhaps because they strut like hoodlums and stare with savage, glinting eyes. In the wild they are wary and engaging, but the habituated hordes at some temples are horrid.

The only nocturnal primate in Thailand is the Slow Loris, a small furry creature with big round eyes and a gentle, endearing expression which creeps along branches in search of food. This benign demeanour belies the ferocious speed at which it snatches and devours its prey of insects, lizards, snails and small birds. In Thai, the loris is known as *ling-lom*, or wind monkey, a name which might reflect its tenacious grip or its acrobatic agility.

Thailand is home to 36 carnivores, which is a truly astonishing number: 2 wild dogs (Asiatic Jackal and Red Dog), 2 bears (Asiatic Black Bear and Sun Bear), 10 mustelids (3 weasels, 1 marten, 2 badgers, 4 otters), 13 viverrids (11 civets, 2 mongooses) and 9 wild cats. All but two of these survive, though most are endangered or threatened. The two in question are the Hairy-nosed Otter and the Otter Civet, both victims of mangrove destruction in the south, although the Otter Civet (a Sundaic species) may have been losing ground already to the otters (which came from the north).

The commonest otters are the Smooth-coated and Short-clawed, the latter being the smallest of this enchanting family and the only one to live in large family groups. Hairy-nosed Otters aside, the rarest otter in Thailand is the Eurasian, ironically also called the Common Otter because that is its status in Europe. These once gambolled about the mountain streams of the north, but have been extirpated by mountain people and their dogs. The only place they are known to occur now is Huai Kha Khaeng where they co-exist with the two commoner species in finely delineated niches.

Domestic dogs are a scourge of wild areas in Thailand. Besides killing and harassing protected species such as otters, they spread non-native parasites, including heart-worm, which can weaken a wild carnivore population. The most vulnerable species are wild dogs because they are so closely related, but wild cats can be infected too. Red Dogs and Asiatic Jackals are strikingly handsome animals, with gleaming coats and long bushy tails.

The nine wild cats inhabiting Thailand range from Asia's largest, the Tiger, to its smallest, the Leopard Cat. They would once have spanned the country, from mountain to mangrove and plain, apportioning prey and habitats between them. Marbled Cats and Clouded Leopards pad evergreen forests at night, looking for small mammals, birds and lizards, often in the trees, while Leopards and Golden Cats may be active during the day, at dawn and dusk, looking for larger prey but are equally at home in more open deciduous forests, as are Tigers and Jungle Cats. In fact, 'jungle cat' is a misnomer, for this small, sharp-eared cat is primarily a grassland species. Fishing Cats and Flat-headed Cats are riverine

Over a dozen species of animals have already vanished from the wild in Thailand, and others are verging on extinction. However, most do survive in captivity or in neighbouring countries. LEFT The elegant Eld's Deer (*Cervus eldi*), or Brow-antlered Deer, was once common in low-lying areas north of Kra. There is now a sizeable captive population in Thailand which will one day be released into an appropriate conservation area. TOP The Sumatran Rhinoceros (*Dicerorhinus sumatrensis*) is one of two rhinoceroses which used to occur in Thailand, the other being the Javan Rhinoceros. Neither has been seen for 20 years, although sightings of the Sumatran rhino are sometimes reported in remote forest areas. CENTRE The Siamese Crocodile (*Crocodylus siamensis*) was once often seen in Thailand's freshwater swamps but it was so heavily hunted that few now survive in the wild. However, both this species and its larger salt-water relative, *C.porosus*, are farmed in great numbers. ABOVE LEFT The White-shouldered Ibis (*Pseudibis davisoni*) was formerly a resident of Thailand but is now extinct in the wild. It is not as yet being bred for reintroduction. ABOVE RIGHT The Sarus Crane (*Grus antigone*) stands nearly two metres (6 feet) tall and used to grace paddy fields and marshlands countrywide. There is now a breeding programme in Thailand which aims to reintroduce them into the wild.

and coastal species respectively, non-retractable claws enabling them to hook their prey from water with a quick flick of the paw.

All but the smallest cats are critically threatened by hunting and habitat loss, which affects them directly and also indirectly through a diminution of prey. Caught alive, large cats are either sold to restaurants to satisfy the decadent demand for power-foods, or they become recreational ornaments for people with something to prove. However, the main trade is in big cat parts for various medicinal purposes, and this threatens to eliminate tigers from Thailand, and from Asia, in less than a decade. The lucrative trade in tiger bones is particularly insidious because hunters do not need to take the risk of killing a tiger themselves as they do if they want the meat or skin. Instead, they bait a fresh carcass with poison within a tiger's territory and return a few days later to collect any bits and bones. This not only threatens tigers all over Asia but other rare animals as well, such as vultures and wild dogs.

As a group, Thailand's marine mammals are neglected although the Dugong and Irrawaddy Dolphin are now attracting public concern. The rest are rarely mentioned. There are 13 species in all: 12 cetaceans (8 dolphins, one porpoise, 3 whales) and a sirenian (the Dugong). All are threatened by the modern fishing fleet which trawls coastal and deep-water seas without controls or catch criteria. Marine mammals are killed for their meat and oil but many also die by drowning in discarded nets.

Perhaps because they are nocturnal, Thailand's bats are even more neglected than the marine mammals, although they are vital to the country's ecological health. One colony of insectivorous bats eats millions of insects a night, thus controlling pests such as rice-hoppers and mosquitoes, while fruit and nectar-eating bats pollinate many forest trees and disperse their seeds. Some wild tree species (such as durian, banana, kapok, sataw and *Sonneratia*) depend exclusively on bats for pollination. Moreover, because they defaecate in flight (which other fruit-eaters do not), bats often scatter seeds over scrubland and degraded forest, thereby helping forest regeneration.

Thailand has 107 bat species (from 45 genera) which is 11 per cent of all bats worldwide and 38 per cent of its own mammal fauna. These figures acquire more perspective when we learn than Britain has only 14 bat species from two genera, all insectivores. Most of Thailand's bats are also insectivores (88 species) but 18 species eat fruit and nectar and one, the False Vampire, is carnivorous. This bat is so called because it does not feed on blood as true vampires do but eats mice, lizards and insects as well as other bats.

One of Thailand's many singular distinctions is being home to the world's largest and smallest bats. The largest is the Flying Fox (*Pteropus vampyrus*) (another misnomer) which is a frugivore that can weigh one kilogram (2 pounds) and has a wingspan of almost 2 metres (6 feet). The smallest bat (and the world's smallest mammal) is the insect-eating Kitti's Hog-nosed Bat (*Craseonycteris thonglongyai,*) also known as the bumblebee bat because its body is that small. It weighs only 2 grams and has a wingspan of under 8 centimetres (3 inches). It has been found in only one small area of western Thailand and is extremely rare.

Other bats are rare, too, because their local range and habitat are restricted. This applies, for example, to the Harlequin Bat which lives in mountain forests of the north, to the Dayak Fruit Bat which lives in rainforest in the very far south and to the Disc-nosed Bat which is apparently endemic to central Thailand and roosts in a limited number of caves. Colonial cave roosting makes bats vulnerable to hunters who net them in the entrance as they leave to feed at dusk. Some Thais eat bats as a delicacy, fried with garlic and chilli, but others protect them assiduously in order to harvest their guano, a high-grade fertilizer. The temple of Khao Chong

Pran in Ratchaburi has a cave which accommodates over two million Free-tailed Bats. Every two weeks, local villagers are allowed to collect a quota of guano and the monks use the income to support a school and other village development projects. As dusk approaches, the bats begin to jostle and the susurration of fluttering wings is interspersed with audible flaps as a few bats leave. Then, within seconds, they start to pour out of the cave and the noise is like the crescendo of a localized typhoon, the rush of wings and air magnified by echoes. From afar they look like a long, black cloud which drifts from the cave for thirty minutes or more, depending on the number of bats. It is an astonishing sight.

Birds

In recent years, Thailand has become a major birdwatching country, not only for visitors but for Thai people too. Those who do not know the country well are sometimes as surprised by this as they are by the discovery that Thailand still has wild tigers. But with 10 per cent of the world's species, Thailand's avifauna is as rich and as remarkable as its other native faunas although it is fair to say that few large birds survive in populated areas.

Because of Thailand's biogeography, its birds can be divided rather broadly into regions or habitats. The north, for example, has a preponderance of colourful montane birds with Sino-Himalayan affinities whereas most southern species are shared with Malaysia and do not extend north of the peninsula. Likewise, the eastern side of Thailand shares birds with Indo-China but there are also birds of seasonal evergreen and open deciduous forest and others of inland plains and lakes, while yet more inhabit coastal mangroves and mudflats. Then there are temporal distinctions, for about 240 species come to Thailand as over-wintering or non-breeding migrants from other parts of Asia and the Palearctic regions and they are found in every habitat alongside resident birds. Thailand is the main flyway for migrant birds to and through South-east Asia.

At least ten bird species have gone from the wild, three of the largest being the Sarus Crane, Giant Ibis and Long-billed Vulture, and others such as Spot-billed Pelicans survive only as non-breeding migrants. They are no longer resident in Thailand. The picture could be bleaker, however, for well over 150 species – one fifth of the country's avifauna – are in danger of extinction if conservation measures are not implemented effectively. Thailand would then lose almost all its storks, most of its pheasants and hornbills, many pigeons, parakeets and birds of prey, several ducks, woodpeckers and pittas and a host of other birds whose range is restricted to endangered habitats such as wetlands and lowland evergreen forest.

Happily, there is reason to hope that such a scenario will not be. Thailand does have an extensive system of protected areas, all of which support birds, and as people adopt more favourable attitudes towards wildlife, more of it may survive in unprotected areas as well. Already there are people who give sanctuary to wild birds. In Phitsanulok, for example, there is a local farmer known as Uncle Tua who lets his fish-ponds serve as a waterfowl reserve. Sometimes his land harbours more ducks than any other site in the country and he is well recognized as a guardian of overwintering waterfowl. In the central plains near Suphanburi, another local farmer, this time an old lady, has let a colony of Open-billed Storks take over the wooded land around her house. This colony was first established by breakaway birds from nearby Wat Phai Lom but now has more occupants than the famous temple site itself.

As stories such as these spread far afield, bringing kudos and support to those who feature in them, other people may follow their example and attitudes will change. But it does take time. A

Outsize Buddhas such as this one on a Phetchaburi hillside have been erected all over Thailand. Many Thai *wats* (temples or monasteries) serve as small wildlife sanctuaries, and some monks actively promote environmental conservation. If they were all to engage in this issue, their impact on wildlife and nature conservation would be inestimable and timely, because they have great influence on ordinary Thais, most of whom are practising Buddhists.

Though Buddhism is not strictly a religion but a philosophy of life, many Thais pray before a Buddha image every day. As yet the ecological teachings of Buddha are less influential than his advice on alleviating personal suffering. Indeed, while some temples encourage conservation, such as Wat Phai Lom, for example, others act against it by allowing the sale of trapped birds and turtles, which are then released 'to make merit'.

pioneering project to save Gurney's Pitta at Khao Phra Bang Kram had many conflicts of interest to contend with before local people and government began to see that a great deal more could be gained by protecting the pitta and its habitat than by destroying it. Birdwatchers already flock to the sanctuary to see its avian rarity and 230 other bird species, thereby helping the local economy; and that project is only five years old. The person who has done so much to teach people about Thai hornbills, Dr Pilai Poonswad, started her project 18 years ago but it is only in the last five years that her work has begun to get the support and recognition it deserves. To some extent this recognition reflects growing public interest in wildlife and its support for nature conservation, but it also reflects Dr Pilai's diligence in studying hornbill behaviour and ecology for years before she put her subjects forward as flagships of forest conservation.

Thailand has 12 hornbills, every one a forest species, all of them threatened. The poaching of nestlings is one threat but a bigger one is habitat loss. Hornbills are not adaptable birds. Their requirements are too specific. To survive in significant numbers, they need huge areas of intact forest with plenty of tall, mature trees because they cannot make their own nesting holes. They rely on finding trees with suitable cavities made by other species such as bears digging for termites. Once they are sure that a hole is not already occupied by squirrels or snakes or other hornbills, they can modify it to suit their needs but if they cannot find a suitable nesting hole, they do not breed. Therefore if a forest becomes too small or if too many tall trees are felled, hornbill populations will decline for want of food and nesting sites.

Many birds are more adaptable – some pheasants, for example. Green Peafowl (the largest pheasants of all) naturally inhabit open forests and grasslands in river valleys or plains but, were they not so assiduously hunted, they would adapt quite well to living in cultivated areas and scrubland as their cousins do in India. As it

is, they have been shot out all over Thailand except in Huai Kha Khaeng where about 300 birds live in the central river valley, protected by the absence of villages and the sanctuary's World Heritage status. Elsewhere, as in Phu Khieo, captive birds have recently been released and may establish wild populations, but reintroductions are notoriously tricky and expensive, and are not feasible for most species. Conservation is the better way to avoid localized extinctions and that is well under way, if belatedly, in Thailand.

Reptiles and Amphibians
Thailand's sizeable herpetofauna includes four types of reptile (chelonians, lizards, snakes and crocodiles) and three types of amphibian (frogs and toads, caecilians and a single salamander). Over 40 species appear to be endemic. Some, such as the Phu Wua Long-toed Lizard and the Spiny-breasted Frog of Khao Soi Dao, are restricted to certain mountains, while others, like Kanchanaburi Pit Vipers and the Siamese Warty Frog, are found within a region. One forest gecko of the north-east, *Cyrtodactylus jarujini*, is named after a leading herpetologist, Mr Jarujin Nabhitabhata. Other names reflect the fact that most early work on Thai amphibians and reptiles was done by western researchers.

The chelonians sub-divide into tortoises, freshwater turtles, marine turtles and softshell turtles. All are emblems of longevity in Thailand. It is possible to find metal or stone turtles carved with mystical signs all over the shell. Turtles are often released into temple ponds by people 'making merit'. Some live for years but many are now poisoned by polluted water, especially at urban temples. Sometimes people put tortoises in ponds, not knowing that they cannot swim.

Tortoises and freshwater turtles do look alike, but tortoises (of which there are three in Thailand) are denizens of forest floors whereas freshwater turtles, or terrapins, live near (but not always in) water. With 14 species, they are the most numerous Thai chelonians. Some, such as Big-headed Turtles and Box Terrapins, like small hill streams but others, including Temple Terrapins and Black Marsh Turtles, prefer shallow waters in lowland ponds, swamps and paddy fields. These habitats also support softshell turtles but the giant species (Asiatic and Narrow-headed) live in large rivers. Softshells are strange looking. They have flat bodies, long snouts and a leathery carapace. They also bite, unlike the trusting tortoise. Narrow-headed Softshells are endemic to the Mae Khlong basin and are the largest of their kind. They can be over a metre (3 feet) long and weigh up to 150 kilograms (330 pounds) but few large ones are found anymore. Like all turtles, they are coveted as food. Marine turtles are just as rare. They are not only killed for food and for their shells, but their eggs are eaten and they get tangled in nets. It is a wonder any survive. Thailand has four species. It used to have five, but the Loggerhead has gone.

Crocodiles have fared even worse. The three Thai species have all but gone from the wild although at least two Siamese ones survive in Khao Ang Ru Nai. They once enlivened the freshwater swamps of central Thailand but are now only numerous in farms, along with larger Estuarine Crocodiles, where they are bred for their skins. The slender-snouted False Gharial used to inhabit southern swamps but has now vanished completely.

There are plenty of snakes in Thailand still – 175 species, of which 25 are marine – but they are rarely seen except in the rains. Most Thai snakes are shy, but some emerge from flooded dens and sodden land to search for dry resting places such as houses. Cobras, racers and rat-snakes visit settled areas anyway because they feed on the rodents that proliferate with man. The same is true of the Reticulated Python, the world's longest snake. It can grow to 10 metres (30 feet) and is more aggressive than the other Thai constrictors. Rock and Blood Pythons prefer forest.

Thais do not like snakes any more than other people and tend to kill those that come too close to home, even though cobras are believed to have been guardians of Lord Buddha. There is also money to be made from selling snakes to travelling dealers who pass them on to accessory manufacturers and specialized food-stalls. These stalls sell food and tonics with fresh snake's blood as the key ingredient. They are drunk by the Chinese to boost vitality and sexual prowess. On top of the flourishing domestic trade, about 100,000 snakes used to be exported from Thailand each year. However, the drastic drop in snake numbers prompted by trade caused such an explosion of rats in rice-growing areas that rodent-eating species, and all pythons, are now protected.

Highly venomous snakes are not protected, however. Over half Thailand's snakes are venomous, but only 56 are dangerously so: the cobras, vipers, kraits and sea snakes. There are three types of Thai cobra: the King Cobra, Monocled Cobra and Spitting Cobra. The King Cobra is the most poisonous snake in the world because it is also the largest, up to 5 metres (16 feet) long, and therefore packs the most poison into one bite. Most Thai vipers are pit vipers. They have heat-sensing organs between their eyes and nostrils to help them detect prey and potential danger. The only true viper in Thailand, Russell's Viper, is responsible for most snake-bites because it is a lowland species which lives on the ground and tends to stay put when approached. Kraits are as poisonous but they are forest snakes.

Of the lizards, the four monitors are the least loved species in Thailand although they are also a favoured food. The largest is the Giant Water Monitor which can measure 2 metres (6 feet) from head to tail. (It is profoundly insulting to refer to someone as a monitor lizard, or *hia*, in Thai. The response could well be violent.) All other lizards – geckos, agamids and skinks – are thought of as good. In fact, no sensible house would be without its *chingchoks*

or *tokkaes* (common geckos with onomatopoeic Thai names) as they feed on noisome insects, including mosquitoes. Adhesive foot-pads enable them to run across ceilings and glass-smooth surfaces without falling. If caught, the tail falls off and continues to wriggle, thereby distracting the attacker. The gecko then grows a new tail. Skinks are inhabitants of forest floors. They are more easily seen in deciduous than in evergreen forest because they make more noise scuttling over dry fallen leaves but, once spotted, they freeze for minutes before daring to move again, their brown bodies blending into the undergrowth.

Frogs and toads are equally hard to see but as soon as the rains start and they begin their search for mates, their presence is very apparent. Some nights, they obliterate all other sound as they croak away together in discordant competition, like a symphony orchestra tuning up. Frogs and toads occur all over Thailand in almost every habitat, including urban drains, but the Crocodile Salamander (the only one of its kind in Thailand) is confined to a few northern mountains. Many frogs are eaten by rural Thais and this, together with the pollution and drying of waterways and lowland forest destruction, threatens some species. Amphibians are especially sensitive to environmental change because they have extra-permeable skins which absorb ambient toxins. Hence they are not as common in rice fields as they were before pesticides were introduced but they do flourish in the conservation areas.

WILD THAILAND AT RISK

Thailand is not particularly well known abroad for its wildlife, yet it has fabulous wilderness areas and a unique natural history. Few countries in Asia can rival its range of habitats and none shares its full flora and fauna. However, a celebration of Thailand's natural treasures must be moderated by the knowledge that the country's wildlife has suffered irreplaceable losses and is still faced with significant threats.

The single greatest change in the last 50 years has been the loss of forest cover. Besides diminishing wildlife, this has also exacerbated flooding, erosion and drought thereby bringing hardship to millions, but wetland reclamation, large reservoirs, intensive agriculture and pollution have done considerable damage too, as has mangrove clearance and over-fishing. Logging, poaching, poverty, mismanagement and corruption are usually given as primary causes of environmental degradation in the tropics, but these are influenced by population size, economic policy and inequalities of opportunity as well as by cultural traits such as a strong social hierarchy and traditional systems of power and patronage. As Thailand converts to an industrialized economy, new standards of aspiration are set by those who can afford them. The rest are disadvantaged, or feel themselves to be. Many will take what they can have free and, in rural areas, the best source is the forest: its land, its trees, its wildlife.

Human Population Growth
Thailand's human population has increased dramatically this century from 8 million people in 1900 to 57 million today. Growth rates have fallen but by the year 2000, Thailand will have 65 million people putting immense strain on its natural resources and environment, especially as urban areas (which use far more of everything than rural areas) are growing at twice the national average.

The Impact of Agriculture and Logging
As the population of Thailand grew, so more and more forest was cleared to make fields. Hill-tribe people are often identified as the

Roads are a necessity of modern life the world over, but their siting is not always entirely appropriate. In Thailand, when a conservation area acquires any sort of status the trend has been to build a major access road, converting a single-lane track to a two-lane highway with a mandatory treeless belt on either side. As well as increasing the volume of traffic, new roads encourage settlers, even in forest reserves. ABOVE LEFT The scenic road was recently built to link Chiang Mai and Mae Hong Son, opening up this remote north-west corner of Thailand. Although it clips off part of the Lum Nam Pai Wildlife Sanctuary, roads such as this are more readily justified than those which run right into a conservation area. Ironically, a metalled version of the narrow forest road (ABOVE CENTRE) is less damaging than the wide mud road (ABOVE RIGHT). A well-enclosed road is less divisive and threatening than a broad open expanse for terrestrial as well as arboreal animals.

principal culprits of forest clearance and they are certainly responsible for some of it, but much more extensive deforestation has occurred in the north-east, south-east, central and southern regions where there are no hill tribes. Forest there was cleared to create farmland for rice, rubber, oil palm, fruit trees, sugarcane and other crops, but many areas were first exploited by logging companies which then let people settle the land instead of allowing the forest to regenerate.

The 1989 logging ban slowed the rate of forest clearance considerably but Thai timber companies simply switched their attention to adjacent areas of Myanmar, Laos and Cambodia. This is likely to undermine Thailand's hydrological health almost as much and will deny it the cross-boundary transfer of species and genes that has enriched its flora and fauna for 40 million years. Logging affects so much more than just trees.

Meanwhile, illegal logging carries on in-country and people still encroach conserved forest land. Deforestation in the north is extra worrying because it affects the headwaters of the Chao Phraya river system upon which almost half the population of Thailand depends for water and irrigation. Northern forest has been cleared by timber companies, agribusinesses (intensive farming of temperate fruit and vegetables) and by subsistence farmers, most of them tribal people. Traditionally, hill tribes

practise swidden or slash-and-burn agriculture. This means felling a patch of forest, burning the debris to fertilize the soil, growing crops for two to three years, then letting the land lie fallow for several years until the soil has revived. Several fields are cultivated in rotation, creating a patchwork of colours and textures across the mountain slopes. This system works well while few people occupy large areas of forest land but, as numbers increase, it becomes less viable.

There is too little forest left now to provide much free food and rice yields are so low that many villagers run out before the next harvest. Yet most hill people, like lowland people, are beginning to want the accoutrements of modern life and buying them requires the kind of cash that only logs, opium, cash-crop farming and tourism can provide. And so the hills and hill peoples are changing. They are no longer as secure or as self-sufficient as they were. Their way of life is nowadays governed by money, as it is everywhere else.

However, some people, both tribal and Thai, are resisting that trend. All over Thailand there are farmers who maintain, and even revert to, traditional systems of farming wherein a variety of useful trees, shrubs, herbs and crops are grown together in such a way as to keep soil fertile, reduce pests and provide food year-round. An advanced form of natural farming is found in the south around Suratthani. There farmers turn patches of forest into managed, but semi-wild, gardens with cultivated plants (including fruit-trees) mixed in with valued native plants.

A similar, but less integrated system, is practised by the Karen people of west Thailand whose way of life is still more or less traditional. They do clear and burn forest for fields, which is a problem in conservation areas, but the plants they grow are mixed and varied and they keep natural forest around villages to harvest for wild plants and protein.

Elsewhere, many Thai villages maintain community woodlands to harvest in similar ways but, by and large, these are small and scattered. Some protect local watershed slopes, others give refuge to small animals and all of them are preferable to plantations from a conservation point of view, but none can substitute for the large areas of natural forest which survive in most conservation areas. They do not protect anything like a full complement of wildlife.

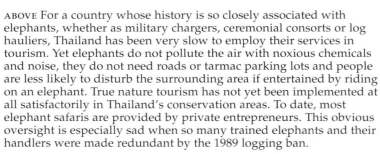

ABOVE For a country whose history is so closely associated with elephants, whether as military chargers, ceremonial consorts or log hauliers, Thailand has been very slow to employ their services in tourism. Yet elephants do not pollute the air with noxious chemicals and noise, they do not need roads or tarmac parking lots and people are less likely to disturb the surrounding area if entertained by riding on an elephant. True nature tourism has not yet been implemented at all satisfactorily in Thailand's conservation areas. To date, most elephant safaris are provided by private entrepreneurs. This obvious oversight is especially sad when so many trained elephants and their handlers were made redundant by the 1989 logging ban.

ABOVE RIGHT One of the least intrusive ways for tourists to explore Thailand's waterways is by canoe. Such small craft can slip in and out of narrow canals causing minimal disturbance to the environment and animal inhabitants.

THE HISTORY OF NATURE CONSERVATION IN THAILAND

Conservation did not really engage the public's interest until the late 1980s when two issues – the Nam Choan hydro-dam and the corruption of concessionary logging – were the subjects of the first national campaigns to challenge the government's right to dictate Thailand's development agenda without reference to ordinary people's interests. Since then, the conservation movement has grown dramatically as the country faces ever more serious environmental problems. But the story of nature conservation in Thailand began many years earlier.

In theory, it should have started in the 1890s when the Royal Forest Department was formed, as that agency was supposed to manage the kingdom's forest reserves in such a way as to ensure that they provided timber in perpetuity. Under a succession of Reserve Forest Acts, lowland and foothill forests were divided into concessions of 30 plots, one of which was to be logged each year, leaving immature trees, gallery forest and some mature trees as seed-banks. Logged plots were to be protected to allow regeneration. After 30 years, the first plot would then have been ready to log again. In fact, this procedure was rarely, if ever, followed. Instead, every tree of value was cut and settlers (often company employees) then took over the land for farming.

Another largely ineffectual conservation act was the Wild Elephant Protection Act of 1921. At that time, elephants were the

only means of hauling logs out of the forest. They were therefore immensely valuable to the logging industry and yet the logging industry was accelerating their decline. Essentially, this act controlled the capture of wild elephants in order to ensure a future supply of them for the domestic market.

More substantive conservation began in the 1960s with the introduction of two radical new laws: the National Park Act and the Wild Animal Reservation and Protection Act. These established the legal basis for national parks and wildlife sanctuaries and, in the latter, regulations governing wildlife trade. One man, Dr Boonsong Lekagul, was largely responsible for their promulgation.

Dr Boonsong was a medical doctor and a keen and practised hunter, as a result of which he got to know and love Thailand's wildlife. After years of travelling the country in search of game, he noticed that many mammals were becoming rare. He therefore took to lobbying government to establish wildlife protection laws and conservation areas. Dr Boonsong also started the first conservation NGO (non-government organization) in Thailand, the Association for the Conservation of Wildlife. Some ten years later, in 1984, this became Wildlife Fund Thailand. In that time, Dr Boonsong produced more books about Thai wildlife than anyone else has done since. In that, he was helped by a succession of young enthusiasts who have gone on to become major contributors to wildlife conservation and public education in Thailand. They included Jeffrey McNeely, Jarujin Nabhitabhata and Philip Round.

Conservation Areas

Khao Yai was the first area to be established in Thailand. It was gazetted in 1962. Since then, 77 national parks and 36 wildlife sanctuaries have been created, together with some 40 non-hunting areas, most of which are wetlands. National parks combine conservation with tourism, whereas wildlife sanctuaries are not generally open to the public. They are meant for research and biodiversity conservation. Non-hunting areas are important sites, usually wetlands, where fish and some plants can be harvested by local people. Altogether, the conservation areas cover about 13 per cent of the total land area of Thailand, a figure that is rivalled by few tropical countries. Forty areas are rather small, but 20 are over 1,000 square kilometres (3,800 square miles) and some of those are contiguous, making quite sizeable areas in total.

The single largest conservation area is the Thung Yai Wildlife Sanctuary, with 3,622 square kilometres (1,398 square miles) but that lies at the centre of nine contiguous parks and sanctuaries which cover some 14,000 square kilometres (5,000 square miles). This is by far the largest such area in mainland South-east Asia and one of the largest in Asia. It also supports one of the richest floras and faunas in the region. In 1991, it became a prestigious UNESCO World Heritage Site in recognition of its 'universal value and importance'. In fact this appellation was applied only to the core areas, Thung Yai and Huai Kha Khaeng, but the areas around are as important and, in the case of Mae Wong as good, because they help maintain the integrity of Thung Yai–Huai Kha Khaeng. Meanwhile, the Khao Yai and Tarutao National Parks have become ASEAN Heritage Sites.

Turning Points

Apart from the pioneering influence of Dr Boonsong, three particular events became turning points in the history of nature conservation in Thailand. The first was the Nam Choan Dam Campaign of the 1980s. Before this campaign, there had been few environmental protests in Thailand, and those were localized. The Nam Choan protest was the first nationwide conservation event to unite the entire spectrum of opposition from government divisions to NGOs, students, local people, the public and media. The issue was whether or not to build a hydro-electric dam inside Thung Yai. The dam would have provided a bit more electricity (about one per cent) but it would have split the sanctuary into two parts and flooded its central valley system, thereby inflicting terminal damage. It would also have increased the probability of a major earthquake in the region. Kanchanaburi province already had three hydro-dams and local people knew what to expect and what promises not to believe. The campaign had several consequences. First it succeeded, and proved that ordinary people could win against powerful odds. Second, it raised the question of government accountability in the use of natural resources and forced powers-that-be to accept that there is more than one way to cost environmental benefits. Third, it made people aware of the issues concerning conservation and development and reasons for worrying about environmental degradation.

No sooner had the Nam Choan Dam been shelved than another threat emerged. A revised interpretation of the Wildlife Act allowed loggers into the sanctuaries. At that time, wildlife sanctuaries were the only properly protected areas, and they covered just 4 per cent of the country; even national parks could be logged. The first victim of this revised ruling was to be Huai Kha Khaeng, the finest single conservation area in the country. But as a fresh campaign started it was pre-empted by cataclysmic floods in the south. It had rained non-stop for a week and then, late one night, the mountain sides of Phipun started to slip. By morning, the entire valley was buried under metres of silt and debris, thousands of people were dead, thousands more were destitute and the damage ran to billions of baht. Here was evidence of the effects of environmental neglect. It soon became clear that the landslides were caused by excessive clearance by legal loggers, and all over the country other loggers had done the same. So the press and public called for a logging ban and, in under six weeks, they got it.

The third most memorable event to date was the death of Seub Nakhasathien. In the last five years of his life, Seub had became one of Thailand's best known and most respected conservationists. He was an official with the Wildlife Conservation Division of the Royal Forest Department and was unusually dedicated, hard-working and honest. He was also unassuming, gentle and kind. He began to get actively involved in conservation campaigning after he managed the Chiew Larn Dam animal rescue project. First-hand experience of the impact of a large dam on wild animals and their habitat had so appalled him that he took a public stand against the Nam Choan Dam, risking official reprimand. Later that year, he also opposed the plan to log part of Huai Kha Khaeng. When that threat subsided, he was asked to take over as warden of the sanctuary. He would have preferred to continue with field research, but he knew and loved the sanctuary well and it was in trouble, plagued by hunters and loggers. His superiors believed that only he could stop them, so he took up the post towards the end of 1989, confident that he would get the help he needed. After months of frustration and opposition he lost all hope of ever helping Huai Kha Khaeng. On 1 September 1990, he shot himself at his house in the sanctuary. His death was mourned by millions, his funeral was sponsored by HM The King, and his banner was taken up by colleagues and friends who collected enough money from admirers nationwide to establish a conservation foundation. Today the Seub Nakhasathien Foundation, though small, is one of the most influential NGOs in Thailand and Huai Kha Khaeng is the flagship of forest conservation.

WILD THAILAND: THE FUTURE

Although every conservation area has problems, more and more people do now value them for their indirect, as well as their direct, benefits. Even so, most people would be surprised to know that just two of the country's some 150 wilderness areas (Thung Yai–Huai Kha Khaeng and Khao Yai) are estimated to yield hundreds of millions of baht a year in indirect benefits. The value of watershed protection alone is US$14 million per year, according to one study. Sadly, such evaluations – beneficial to the country as a whole – do not stop individuals from orchestrating forest exploition for their own gain.

However, Thailand does have two great advantages over most countries in Asia: it has a relatively free and prolific press and it has some courageous and effective NGOs. To some extent, that is why it has unflattering, as well as flattering, reputations. People know more about what is going on in Thailand than they do about other countries in the region where customs are similar but information is suppressed. It is very much to Thailand's credit that this is so. It may also be its saving grace, for the media and NGOs not only keep the government in check, they also push for change. Without them, Thailand would not have made the remarkable progress it has in conserving nature in the last ten years.

The country's many Buddhist monks may also contribute to conservation in future. Buddha's teachings make many references to nature and the need to maintain the natural balance – a principle known as *silatham* – but, to date, only a few monks have been actively engaged in promoting conservation. One of the most respected is Ajarn Pongsak. This beatific man was the abbot of Wat Prathat on Doi Suthep when he founded the Dhammanaat Foundation, a small charity which teaches self-help conservation to villagers using Buddhist principles of harmony and restraint. The more his teachings took effect, the more opposition he aroused among those with commercial interests in the area. He preferred to leave the monkhood altogether rather than become involved in unseemly dispute over attempts to discredit him. Now wearing white instead of yellow robes, he continues his work with an undiminished following.

The Mixed Blessings of Tourism

Thailand is a wonderful place for a holiday. The people are friendly, the food is delicious, the culture is varied, the wild places are wonderful, the weather is warm and most of the beaches are

FAR LEFT Uncontrolled hunting is still a major threat to Thai wildlife in spite of protection laws. All kinds of methods are used, from shooting to trapping and poisoning. Here a captive Grey-headed Parakeet will be used to lure a wild member of its species to a limed trap placed in a tree. LEFT Brightly plumaged birds such as this are popular as cage-birds and some species have become rare as a direct result of the trade.

LEFT Wild animal parts are available to determined buyers anywhere in Thailand, but are rarely as conspicuously displayed as this except in border markets where policing is more difficult. This shop has been set up on the Myanmar side of Mae Sai, out of reach of Thai law enforcers but accessible to Thai buyers. In this one shop alone there are python, tiger, leopard and clouded leopard skins (SEEN ABOVE) as well as hornbill casques, serow heads, bears' paws, tiger teeth and penises, tortoise shells, dried pangolins, every kind of horn, and other animal parts. It is well-nigh impossible for Thailand's conservation authorities to police thousands of kilometres along the border without the help of every government agency and co-operating citizens. Nor does it help that the legal penalties are often cheaper than the goods themselves.

LEFT Marine fishing has long governed the way of life of coastal communities in Thailand. Traditionally, fishermen used low-impact methods to catch the fish they needed. But fish stocks in Thai seas have now been severely depleted by the commercial fishing fleet which uses intensive trawler nets, catching (and killing) unwanted species and immature and undersize fish as well as those of market size. In the last 30 years, Thailand's trawler fleet has grown from 100 boats to over 12,000, causing untold damage to the country's marine resources and to traditional fishing communities. The severity of this problem is well recognized and there are regulations governing net size, but policing has not yet proved effective.

RIGHT Forests regulate the flow of water better than any man-made reservoir or barrage, so denuded slopes such as these in the north-west province of Mae Hong Son, cleared by farmers using the slash-and-burn method, are cause for concern. Forests have been cleared this way all over Thailand, but the problem is especially worrying in the north because it is being cleared by both lowland and hill people, with the result that the watershed slopes of the Chao Phraya river are doubly threatened, from above and from below. The impact of this is already being felt in the central plains and in Bangkok, where water is no longer assured year round and flooding is ever more erratic.

BELOW LEFT Timber used to be one of Thailand's most lucrative export commodities. Unfortunately, the selective felling system as required by law was not implemented, with the result that this supposedly sustainable resource was seriously depleted by the 1980s and the impact of indiscriminate logging was evident. A nationwide ban in 1989 cancelled most legal logging overnight, but it has not stopped illegal felling although it must have reduced the scale of it. The logs shown here lay just outside a conservation area.

BELOW RIGHT Thailand is plagued by fires every single year. Few, if any, are natural, and most are uncontrolled. They are lit to clear old crops, to keep scrub down, to facilitate hunting, for convenience or by accident. Inevitably, they spread into deciduous forest and scrub, not only impeding forest regeneration but weakening mature forest stands. Dry dipterocarp forest is fire-resistant but mixed deciduous forest is not: so fire encourages the conversion of the richer forest type into its poorer counterpart. As fires become more frequent and more forceful they reach into the evergreen formations, thereby undermining them as well and threatening dependent species. Many ecologists believe that fire poses the greatest long-term threat to forest and wildlife conservation in Thailand.

Conservation in Thailand, as in many other countries, calls for tireless dedication and commitment. ABOVE LEFT Forest rangers are among those prepared to accept daily risks but in recent years have seen improvements to their service with the provision of better equipment and training. LEFT Their greatest advocate was Seub Nakhasathien, one of Thailand's most diligent and knowledgeable wildlife champions. His untimely death in September 1990 shocked not just his fellow conservationists but the general public, for whom he became a national hero. ABOVE RIGHT The twice life-size bronze statue which stands beside the house in which he died in Huai Kha Khaeng Wildlife Sanctuary has become something of a shrine, where people come to honour his memory.

OPPOSITE PAGE Huai Kha Khaeng, pride of Thailand's protected area system, owes much to Seub Nakhasathien, who helped to make the sanctuary a World Heritage Site.

magical. Little wonder, then, that the country has become a major tourist destination. The number of visitors grew from under two million in 1981 to over five million in 1990. Revenues also increased and tourism is now the leading source of foreign exchange. Predictably, this influx of visitors has also caused problems, some social (such as the disruption of hill-tribe villages), some aesthetic (such as obtrusive seaside construction) and some environmental.

Tourist development in Thailand has not adhered to the Buddhist principle of *silatham*, or balance. The sea off Pattaya is now so polluted by human waste that it is unsafe to swim in. The wells of Phi Phi island, a national park, are similarly contaminated. Many coral reefs are so badly damaged by the anchors of tourist boats and by curio collectors that some have died. And no national park has yet implemented effective nature tourism.

To date, nature tourism in Thailand means tourism in areas of natural beauty, not tourism that is managed in sympathy with nature, to do no harm to wildlife. As a result, there are no controls and facilities are often inappropriate, witness the link-road that runs right through Khao Yai. And yet nature tourism, properly managed, could be a tremendous force for good without doing very much harm. It would earn the parks much-needed revenue, it would involve more local people in park management so that they, too, had an interest in the survival and improvement of parks as conservation areas, and it would make people more aware of Thailand's fabulous natural heritage. Above all, it would encourage urban Thais to become better acquainted with the natural character of their country. The more they learn to love it, the more secure its future will be, and the greater the chance that the stunning beauty of wild Thailand will survive for future generations to enjoy.

Focus on
NORTH THAILAND

Conjure up an image of an accordian with its pleats and you have some idea of the contrasting peaks and troughs that run the whole way across northern Thailand and adjacent parts of Myanmar (Burma). The north is essentially a series of mountain ridges folded between two mighty offshoots of the Himalayan Range: the Dawna-Tenasserim and the Annamitic Chain.

This huge region makes up roughly 20 per cent of the country's land area. Not only the most mountainous, it includes Doi Inthanon, the country's highest mountain, located some 60 kilometres (37 miles) south-west of Chiang Mai. (*Doi* is the northern Thai word for mountain.) The town of Chiang Mai is the only one in Thailand to have a national park, the forested Doi Suthep, by its back door.

The northern border is sealed by both mountain ranges and rivers and this boundary follows the line of one, then another. Starting from the colourful, multi-ethnic town of Mae Sot, just 5 kilometres (3 miles) from Myanmar in the west, travelling northwards, the border is confined by the Moei and Salween rivers and then by the Daen Lao Range which links some of the country's

highest peaks including Doi Ang Khang, Doi Pha Hom Pok and Doi Tung. The border joins a tributary of the Mekong at the frontier town of Mae Sai, Thailand's most northerly point, and then the mighty Mekong itself.

The Mekong, in fact, forms the national boundary in the north for less than 100 kilometres (60 miles) before it veers west into Laos, past the former royal capital of Louang Prabang, and then flows south to frame Thailand's north-east frontier. The rest of the north's border runs as a vertical line along the Louang Prabang mountain range, the upper part of the Dong Phaya Yen Range dotted with *dois* of 1,800 metres (5,900 feet) and more. When it meets the Mae Heung, another tributary of the Mekong, it passes from the north to the country's north-east.

Between the Thanon Thongchai and the Louang Prabang ranges which divide the drainage of the Salween and Mekong rivers from the rest of northern Thailand, three other ranges squeeze into this folded landmass: the Inthanon Range which boasts Thailand's highest mountain and lies due west of Chiang Mai; the Khun Tan Range which includes Doi Mae Tho and lies due east of Chiang

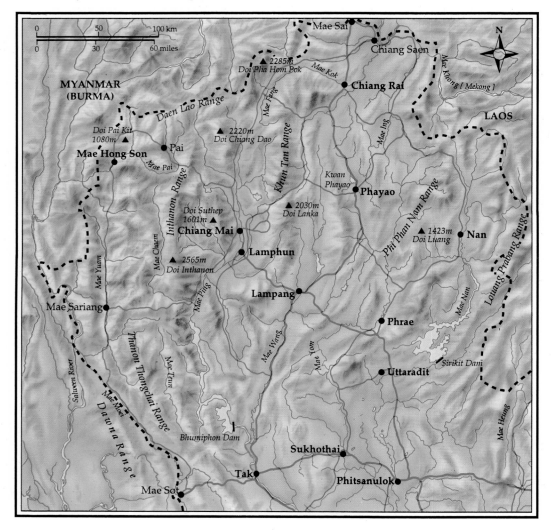

OPPOSITE PAGE Makeshift shelters are scattered in fields of rice, maize and banana trees against the verdant background of tall, evergreen forests that cover the higher altitudes of northern Thailand. This sloping terrain between Chiang Mai and Mae Hong Son presents a typical view of the north. Like other forested mountain ridges of the region it is occupied by hilltribes whose villages tend to be some distance from their cultivated fields, hence the shelters against the harsh sun or heavy rains. For those who visit Thailand, the north is a feast for the eye. For those who live there, and that includes most of the country's minority hilltribes, the forests and many river valleys that flow south are their economic and cultural lifeblood. The hilltribes naturally gravitate to where the soil is best for cultivation and that happens to be the best forest areas. Trees are cleared to plant crops, which is an especial problem for the north because the region is the well-head of Thailand, the mainstay of the country's water system. The forest canopy catches the rain and filters it down to the root system which acts as a natural reservoir, regulating the release of water down the slopes that feed eventually into the rivers. Without this forest 'watershed' the rains would simply run away, taking the topsoil with them, and the rivers would swell quickly. Deforestation therefore leads to the double catastrophe of floods in the rainy season and drought in the dry season. So in the north, more than in any other region of Thailand, the country must reconcile the demands of upland and lowland people with the conservation of nature.

Mai; and the Phi Phan Nam (meaning 'ghosts of a thousand waters') which has Doi Luang and lies further east again. These five ranges separate the four main rivers of the north, the Mae Ping, Mae Wang, Mae Yom and Mae Nan. When these rivers unite just north of Nakhon Sawan, they form the great Chao Phraya river, Thailand's vital lifeline into Bangkok and the rice bowl of the central plains.

All these rivers rise within north Thailand and, at present, only the Mae Yom survives undammed. The other three have dams built to control flooding and to supply water for rice cultivation in the central plains and to the metropolis of Bangkok. The Mae Yom thus has added ecological value as the only major waterway in the upper Chao Phraya Basin that still harbours native fish which migrate upriver to breed.

The folds of rivers and ridges that mark out the north of Thailand are thinly populated by picturesque peoples who make up the assorted hilltribes collectively called *Chao Khao*, Thai for 'Mountain People'. The true natives are Lanna Thai, *Lanna* meaning 'Million Ricefields'. They are descendants from the old kingdom that was ruled from Chiang Mai from the thirteenth to the sixteenth century. The hill peoples' distinctively embroidered and decorated costumes help to identify respective 'tribes' and find a ready market among tourists.

One of the best-known landmarks in the far north is the

infamous Golden Triangle, the region that encompasses the border highlands of Myanmar, Laos and Thailand and produces much of the world's opium (mostly in Myanmar). This dark, sticky resin is worth its weight in gold. Even though its cultivation is banned in all these countries, the opium poppy is still cultivated on some slopes above 1,000 metres (3,280 feet). At these high altitudes, which pose no problem for the plant, it is grown beyond the reach of the law. Most of the area comprises remote, uncharted uplands covering several thousand square kilometres.

Official sources claim that roughly half the north is covered with forest, therefore retaining more forest cover than other parts of Thailand. In reality, however, much of it is degraded and northern forests are under threat to much higher altitudes than elsewhere since they are home to mountain peoples as well as to lowland Thai and Karen.

The forest settlers' reliance on slash-and-burn farming, or shifting cultivation, has had an increasingly harmful impact on the region's once-abundant forests. It is a low-intensity form of farming where forest is cleared through burning, cultivated for a few years to grow rice, vegetables or sometimes opium, and then left to grow again over 10 to 30 years. In the meantime the farmers clear another tract of forest. Secondary forest, typically lower growing and less dense, gradually reclaims the clearings. This pattern of agriculture is revealed in hillside patchworks made up of abandoned clearings, secondary and primary forest. If the populations are small this system does not cause serious disturbance. But populations have grown and, as the forest settlers are farmers who naturally prefer land with good soil and water, they have moved into lowland areas with mixed deciduous forest and evergreen strips following the lines of streams. In the uplands, they have concentrated on the seasonal evergreen forests rather than the poorer vegetation of higher altitudes.

This has meant that the forests that are cleared first are those with the highest biological diversity, for soils that give higher crop yields are also those that support more life. The forests have also suffered from the preferential logging of teak from mixed deciduous forest, the subsequent harvesting of hardwoods from all timber-rich formations, the steady increase in lowland Thai farmers, the fires that have swept through many forests each year and the hunting that has accompanied such encroachments. Add all these incursions together and the threat to the north's natural environment becomes clear.

In the wild north today many plants and animals verge on local, if not absolute, extinction. Of the 1,300 species of orchid in Thailand there are two species found exclusively in the north, including *Vanda coerulea*, better known locally as *Fa Mui*. Such plants are especially vulnerable, as are many bird species including pheasants, vultures, wood ducks and most of the hornbills. Outside the conservation areas, few large mammals now survive. Goral and Serow goat-antelopes cling on in small numbers because they inhabit inhospitable mountain terrain and are surer-footed than human hunters. Black Bears are nocturnal and secretive so some still snuffle around the higher evergreen forests, but few gibbons live there with them anymore. Barking Deer and boar breed twice a year, maintaining small numbers that way. Tigers have been hunted to virtual extinction as have the wild Banteng cattle. Elephants are reduced to one tiny wild population in the Omkoi Wildlife Sanctuary. Their story of survival is perhaps the saddest of all, for they helped the logging industry that brought about their demise in the wild and now does not need them, so their captive numbers have plummeted as well.

The logging business began in the north because that is the only part of Thailand that ever supported teak. Teak is a hardwood with exceptionally high resistance to pests and disease and a fine

Stilted houses of the Karen tribe perch on dry slopes near the Mae Moei river which forms the boundary with Myanmar, the Karen's original homeland. The Karen are the largest tribe in Thailand with over a quarter of a million living in the north; another 3 million live in Myanmar.

grain that is easy to carve. This makes it the most valued wood for buildings and furniture. In the past teak was the only timber taken but it was never especially plentiful, for although it grew throughout the north, it was confined to rich, moist soils in the deciduous forest belt below about 750 metres (2,500 feet). By the 1960s, no teak forest remained pristine and today it is an endangered forest type. The best surviving stand of it is in the Mae Yom National Park.

Mae Yom is one of 24 conservation areas in the north that all together cover some 14,730 square kilometres (5,685 square miles), or 13 per cent of the total land area and about 24 per cent of remaining forest cover. This compares well with the rest of Thailand and, indeed, with most other countries in Asia. Six conservation areas are over 1,000 square kilometres (386 square miles), all but seven cover 400 square kilometres (155 square miles) or more, and ten are contiguous (made up of five pairs). Sadly, few are free of human settlement and the damage this can cause.

Nevertheless these conservation areas do help to protect a remarkable array of forests and wildlife. Some forest types can be found elsewhere in Thailand, but the higher range of altitudes and temperatures, with the more sheltered slopes and deep colluvial valleys, endow the north with vegetation unique to the region. Slope, soils and altitude determine which forest grows where, but the main natural vegetation types of the north are deciduous forests and seasonal evergreen forests with a variety of coniferous and broadleaf formations. The north has three vegetation types found only in this region: mixed deciduous–teak forest; a montane scrub found only on Doi Chiang Dao; and upper montane forest above 1,800 metres (5,900 feet) where there is a prevailing belt of mist or cloud. The best example of the last type is the dense tract that occurs on the shoulders of Doi Inthanon above 2,200 metres (7,215 feet).

Among the Sino-Himalayan mammals seeking refuge in the northern highlands, the largest are Goral and Black Bear. Chinese Porcupines, Siberian Weasels, Père David's Vole and the Harlequin Bat are some of the smaller mammals found there. But mammal numbers are insignificant compared to the plants, birds and insects that are found only in these northern peaks. At least 58 species of breeding birds are found only in the higher habitats of this region. Only five resident lowland birds are confined to the north, among them the Pale-headed Woodpecker of evergreen forests by the Mekong, and the Black-backed Forktail of rocky streams in Mae Hong Son.

For reasons that are not clear, the Khun Tan Range acts as a barrier for some resident birds. It runs roughly down the centre of the north, east of Chiang Mai, from Doi Pha Hom Pok to the Bhumiphon Dam. A few lowland species found due west of it, including Kalij Pheasants, are of Indo-Burmese origin while others found due east, such as Siamese Firebacks and Coral-billed Ground Cuckoos, originate from Indo-China. Even some montane birds do not occur west of the Khun Tan Range.

Despite the predominance of forests and mountains, north Thailand also has important plains wetlands which give refuge to thousands of waterbirds. The ploughed paddy fields and reed beds of the Tha Ton marshes, above where the Mae Kok and Mae Fang rivers meet, teem with migrants at the end of each year. The ponds in the Chiang Saen Basin and nearby banks of the Mekong are a staging-post for species flying south and a base for over-wintering shorebirds and ducks as well as riverbank residents. In one year alone 76 species were recorded here including Spot-billed Ducks, the only site this bird is ever seen in Thailand.

Golden light over the Golden Triangle. The Mekong river in the foreground touches the northern Thai border here and links the borders of Myanmar, Laos and Thailand. In the higher, more inaccessible reaches above 1,000 metres (4,000 feet) the opium crops are grown, making this the world's major opium-producing area.

Doi Suthep–Doi Pui

This national park of 261 square kilometres (100 square miles) is the pride of Chiang Mai, Thailand's second largest city. Few modern cities can boast such a splendid backdrop. The park is named after two forested mountains immediately west of the city, Doi Suthep and Doi Pui,which rise majestically from suburban foothills at 360 metres (1,180 feet) to the highest peak of Doi Pui at 1,685 metres (5,527 feet). Doi Suthep is a park of great significance because it supports a remarkable flora with over 2,000 flowering plant species – far more than any other studied area of seasonal tropical forest – some of which are not known elsewhere. The forest itself is a mix of deciduous and evergreen, with evergreen dominating at around 900 metres (2,952 feet), although semi-evergreen forests fill gulleys and waterways at lower elevations. These forests are filled year-round with flowers and a profusion of exotic birds, butterflies and small mammals, and are home to an endemic warty frog.

It is vital that Chiang Mai learns to value this extraordinary public asset, particularly as human encroachments such as the 14,000 tribal settlers (90 per cent of whom settled within the last decade), government buildings and poorly managed tourism have done much harm. Already the park has lost most of its primates as well as the hornbills that once dispersed one-tenth of its forest tree seeds.

The complementary colours of the flowering deciduous forest on the lower slopes of Doi Suthep provide a fantastic backdrop to Chiang Mai. The park is recognized as one of the city's greatest assets.

RIGHT A splash of blue in a sea of green, the audacious Blue Magpie (*Urocissa erythrorhyncha*) is attracted to areas used by humans so, although rare, it is seen in the highly visited Doi Suthep park, especially on the forested slopes below the temple of Wat Phra That.

BELOW LEFT Eye-catching 'snake-head' wing-tips identify two mating Giant Atlas Moths (*Attacus atlas*). The unusual mirror-image patterning is believed to act as a deterrent to predators such as squirrels. As its name suggests, the moth has a large wing-span reaching up to 330 millimetres (13 inches), and is the largest of the three species of atlas moth found all over Asia in untouched deciduous and evergreen forests. It is a member of the silk moth Saturnidae family which make silken cocoons.

BELOW RIGHT The smaller male Giant Atlas Moth hangs from the larger female during mating. The male can be recognized also by the antennae which detect the pheromone emitted by the female.

Doi Inthanon

Doi Inthanon was made a national park to protect Thailand's highest mountain as well as four of the Mae Ping's main tributaries. The towering centrepiece of this 482-square-kilometre (186-square-mile) park is the eponymous granite massif of 2,565 metres (8,415 feet) named after Chiang Mai's last ruling prince. Being 300 metres (984 feet) higher than any other Thai mountain puts it in a conservation category of its own: for it is the only place in the country high enough to support a sizeable tract of upper montane forest. This dense evergreen forest has oaks, chestnuts and magnolias more usually associated with temperate climes; but here the trees are festooned in epiphytic flowering plants, ferns, lichens and mosses which like the cooler temperatures and high humidity.

The mountain is often cloaked in cloud but this does not conceal the brilliant colours of many local birds such as Blue-winged Minlas, Green Cochoas and Red-headed Trogons. The summit has a sphagnum bog, the only one in Thailand, where Green-tailed Sunbirds congregate to feed. These birds are unique to Doi Inthanon. Other birds like the Ashy-throated Warbler, and mammals such as the Szechuan Burrowing Shrew, are also confined to this mountain, as are many Palearctic birds which take refuge during their annual migration. Despite many threats, this park remains a paradise for birdwatchers and fertile ground for students of ecology.

The view from the summit of Doi Inthanon presents a landscape of tree-top diversity. This mountain is higher than any other in Thailand and harbours many high-altitude plant and animal specialities. In the foreground lies hill evergreen forest while lower down dry evergreen forests take over. It is the middle elevations between 1,200–1,500 metres (4,000–5,000 feet) that have been most depleted by human encroachment; great swaths cleared for agriculture can be seen in the distance. Thankfully the conservation efforts of recent years have put some brakes on deforestation.

ABOVE Many of Doi Inthanon's surviving mammals are nocturnal, including this Common Palm Civet (*Paradoxurus hermaphroditus*). This masked hunter is a forest animal but adapts well to areas of human habitation where it feeds on mice and cultivated fruit.

BELOW LEFT Sharp quills some 200 millimetres (8 inches) long protrude from the hindquarters and tail of the aptly named Long-quilled Porcupine (*Hystrix brachyura*). When threatened, it stamps its feet, snorts, and rattles its tail. If that fails to deter a would-be predator, the porcupine will charge backwards with quills raised to stab its assailant.

BELOW RIGHT A mating pair of White-eyed Toad-frogs (*Leptobrachium chapaense*), found in the higher reaches of Doi Inthanon above 1,000 metres (3,280 feet). There are around 40 species of amphibians alone in the streams of this park.

ABOVE The spectacular Vachirathan waterfall on the Mae Klang river has a sheer drop of 50 metres (164 feet). Located half-way up Doi Inthanon, it is one of the park's most stunning sights. The river not only attracts sightseers but also a variety of birds which favour rocky rushing streams, such as the dark slaty-coloured Plumbeous Redstart with its reddish-chestnut tail and the River Chat with its striking chestnut-red rump and tail ending in a distinctive black band.

RIGHT The Mae Klang is one of several important tributaries of the Mae Ping, and one of the first sights to greet visitors to the park. The public road up Doi Inthanon overlooks this river through much of its course as it winds its way from deciduous to evergreen forest.

LEFT A Changeable Hawk Eagle (*Spizaetus cirrhatus*) eyes the forest floor intently. It is a mountain species, most often seen along the western border of north Thailand, although it is nowhere common. Fortunately, birds of prey are not yet significantly threatened in Thailand (with the exception of vultures) as they are not commonly hunted or kept in captivity. Most of them are forest birds of high mountain areas where they suffer less from human interference than coveted low-altitude species.

BELOW LEFT In contrast to birds of prey, pheasants are widely hunted in Thailand for food and for the captive bird trade. Consequently the striking Silver Pheasant (*Lophura nycthemera*) is likely to be seen only in well-protected conservation areas of north and north-east Thailand. It is found on the higher slopes of mountain ridges, such as Doi Inthanon, foraging in the evergreen forests between 700 and 2,000 metres (2,300–6,500 feet).

BELOW RIGHT A bright red face instantly identifies the rare resident Red-faced Liocichla (*Liocichla phoenicea*). This bird dwells only near the summits of the very highest mountains of the extreme north. Isolated mountains, such as Doi Inthanon, are equivalent to islands and this explains the scattered distribution of such song-babblers. The northern mountain parks and sanctuaries are extremely important in protecting both resident and migrant mountain birds.

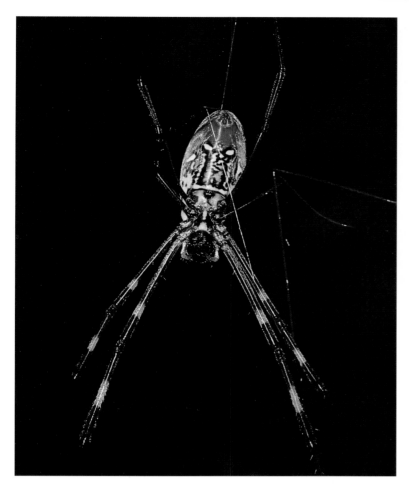

ABOVE The strongly contrasting yellow and black stripes of this timber beetle (*Eurybatus formosus*) appear to mimic the warning coloration of a stinging wasp. The female is thought to use her long sensory antennae to gauge the width of a trunk or branch before laying her eggs. The larvae bore further into the centre of the wood and adults will later emerge using their powerful jaws to gnaw their way out. This is one of 35,000 species of timber beetle found worldwide.

ABOVE The striking yellow spots and strong red marking identify this female Golden Orb Weaver (*Nephila maculata*). This species of spider is widely distributed over the north of Thailand and indeed over the whole of Southeast Asia.

RIGHT On the higher reaches of Doi Inthanon above 2,500 metres (8,200 feet) pink and white orchids drape the moss-covered branches of a hill-evergreen tree. The pink orchid on the left is *Pleione praecox* and the white orchid to the right is *Dendrobium wattii*.

ABOVE The trumpet-shaped flowers of this red *Aeschynanthus* species show the long stamens typical of plants that deposit pollen on the back of pollinators, such as sunbirds, which hover while they insert their long curving beaks into the flower to extract the nectar. Like the Golden Balsam (ABOVE LEFT) this plant is rare and confined to the upper montane forests of the north.

ABOVE LEFT Commonly known as Golden Balsam, *Impatiens longiloba* is a rare species found in the moist hill-evergreen forests of the north.

LEFT Another rare inhabitant of the hill-evergreen forests of the north is the *Agapates hosseana* shrub which is an epiphyte belonging to the heather family. The summit slopes of Doi Inthanon are an important conservation area for all the plants featured here.

LEFT Many flowering plants found near the summit of Doi Inthanon are more typically associated with south China and the Himalayas. This yellow cup belongs to the threatened species *Hypericum garrettii*.

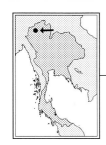

Doi Chiang Dao

Doi Chiang Dao is the largest limestone massif in Thailand and its main peak is, at 2,220 metres (7,282 feet), the country's third highest mountain. It rises dramatically at an angle of 60 degrees to face the rising sun. Not surprisingly, perhaps, its Thai name means 'the mountain that meets the stars'. Doi Chiang Dao in fact contains 17 peaks and ridges above 2,000 metres (6,560 feet) that curve, like a horseshoe, to form a jagged 10-square-kilometre (4-square-mile) crest. Its poor, porous soils, exposed rocks and limited surface water make it a harsh, unforgiving habitat in which, none the less, over 50 exciting plants and insects known only in these parts – a record for endemicity in Thailand – can be found. Also confined to this mountain is a Four-fingered Skink.

Mossy montane forest is the main cover at about 1,000 metres (3,280 feet). High up near the barren, windblown summit, the vegetation, called upper montane scrub, is unique. It contains many temperate herbs and shrubs that have colonized cracks and crevices in the limestone and give the appearance of a sub-alpine rock garden. The muted background of grey, taupe and ash-green is relieved by the pinks, purples and yellows of primulas, delphiniums, gentians and saxifrage. The stark but striking summit habitat of Doi Chiang Dao is not directly threatened by humans, but it is under threat from fire, and the plants now clinging to the crags are the survivors of populations that fire has gradually replaced with commonplace grass.

Harsh limestone peaks pierce the skyline at Doi Chiang Dao. The palm on the left (*Trachycarpus martianus*) is typical of the upper montane scrub that is unique to this mountain, while the hardy alpine rhododendron to the right (*Rhododendron ludwigianum*) is the only one known to grow in alkaline soil.

ABOVE A rosy-pink face distinguishes this otherwise well-camouflaged male Blossom-headed Parakeet (*Psittacula roseata*) that is found in the deciduous forests of Doi Chiang Dao. The female's head is more bluey-grey.

BELOW LEFT This little gentian (*Gentiana australis*) is one of many species from temperate plant families which characterize the unique montane scrub of Doi Chiang Dao.

BELOW CENTRE Here extracting moisture from a wild raspberry, this moth (*Anomis fructusterebrans*) is one of many tear-drinking species. Others siphon water from around the eyes of mammals such as cattle and deer.

ABOVE This Sino-Himalayan pheasant (*Syrmaticus humiae*) was named after the wife of the British ornithologist who spotted its feathers on the headdress of a Manipuri official sent to join him on a field trip in Myanmar. Hume's Pheasant is found on a few of Thailand's northern mountains with Doi Chiang Dao being its only protected site.

BELOW RIGHT The Crocodile Salamander (*Tylototrition verrucosus*), also known as the Himalayan Newt, is the only surviving salamander in Thailand. It is confined to the moist areas of the north's highest peaks. Too many have been collected both by amphibian enthusiasts and by medical scientists seeking to learn how it regenerates its limbs.

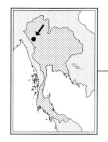

Omkoi and Mae Tuen

Covering 2,397 square kilometres (925 square miles), these adjoining sanctuaries together make up the largest conservation area in north Thailand, and one of its most important. Omkoi and Mae Tuen both still manage to support two of Thailand's rarest large mammals, elephant and Goral, though the elephants are threatened by cattle encroachment and the fires that villagers light annually to improve grazing, and the Goral by hunting and harassment. The elephant herd, the last wild population in north Thailand, may number less than 30. No one knows the size of the Goral population for the man who started to study them, Seub Nakhasathien, died in 1990 and his work has not been continued. It is a challenge, for these shy goat-antelopes hide on high-altitude crags and are hard to distinguish from the mottled colours of their habitat. In Omkoi they live on Doi Montjong, a 3-kilometre (1-mile) ridge with a sheer west-facing slope of rocks, grass and gnarled rhododendrons and a gentler eastern face of moist hill evergreen forest. The contrast is astonishing – a superb illustration of how aspect and soil influence vegetation.

Happily the yearly fires do not threaten the sanctuaries' rare resident birds – the Rufous-throated Partridge, Purple Cochoa and Burmese Yuhina. They all live in hill evergreen forests above 1,200 metres (about 4,000 feet). The Burmese Yuhina is not recorded at any other site in Thailand.

Omkoi's most striking feature – the distinctive lion's head ridge of Doi Montjong. Its sheer southern face is so eroded by the elements that little survives except grass and pockets of woodland.

LEFT North Thailand supports the most easterly population of this attractive little goat-antelope, the Goral (*Naemorhedus goral*). It inhabits the higher reaches above 1,000 metres (3,280 feet) and seems to prefer more difficult, exposed rocky terrain against which it blends perfectly. Such rocky outcrops are inaccessible to most predators except the Asian Golden Cat (known locally as the Firecat) and hunters with rifles. Omkoi protects the only sizeable population of Goral in Thailand.

OPPOSITE PAGE, ABOVE The last survivors of their kind in northern Thailand, a herd of wild elephants occupy the grasslands, river valleys and forests of Omkoi and Mae Tuen, the only sanctuaries in the region left to these creatures. In the past they were victims of the teak logging industry and the takeover of their habitats. Even now the elephants are not safe as settlers have arrived with several thousand cattle and they compete for food. With over 2,000 square kilometres (772 square miles) the sanctuaries could be supporting several hundred elephants but possibly only 30 individuals roam the forest and grasslands. Encouragingly, though, the matriarchal herd of 16 includes seven youngsters. With suitable protection this herd will survive and expand as several babies have been born and raised successfully in the wild.

BELOW The ancestor of the domestic chicken, the Red Junglefowl (*Gallus gallus*) is a common inhabitant of Thailand's forests. Some populations have a distinct white ear-patch, evident in this pair. Junglefowl can be distinguished from domestic chickens by their slate-grey legs (a chicken's legs are pale) and, in the male, by a white patch at the base of the tail. The *cock-a-doodle-doo* call, however, is no different from the familiar barn-yard call and can strike a rather incongruous note in remote forest areas.

BELOW Described as sounding like 'the squeaky hinge of a metal gate', the loud jangling call of the Black-collared Starling (*Sturnus nigricollis*) advertises one of Omkoi's most common resident birds. It is among the 200 or so avian species found in the sanctuary. Like the Red Junglefowl it is widespread throughout the country and is usually found in both deciduous and evergreen forest and scrub below about 1,500 metres (5,000 feet).

BELOW Known locally as the 'thousand-year-old rose', this vibrant wine-red rhododendron (*Rhododendron delavayi*) blossoms along the weathered slopes of Doi Montjong. This plant is endemic to the mountainous regions of northern Thailand.

BELOW Yellow male flowers surround the ochre-coloured female flowers on this parasitic plant *Balanophora fungosa*, which feeds off the roots of evergreen trees. Wax obtained from the tubers is used by locals to make birdlime – a sticky substance spread on perches to trap small birds.

These attractive flowering trees all flourish in the deciduous valleys and foothills of the adjoining sanctuaries of Omkoi and Mae Tuen. While the mountain areas of north Thailand remain chiefly evergreen, the combined effects of deforestation, drying and fire appear to be encouraging the spread of deciduous forests at the expense of evergreens on the lower slopes. OPPOSITE PAGE The Orchid Tree (*Bauhinia variegata*) is so named because its pretty pale pink flowers resemble orchids. The genus *Bauhinia* includes climbing shrubs and vines as well as trees and they are all common in Thailand's deciduous forests. RIGHT This yellow-flowering tree is associated with the deciduous forests of north and north-west Thailand. BELOW The rare *Engelhardia spicata* is found high up in hill-evergreen forests and is known to be a good host of epiphytic orchids. BELOW RIGHT This red-flowered *Cassia* is a common tree of deciduous forests throughout Thailand.

Lum Nam Pai and Namtok Mae Surin

These two conservation areas take their names from the rivers they give rise to, the Pai and the Surin, and both very much help to preserve some of the prettiest countryside in Thailand.

Lum Nam Pai is a wildlife sanctuary that covers 1,194 square kilometres (460 square miles) in the shape of a lop-sided triangle linking three peaks and three rivers, including part of the Pai. Sadly, the valleys' river-hugging habitats are given inadequate sanctuary as only one bank is protected, so people hunt there with impunity. One casualty is the peafowl population. However, smaller inhabitants of these valleys do survive and higher up, where the forest turns to broadleaf evergreen and pine trees, there are boars and bears and both Goral and Serow goat-antelopes, as well as masses of bats. For this is limestone country and the mountains are pitted with caves, a haven for speleologists and associated scientists.

Namtok Mae Surin is a small 397-square-kilometre (153-square-

mile) national park just south of Mae Hong Son. It has similar features to Lum Nam Pai but also boasts a scenic waterfall. It lies at lower altitude with a small central plateau surrounded by rolling hills where edible mushrooms abound in the rains and attract thousands of collectors. In winter (late November to early January), the low-lying hills that have lost their forest cover, in and beyond the park, are inflamed by ranks of yellow flowers that blur into an undulating sea of gold. These areas are known as 'fields of golden lotus', though they are not, in fact, lotuses but non-native sunflowers from Mexico.

Pine-oak forest on Doi Pai Kit – a feature commonly associated with poor mountain soils in northern Thailand – gives way to a spectacular view of Lum Nam Pai Wildlife Sanctuary. Here forested valleys surrounded by mountains provide some of the prettiest views in Thailand.

ABOVE LEFT Speckled with lichen, this bark provides much environmental information, because in tropical forests lichens are specific to one kind of habitat, are tenacious once established and susceptible to fire and drought. Identify the species in a community of lichens and you have for the most part a living documentary of that area's past 50 to 100 years. For example, there are eight species growing on this trunk and their identities reveal that the tree is a slow-growing species in a seasonal evergreen formation which has not been disturbed as yet by fire. The Royal Forest Department, Chiang Mai University and the British Natural History Museum have undertaken a pioneering study in Thailand to establish exactly how to use lichens as indicators of environmental change and this is now yielding dramatic and exciting results.

ABOVE RIGHT In sharp contrast to the dull-coloured branch on which it finds support, this epiphytic flower (*Aeschynanthus hildebrandii*) displays beautiful red petals. Like many attractive plants in the region it is threatened by habitat destruction and over-collection.

RIGHT Equally beautiful, the orange bracts of this ginger plant (*Hedychium coccineum*) frame its red fruits quite clearly. This plant, like the *Aeschynanthus*, is also confined to the upper evergreen forests of northern Thailand.

LEFT A formidable stalagmite formation rises up in a limestone cavern in the Tham Lot cave of Lum Nam Pai, north-east of Mae Hong Son. Most of Mae Hong Son and indeed Thailand's western mountain ranges are limestone, and therefore pitted with caves throughout. Few of these extensive and spectacular caves have been properly studied and may still contain a multitude of undiscovered creatures many of which will be exclusive to individual cave systems. ABOVE This cave hunting spider of the *Heteropoda* species is just one such unknown variety lurking in the shadows of Tham Lot.

OPPOSITE PAGE The wild mountain landscape of north-west Thailand fortunately remains unspoilt, despite a new road running from Pai to Mae Hong Son. This view from the roadside shows that the natural vegetation has not been affected.

The insects of Thailand also remain under-studied, including the myriad dragonflies and damsel flies that frequent the many streams of Mae Hong Son. BELOW LEFT This blue-bodied dragonfly of the Libellulidae family is identified as a male by the pincers which are used to clasp the female during mating. BELOW CENTRE A female damsel fly of the Calopterygidae family. BELOW RIGHT A male damsel fly (Platycremididae) expands its legs in a threatening display to deter other males.

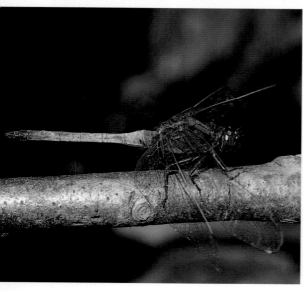

Mae Yom

Mae Yom was, until recently, largely unknown to nature lovers and scientists and this may explain its unwarranted neglect, because this national park supports by far the largest natural teak forest – about 280 square kilometres (108 square miles) – surviving in Thailand. Moreover, it is the only national park in the north that includes a major forested lowland river, the Mae Yom, within its boundary; every other river of equivalent size in the north is dammed. The richest, most exciting part of the park lies here with the tallest teak forest 30-40 metres (100-130 feet) high, the best nature trails, the richest lowland flora and the river itself the finest for fish in the upper Chao Phraya Basin. Here too dwell several highly threatened species including Red Dog, Golden Cat, White-rumped Falcon and Green Imperial Pigeon. Despite this impressive list of natural fauna and flora, the park is by no means pristine and has been poached and robbed of its teak for years, though none of it is so degraded that it cannot recover. If the park were properly protected and its wildlife restored, it could become a conservation area of international significance. However, unbelievably, Mae Yom is now threatened with a dam as well. Named after one of several stretches of small, white-water rapids, the Kaeng Sua Ten Dam would create a reservoir of 65 square kilometres (25 square miles) and would inundate the best part of the park.

Part of the largest surviving tract of teak forest in Thailand which is protected by the Mae Yom National Park. This park does not just help to conserve the ecology and genetic diversity of this most valuable of timbers, it also protects the only remaining undammed tributary of the great Chao Phraya river.

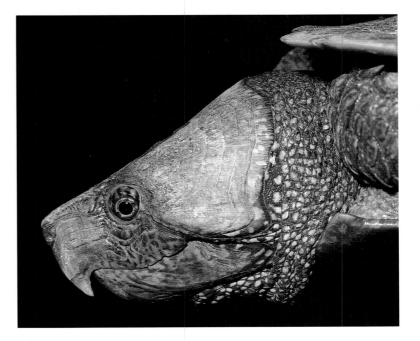

ABOVE AND ABOVE RIGHT The aptly named Big-headed Turtle (*Platysternon megacephalum*) is a rare sight in Thailand as it is widely hunted for food like other turtle species. Its unusual hooked upper lip and long tail also help to identify this turtle, which survives in the undisturbed and undammed hill streams of Mae Yom and other mountain forests of the north.

RIGHT A distinctive scolding cackle and a bright white crest lend this bird its name: the White-crested Laughingthrush (*Garrulax leucolophus*), seen here searching for food on the forest floor. It is most commonly found in mixed lowland deciduous and evergreen forests of northern Thailand such as those on the Mae Yom river basin.

BELOW LEFT Although this tree, *Careya sphaerica*, is not native to Southeast Asia, it is now naturalized in the deciduous forests of continental Thailand including those at Mae Yom. The filamentous flowers open at night and are thought to be pollinated by moths. The leaves, when young, are used as a vegetable.

BELOW RIGHT Coiled and alert, this Keeled Slug Snake (*Pareas carinatus*) feeds on the slugs and snails that also inhabit its native forests. It measures up to half a metre (1½ feet) long and the species as a whole is fairly widespread.

Focus on
NORTH-EAST THAILAND

On the face of it the north-east region, or Esarn as it is also known, seems far less dramatic or wild than other parts of Thailand. It comprises a vast, not very diverse plateau, called the Khorat Plateau, that makes up one-third of the entire landmass of Thailand. It is effectively the country's 'outback' with the harshest environment, few forests, and general poverty among its 20 million inhabitants. All this does not add up to a picture of nature in abundance (and very few tourists travel here as a result) but, in fact, the region is well blessed with conservation areas, especially wetlands, and some awesome scenery as well as with rare animals, birds, plants and stunning archaeological discoveries.

Esarn is almost square: the Mekong river encircles the north and east. Two river basins, the Sakhon Nakhon Basin of the river Songkhram and the Khorat Basin with the rivers Chi and Mun both drain into the Mekong. They are wedged in by mountains – the Phanom Dongrak and Phetchabun Ranges. These two rivers and mountain ranges form the western and southern rims of Esarn. A third river, the Pasak, runs down the western side between the Phetchabun Range and its shadow, the lower range of Dong Phaya Yen, before veering west to join the Mae Chao Phraya. The looped meanderings of these main rivers show how Esarn's saucer-shaped plateau slopes gently south-eastwards from the highest in Phetchabun peaks at 1,000–1,600 metres (3,280–5,250 feet) to the riverbanks of the Mekong at around 150 metres (500 feet).

The Mekong itself – the name is a contraction of *Mae Nam Mae Khong* meaning 'Mother Water Khong' – forms the long Thai–Lao boundary throughout lowland Esarn. At this stage it is a bigger, more muscular river than in its higher reaches when it defines the north's border. Between September and October the monsoon rains sometimes swell the Mekong's banks to overflowing, replenishing nearby rice fields. When the water level drops small islands and sandbars appear in midstream. The confluence of the Mekong and the Mun near Khong Chiam is known locally as 'Two-colour River' because of the contrast between the Mekong's muddy colour and the Mun's comparatively clear water. At Pha Taem, the Mekong cuts through a deep gorge where impressive sandstone cliffs are home to a natural gallery of prehistoric rock paintings showing elephants, fish and turtles.

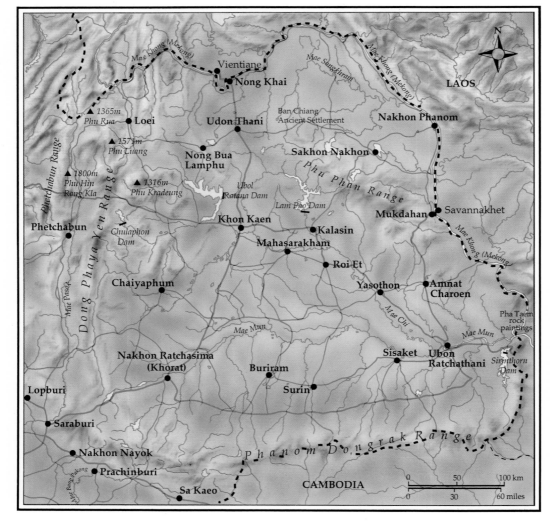

OPPOSITE PAGE This stark but colourful image is symbolic of Esarn today. Esarn is the single largest region in Thailand, with one-third of the country's land area and a third of its human population. It also has the poorest soils as well as the lowest rainfall and yet it was the first region to be settled by agricultural man some 6,000 years ago. This history of occupation in an area of natural fragility has created a degraded land where economic and environmental poverty are matched by cultural colour and resourcefulness. Most of Esarn consists of grassland scrub and ricefields with some cultivated trees, the most notable being mulberry. These feed the caterpillars whose silken cocoons are turned into the region's most exquisite artefact, hand-woven silk.

Some 50 million years ago Esarn was an inland basin periodically engulfed by the sea; but during periods of tectonic movement it rose to its current elevation of 200 metres (650 feet) above the waterline when the Indian Plate slid under the mainland of Laurasia. As the plates collided, the plateau itself also buckled in a fault-line that links the northern Dong Phaya Yen mountain range with the eastern Phanom Dongrak, giving rise to a low ridge of hills some 300–500 metres (1,000–1,650 feet) high, known as the Phu Phan Range. These mountain ranges are the visible evidence of two dramatic fault-lines that splice the region's sedimentary bedrock. Pressure points along these fault-lines can be seen today in the precipitous escarpments (the most notable bordering

Cambodia) and by outcrops of volcanic rock, including the basalt hills of Buriram and Sisaket from which the finest Khmer temple in Thailand, Phanom Rung, was made. This twelfth-century temple hints at what Angor Wat over the border in Cambodia must be like.

Indeed, the region was once claimed by the kingdoms of Cambodia and Laos: Esarn is bordered by Laos and Cambodia on three sides. Present-day inhabitants speak a Lao dialect in the north and Khmer in the south, both languages similar to Thai. They are also among the most hospitable and accommodating people in Thailand, perhaps a legacy of good-natured subjugation to alternating powers. They are also some of the poorest people in

Cultivated fruit trees and a few wild trees are sprinkled over the dry grassland of the north-east.

Thailand – a poverty stemming, in part, from the older legacy of Esarn's life as a shallow inland sea.

Sandwiched between strata of sandstone and shale there are three layers of rock salt deposits which formed when sea water evaporated. The oldest salt layer is 800 metres (2,625 feet) deep, the youngest barely 30 metres (100 feet) deep. These layers add up to poor soil fertility and the soils are getting saltier. The north-east has a hotter, longer dry season than other parts of Thailand and, at its centre, it gets less than 100 millimetres (4 inches) of rain a year where other regions get 130–400 millimetres (5–15 inches). This bedrock, together with Esarn's more savanna-style climate, greatly affects the region's wild places. Only the least diverse vegetation type, dry deciduous forest, survives in most areas. In the hills, however, evergreen forests prevail and remain in quite good condition because Esarn has no highland peoples.

Despite its harshness today, the north-east must once have been a promising place to live for its population is higher than anywhere else in Thailand (apart from the central plains), and it is home to the oldest human settlements in the country. The ancient villages of Ban Chiang and Ban Na Dee in modern Udon Thani were founded around 4000 BC (long before the time of Buddha or Christ) and survived till AD 500. These settlements are best known for their distinctive clay pots which are the earliest examples of fired earthenware anywhere in South-east Asia. Indeed, imprints of rice in some pottery shards also indicate that this native Asian grass was being cultivated in the region some 6,000 years ago – earlier than anywhere else.

Certainly wild rice is abundant in the Sakhon Nakhon Basin today along with other grass species. In fact grassland cultivated for dairy and beef-stock grazing, ricefields and cassava have replaced most of Esarn's deciduous forest. With only 15 per cent

forest cover, and that mostly on mountains, it is the most denuded region of Thailand. Deforestation accelerated between 1973 and 1982 when half the surviving forest was lost in just ten years as the Thai army waged war against Communist sympathizers. Today, a typical overview of Esarn is not the knobbly knit of forest canopy but the rippling velvet of green or golden grass, depending on the season. It is an attractive landscape, none the less, despite being semi-natural.

Ironically, there are natural features of Esarn which seem to be most 'unnatural'. This is true of the 'living rocks' that occur in some provinces, most notably in Mukdahan, Chaiyaphum and Loei. In these areas tough sandstone overlays a softer sedimentary rock which has weathered away leaving 'sculptures' that look like tortoises, toadstools, cows and mythical midgets with descriptive local names. This sandstone is also the source of less mythical but no less mysterious fossils, those of Thailand's dinosaurs.

Thailand was home to at least two dinosaur species 150 million years ago: a plant-eating sauropod over 18 metres (60 feet) long, and the meat-eating Allosaurus 10 metres (30 feet) long. Their fossils are found only in Esarn because the sedimentary sandstone of this former inland basin has sealed them for posterity. Their monstrous footprints are a feature of the Phu Luang Wildlife Sanctuary, but their bones are preserved at Phu Wiang National Park which was created specially for them.

In their day the dinosaurs must have dominated the skyline of the Khorat Plateau for the landscape then was flat. Now the skyline is defined by fabulous flat-topped mountains called mesas. They consist of thick horizontal layers of sandstone over shale, with steep striated screes stretching down several hundred metres until they broaden into forested slopes lower down. Most conservation areas in the western highlands of Esarn have mountains like this, Phu Kradeung being the best known. *Phu* is the Esarn word for mountain and *Kradeung* describes its 'bell'-shape. It now forms part of a small but exquisite national park.

The level top of Phu Kradeung is a feature in itself, an undulating plateau of 60 square kilometres (23 square miles) with stunning views of the valleys below. It is also home for Esarn's high-altitude plant communities. Some plants are also found in the north but many others, including two rhododendrons, several orchids and a small violet gentian are found only on the sandstone soils, high plateaux and crumbly screes of this region.

Moreover, some localized plants are so dependent on one another that conservation efforts have to focus on whole communities rather than on individual species. One striking example is the relationship of a small resilient *Agapates* shrub and two elegant ground orchids with the lichens that make their stony environment habitable. These orchids and the shrub are threatened by collectors and by tourists who tread on the lichen-coated rocks and unwittingly kill the bedding that supports the three plants. For this reason Phu Kradeung is closed for three months each year, as are other parks and sanctuaries in north-west Esarn.

Despite such human encroachments, Esarn is well blessed with a total of 29 conservation areas. True, they cover only 8 per cent of the region and, in some cases, are rather small, being under 400 square kilometres (155 square miles), but three parks and one sanctuary are well over 1,000 square kilometres (386 square miles).

Thap Lan and Pang Sida, two adjoining national parks, together cover a vast 3,084 square kilometres (1,190 square miles), making up the largest and therefore one of the most important protected areas in the region. This fact comes as quite a shock because neither park is known as a priority conservation area and both have been largely neglected as a result. Yet they still support sizeable tracts of the lowland evergreen and deciduous forests that once covered 80 per cent of Esarn, whereas all other parks and sanctuaries in the north-east are located on mountains and minor hills and protect montane habitats.

Thus of anywhere in Esarn, only Thap Lan and Pang Sida could now support Kouprey, the rare wild ox that once roamed the open lowland forests of northern Cambodia, Esarn and adjacent parts of Laos. Kouprey have not been reliably sighted anywhere in these parts since the Vietnam War, and the Khmer Rouge occupation of Cambodia. But if any were to be sighted in Thailand, they would have to live in Thap Lan and Pang Sida because nowhere else has large enough areas of Koupreys' natural habitat free of anti-personnel mines.

Mines litter the forests of the Phanom Dongrak Range. They were laid by Thai, Khmer Rouge and Cambodian soldiers alike to hinder the progress of one another. Sadly, they must also have taken their toll on large mammals like deer and wild pigs that walked the forest trails. But they have also deterred civilian hunters and loggers and have therefore kept border forests intact along with their tree-dwelling inhabitants, including the rare White-winged Duck.

This large and elusive duck, with its dark body and speckled white head, lives beside sluggish streams, ponds and swamps in the level evergreen forests of flatlands and plateaux. It was once widespread in Thailand, but most of its habitat has long since gone and so, it was thought, had the bird. But in early 1986 three ducks were taken from a farmer in Ubon Ratchathani who had trapped them in his ricefields near the Phu Jong Nayoi National Park. The White-winged Duck was thus rediscovered in Thailand after a gap of almost 30 years. It has since been seen in the Thung Yai and Phu Khieo Wildlife Sanctuaries as well, but is nowhere numerous. However, this endangered bird is at least found in larger numbers than the Comb Duck, once a resident of Esarn's many lakes and marshes, which now comes only to over-winter. Like so many lowland animals, it is a casualty of the hungry human population that ekes out a living on this huge impoverished plain.

In contrast, many thousands of migrant waterbirds, including herons and storks as well as waders and raptors, are located on the freshwater lakes and marshes of Esarn each year. Such wetlands are vital in helping to maintain the region's biodiversity and 13 of them are listed as being of international importance. A further five are protected against hunting. Although the region is notoriously dry and hot, it is prone to annual flooding, mostly along the major river systems. This helps to sustain the variety of marshes, lakes and streams that provide many important birdwatching sites in Esarn.

Not surprisingly called Turtle Rock, this impressive natural sandstone sculpture has been weathered and shaped by the sun, wind and rain over millennia. Such formations are scattered over Esarn, particularly in Mukdahan, Loei and Chaiyaphum provinces, as it is the only predominantly sandstone region of Thailand. Sparse rainfall, and relentless heat, particularly at the end of the dry season, have contributed to a harsh, semi-arid environment. But the Khorat Plateau, to give the north-east its other well-known name, still has much to offer, including some surviving stands of evergreen forest as well as upland fields that erupt into greens and golds. There are also refreshing montane areas guarding the resplendent yellows, pinks, purples and reds of rare orchids and other flowers, while the mighty Mekong river runs through the region bringing its own natural, spiritual and economic wealth.

Thung Salaeng Luang

Most people who go to Thung Salaeng Luang are surprised and delighted by the spectacle of rustling open fields encircled by dry oak forest and stately pines, in winter beautifully offset by a brilliant blue sky. *Thung* means 'field' in Thai, though the fields in this national park lying in the Phetchabun Range are neither fully cultivated nor totally wild. They are instead man-made grasslands of 5–15 square kilometres (2–6 square miles) which were cleared for cultivation and are now prevented from reverting to their forest state by the fires that engulf them each year.

Winter is the time to go there, from November through to March, for this is when the savannas erupt in flower. The flowers belong to a variety of gingers, ground orchids, sedges and shrubs with highly evocative local names such as 'running horse orchid' and 'monkey's pots and pans'. Their exuberant colours are further enhanced by the multitude of insects that feed from them, most of them still unnamed and their relationship with the plants still unknown. So small it could be mistaken for an insect, albeit a bulky one, the Short-tailed Parrotbill skulks around the grasslands looking for edible stems. This bird is rarely seen in Thailand outside Thung Salaeng Luang and even there it is scarce. On a much larger scale, elephants still live here, along with tiger and deer. But hunting has taken its toll on wildlife, so large animals are rarely seen. As a result it is the scenery, not the species, which makes this 1,262-square-kilometre (487-square-mile) park special.

Although Thung Salaeng Luang is best known and most visited for its grasslands, these cover only a tiny proportion of its total area. Most of the park consists of forested slopes, with waterfalls and rocky ravines.

Pockets of grassland surrounded by open pines with tropical oaks and dipterocarps are a distinct feature of Thung Salaeng Luang. Such areas are indicative of poor porous soils. Nevertheless, in the cool season (November to March) these grasslands blaze with colour from a splendid variety of wild flowers. The whole park itself is large, covering 1,262 square kilometres (487 square miles) in the Phetchabun Range, and most of it remains as forest.

A dramatic site provided by the Khaeng Sopha waterfall, one of three spectacular staircase waterfalls in Thung Salaeng Luang, which thunders down a series of steps before succumbing to the calm of the savanna forest below. The park consists of limestone with sandstone and the distinctive layering of sandstone slabs is clearly evident here. The waterfall drops from the limestone spine that runs down the middle of the park and feeds a tributary of the Mae Nan. This is one of the few rivers of the north-east that belong to the Chao Phraya Basin rather than the Mekong river basin. The other streams of Thung Salaeng Luang feed into the Mae Pasak, a major river which runs north-south between the parallel ranges of Phetchabun and Dong Phaya Yen and joins the Chao Phraya just north of Bangkok. Today, the waterfalls attract thousands of Thai visitors, especially from urban areas (Esarn is the most populated region in Thailand) where there are few public parks and little opportunity for outdoor recreation. Visitors in the future could be hugely disappointed since, in recent years, even this large river has become dangerously short of water due mainly to excessive forest clearance. Ambitious plans to divert water from the Mekong to correct the shortfall could threaten nature's age-old equilibrium that benefits the whole of Indo-China from the breeding grounds of the middle Mekong to the fertile floodplains of the Thonlé Sap and the fabulous fishing grounds of the Mekong Delta.

ABOVE LEFT A *Livistona* fan palm luxuriates in a strip of seasonal evergreen forest. Most palms, however, are associated with the rainforests of the equatorial belt.

ABOVE The striking blue bands of this bee identify it as an *Amegilla* mining-bee, a non-social species which burrows into the soil to nest. This one is feeding from, and pollinating, a mallow flower (*Pavonia* sp.), a relative of the hibiscus. Both plant and pollinator occur widely in open areas of South-east Asia.

LEFT A widespread climber of the evergreen forest is *Celastrus paniculatus*.

FAR LEFT Thung Salaeng Luang is famous for its flowers, some of which are rare and localized, like the pink and white ginger *Alpinia assimile*. All *Alpinias* grow enormous rootstocks, one of which is sold as galangal for culinary and medicinal use.

LEFT The purple *Canavalia* is a member of the pea family. This pretty exotic, generally referred to as a weed, is fairly common in the region.

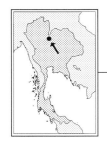

Phu Hin Rong Kla

This national park covers a mere 307 square kilometres (118 square miles) but offers a welcome change of scenery and temperature from the plains to the east and west. It rises to 1,800 metres (6,000 feet) with tropical mountain forests and numerous orchids and lichens tucked between its wooded slopes and deep ravines. When the army cracked down on Communist dissidents in the 1970s, Phu Hin Rong Kla became the stronghold for hundreds of young educated urban Thais. Today their huts, water mills and graves are preserved as sites of historical interest in a quiet woodland grove at the bottom of the hill. Most large animals were eaten during the insurrection so today only smaller species survive.

However, the park does have some superb examples of the forces of nature at work. On the south side of Phu Hin Rong Kla looking along the Phetchabun Range, there are several horizontal slabs of smooth rounded cobbles which are moulded from sandstone by centuries of wind and rain. Further west and lower down at the edge of the park, a level tract of shrubland is pitted with caverns and cracks which opened when subterranean tremors wrenched the surface rock apart. Now lined in lichen, moss and mulch and heavily shaded by ferns, these caverns are effectively hidden mini-habitats waiting to be found. In contrast to these silent mementoes of natural power, the inaccessible Mon Daeng Waterfall crashes down the 32 steps it has chiselled in the mountainside over many hundreds of years.

Facing south from the top of Phu Hin Rong Kla, there is a long, lingering view of the Khao Kor valley where Thai troops flushed Communist rebels from their hideaway in the 1970s, felling the forest as they went. Today the valley's gentle contours are exposed, forever revealing the violence of its past.

ABOVE Exposed blocks of sandstone in the Phu Hin Rong Kla National Park demonstrate the extraordinary effects of weathering by sun, wind and rain over thousands of years. Erosion has exposed these button rocks.

BELOW Hardy low-statured shrubs such as this attractive white heather *Lyonia foliosa* characterize the sandstone mountains of the north-east. Many of these plants are found only in this region of Thailand.

BELOW Some 5 metres (16 feet) of coiled snake is always an alarming sight to encounter, although this Rock Python (*Molurus bivittatus*) is the most passive of Thailand's three python species. It lives in forest and wooded grassland and feeds on warm-blooded prey such as deer, pigs and monkeys, which it kills by constriction.

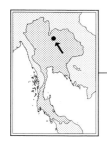

Phu Luang

This mountainous royal wildlife sanctuary (*phu* means 'mountain', *Luang* is a royal title) is a haven for rare orchids and other flora. It is shaped like a cloven hoof with a 'V' cut away by a waterfall and a heel that is broad and flat. The skirts of the mountain are forested with deciduous and evergreen formations, but the most rewarding part is the 100-square-kilometre (38-square-mile) plateau on top. A gruelling 8-kilometre (5-mile) trek through tall, humid forest is just the beginning of the arduous route to the plateau, during which a glimpse may be caught of a Gaur or Serow. Approaching the plateau, the vegetation changes to short, open woodland underlaid with grasses and pygmy bamboo. At 1,571 metres (5,154 feet) the plateau itself is a riot of colour from February to May when its shrubland flowers are in bloom, and the lichen-covered rocks are interspersed with pink rhododendrons, white heathers, magenta balsams, blue gentians and orchids of many hues. Together they create a beautiful but fragile oriental garden where Golden-throated Barbets and Black-throated Parrotbills also reside – birds as yet unseen elsewhere in Esarn. Phu Luang is one of the most crucial sanctuaries for orchids in Asia, for within its 848 square kilometres (327 square miles) it supports 160 species, all of them rare and some of them unique to north-west Esarn.

The bright blooms of *Rhododendron simsii* provide a vivid foreground to this view from the top of Phu Luang showing the classic mesa mountain outline in the distance.

ABOVE A modern-day reminder of the dinosaurs that once roamed Esarn 150 million years ago, this highly agile Yellow-headed Monitor Lizard (*Varanus bengalensis*) keeps a sharp look-out for prey. It is remarkably adept at climbing trees in search of food, including birds' eggs and fledglings. It is the smallest of Thailand's four monitor lizards, but even so can reach lengths of over a metre (3 feet).

BELOW Possibly some of the oldest footprints in the world. These dinosaur prints are over 3 metres (10 feet) long and belonged to the carnivorous Allosaurus. They are one set of several that can be seen at Phu Luang and dinosaur fossils generally are a feature of the north-east region where the stable sedimentary substrates have helped to preserve them for posterity. The other dinosaur that dominated the prehistoric plateau was a plant-eating sauropod.

BELOW The pretty flowers of *Rhododendron simsii* which is endemic to the cool upland plateaux of the north-east region. Many rhododendrons are strictly terrestrial plants but some tropical species are epiphytic; a few can adopt either habit.

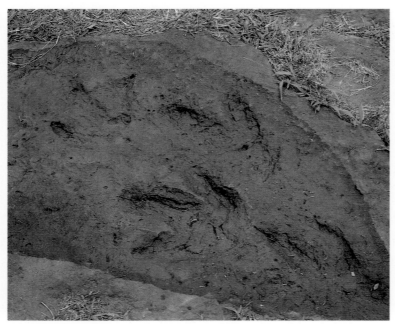

Phu Luang is one of the most crucial sanctuaries for orchids in Asia. The sanctuary is equidistant, about 50 kilometres (30 miles), from four other protected areas (Phu Rua, Phu Kradeung, Phu Hin Rong Kla and Nam Nao), all with commendable qualities but none more so than Phu Luang harbouring 160 species of orchid. The yellow *Dendrobium gibsonii* (RIGHT) has a distinctive arrangement of alternate leaves and corresponding flower clusters. *Sunipia minor* (ABOVE) grows on trees and has small discreet flowers. Two other orchids, *D. infandibulum* (BELOW CENTRE) and *Cymbidium insigne* (BELOW RIGHT), have evolved as floral mimics of the rhododendron *Rhododendron lyi* (BELOW LEFT) a prominent shrub of the plateau. All three plants are pollinated by the bumblebee *Bombus eximius* but only the rhododendron gives it nectar in return. The orchids simply dupe the bee into thinking they are rhododendrons by producing flowers which look remarkably similar. When a bee goes into them, the orchids place a pollen pack on its back but each orchid puts its pollen on a different part of the back, thereby avoiding reproductive confusion. This evolving deception continues even now, for *C. insigne* has two morphs on this mountain, one pale, one stripy. The latter is the original form found elsewhere. The pale one is found only here for it is the rhododendron mimic. This astonishing deception was discovered by researchers from the Royal Botanic Gardens at Kew and Copenhagen University.

Nam Nao and Phu Khieo

Nam Nao is a national park of 966 square kilometres (373 square miles) while Phu Khieo is a wildlife sanctuary covering 1,560 square kilometres (602 square miles). Together they make up the second largest conservation complex in Esarn. More importantly, they encompass five mountains which makes them a vital natural reservoir for the Chi and Pasak rivers. Their value as rainwater regulators to this mostly arid region is reflected in their Thai names: *nam nao* means 'cold water' and *phu khieo* means 'green mountain'. Both Nam Nao and Phu Khieo are in danger of being devalued by the Chulabhorn Hydro-dam which has drowned their common lowlands and given easy access to loggers. Nam Nao is also spliced by Highway 12, a busy road that has led to much encroachment in the northern part of the park.

However, the contiguous forests of these conservation areas support a rich variety of deciduous and evergreen forest birds including babblers, thrushes and flycatchers, while also providing a much-needed haven for large mammals including bears, gibbons and Golden Cats. Several animals that were previously decimated are being re-introduced to Phu Khieo. The first to be released was the Hog Deer, a pretty little deer in spite of its name, which, together with numbers of Sambar Deer, hangs around the park visitor centre appearing to prefer the more protected, well-tended grasslands to the wilder areas of open forest. The sanctuary's most elusive mammal is a rhinoceros that hides in the deepest, densest forest. In spite of several expeditions, no proof has been found of its existence apart from tracks that were sighted five years ago.

This is a typical *thung* (Thai for 'field') and a striking feature of the Phu Khieo Wildlife Sanctuary. Such land, and the lake beside it, attracts many birds and animals, including deer, which have been reintroduced from captivity.

ABOVE Viewed across the mixed deciduous forest of Nam Nao National Park, the tabletop mountain of Phu Kradeung rises to 1,300 metres (4,265 feet) in the far distance. Phu Kradeung is the best-known mesa mountain in the region and is itself part of a national park.

RIGHT A more open canopy than one would normally expect from montane evergreen forest indicates that trees have been felled in the past here in Nam Nao National Park. Banana plants and the foreground tangle of creepers can only proliferate where there is abundant light, again a tell-tale sign of man's encroachment, in this case a road.

An upland lake (ABOVE AND LEFT) is located in the central plateau of the Phu Khieo Wildlife Sanctuary. The lake is bordered by both forest and open savanna and the woodland edge especially provides a significant site for wetland birds including the Spot-billed Pelican (*Pelecanus philippensis*),shown here. There are few surviving woodland lakes left in Thailand so the need to conserve them can never be overstated. Some 20 years ago, for example, this was a breeding site for the stately Sarus Crane (*Grus antigone*) with its distinctive bare-red head, but the bird was wiped out by hunters. Now, thankfully, it is being reintroduced into this sanctuary where it can join the extremely rare and endangered resident White-winged Duck (*Cairina scutulata*). This large black-bodied bird with white head and neck prefers such waters on plateaux up to 1,500 metres (4,920 feet).

OPPOSITE PAGE The tree-covered slopes of both Phu Khieo and Nam Nao contain some impressive pine trees such as *Pinus merkusii*.

An alert Hog Deer (*Cervus porcinus*) shows natural wariness. This species has lost much of its habitat to rice cultivation and has suffered from hunting, but today has prime feeding grounds in both Phu Khieo and Nam Nao afforded by the open grasslands in these conservation areas. The Hog Deer which now roam these grasslands are descended from a herd that was rounded up in 1986 from Koh Kradat, a dead-flat island off the south-east coast, south of Koh Chang.

The Sambar Deer (*Cervus unicolor*) is the largest deer in Thailand, being almost as large as the European Red Deer. This is a hind (the buck has antlers). Although it is primarily a forest-dwelling deer, preferring to browse rather than graze, it does come to feed on grasslands. Its principal predators include tiger, leopard and man, and the last, particularly, has contributed to its dramatic reduction in numbers across Thailand. This deer is now common only in well-protected conservation areas.

ABOVE A bizarre sight at Phu Khieo, this aptly named strangler vine is constricting the trunk of its host.

ABOVE RIGHT Amid the dry leaf litter of a deciduous forest floor, the wild amaryllis (*Lycoris*) provides an attractive contrast. This plant is not native to Thailand but has settled in and is spreading of its own accord.

RIGHT Clinging to the trunk of a tree, this succulent creeper, *Hoya potsii*, does not extract nutrients from the living tissue of the trunk or branch on which it perches and therefore does no harm to its host.

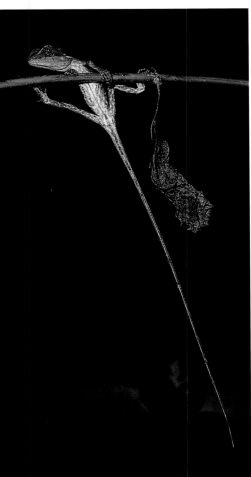

FAR RIGHT This acrobatic lizard (*Calotes emma emma*) performs a high-wire balancing act deep in the forest of Phu Khieo. Lizards prey on insects but some species also devour mice and small birds.

RIGHT A spectacular aerial ant nest built around a slender tree trunk.

The Mekong

This mighty river touches the northern tip of Thailand after a heroic journey of some 2,000 kilometres (1,242 miles) from its source in eastern Tibet. It forms the border of the north-east region for a few hundred kilometres and is within easy reach of several national parks in the Phetchabun hills.

The river changes dramatically in time and place. In the rains it is a seething, muddy torrent. In the dry season it may drop as much as 15 metres (50 feet) becoming quite benign as it leaves aloft its seasonal islands and sandbanks. By the provincial capital of Mukdahan, a gateway to Laos, it encounters the first of several rapids, the Lipi Falls. These, and the Khone cataracts further south, have been a barrier to human navigation but do not impede the myriad fish which migrate upriver to breed. Of these the most extraordinary is the giant Mekong Catfish which can grow 4 metres (13 feet) long and weigh 300 kilograms (660 pounds). In days gone by great shoals

of them battled up-river each year, but now very few of them do the run; too many were fished too often. Other fish seeking refuge in the Mekong's waters include the Striped Featherback, Mae Khong Herring, Laotian Shad and the freshwater Dorab.

What wild countryside remains beside the Mekong is conserved in a few small parks and sanctuaries and these are locally important. But the Mekong itself is unprotected although it is the life-line of every country in Indo-China.

The great Mekong river has for centuries been the lifeline of every country in Indo-China, both as a source of food and water and as a communication route.

ABOVE This view from the Patem cliffs across to Laos shows the Mekong river in its wider somnambulant phase. This middle section, and the tributaries which branch into north-east Thailand, form vital stretches for migratory fish which return to breed here during the rainy season.

RIGHT *Lagerstroemia speciosa*, also known as the 'Queen's Flower', is a widespread tree of open scrubland and deciduous forest. It is widely planted as an ornamental because of its attractive pink blossom and hardy character.

A pattern of mudflats and sandbanks exposed in the dry season conveys something of the Mekong's mystical qualities as a locally revered river and one that epitomizes the Thai epithet of 'Mother Water' (*Mae Nam*). Such seasonal riverine 'islands' provide an important habitat and food source for breeding and wintering waterfowl including ducks and waders like the Little Ringed Plover (*Charadrius dubius*) and Small Pratincole (*Glareola lactea*). An awesome river, the Mekong is imposing in its grandeur, inspiringly beneficent, always, to date, unshackled and free. It grew out of Asia's evolution, one of five rivers that rise in the eastern Himalayas, the seventh longest in Asia, the twelfth longest in the world.

ABOVE In between serene stretches of water, the middle Mekong and its tributaries are scattered with rapids, such as these on the Mun river. Rocky areas are extremely important to the health of a river because they not only aerate the water but also provide refuge for small fish and fry.

BELOW Northern Pintail ducks (*Anas acuta*) are among the many waterfowl migrants which overwinter on the ponds and marshes lining the Mekong in the north-east. The drakes have distinctive white forenecks and breasts. The pointed tail also helps to identify this species. The middle Mekong basin, of which Esarn is the major part, has a variety of important seasonal and permanent wetlands.

BELOW Drawn on stone over 2,000 years ago, these rock paintings at Pha Taem, beside the Mekong, depict a giant catfish (a species which still inhabits the river) and a giant soft-shelled turtle as well as several fish traps. The red paint is a mixture of soil, fat and tree gum and it is the handiwork of ancient rice-cultivating settlers. The images cover a 170-metre (560-foot) stretch and are located on a sheltered rockface.

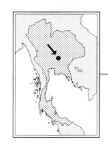

Khao Yai

Khao Yai is the flagship of Thailand's national parks. It was the first one to be established (in 1962), it is the most visited, and it remains one of the largest at 2,168 square kilometres (837 square miles). Above all it is one of the best refuges in the country for animals and birds in the wild, and remains the most likely spot in Thailand to see a wild tiger or elephant. The park occupies the end of the Phanom Dongrak Range in the south-west corner of Esarn, barely 180 kilometres (112 miles) from Bangkok. Contrary to the image of its name ('big mountain') it does not contain a single mountain but several rising above 1,000 metres (3,280 feet), and the highest reaching 1,351 metres (4,432 feet). These support hill evergreen forest, but most of the park is plateau from roughly 600–800 metres (2,000–2,600 feet) above the sea. At lower altitudes, it harbours some fine old tracts of seasonal evergreen forest, some of which is unusually wet. Orchids and other epiphytic plants are in abundance and there are several plants unique to the area such as *Burmannia distacha*.

The park boasts over 20 species of large mammals such as Hog Badgers and Leopard Cats, and 300 species of birds including Scarlet Minivet and Vernal Hanging Parrot. Its wonderful trails, originally made by elephants, wind through forests, streams and grasslands, passing huge buttressed trees, strangling figs, wild boar wallows, mushroom clusters, hornbill nests and salt-licks with quivering mud-puddling butterflies, and possibly a hidden tiger.

Natural power and danger are evident in Haew Narok (Thai for 'Devil's Gorge'), the most impressive of several waterfalls in Khao Yai National Park. Even elephants have succumbed to its force.

LEFT The evergreen and deciduous forests of Khao Yai are threaded with wilderness trails ranging from 2–20 kilometres (1–12 miles) which are remarkably rewarding and empty given that the park sees 700,000 people a year. This magnificent park is threatened on every side and yet it remains Thailand's showcase national park, partly because it was the first to be created, partly because it is so close to Bangkok (2–3 hours by road) and partly because it is an extremely important conservation area. The last distinction derives from the fact that the park is unusually moist for an area of Esarn, receiving up to 3,000 millimetres (118 inches) of rain each year. This explains the predominance of evergreen forest and the super-importance of its forested slopes, for they supply water to the streams which feed the rivers of the park's four adjoining provinces. Because of its premier status over the last 20 years, Khao Yai has been the site of two of the most significant research projects in Thailand involving hornbills and gibbons. Two more long-term projects have recently been started to study elephants and forest dynamics. It is rare for researchers in Thailand to get support for such projects even though these yield some of the most useful ecological information. Those undertaken in Khao Yai bear witness to its status as an ASEAN heritage site but, in spite of this prestigious billing, the park's integrity is threatened by resort developers, dam builders, corrupt officials and loggers. Happily, supporters greatly outnumber adversaries and Thai people would mind if this park lost any more of its natural value.

BELOW This earthball, *Scleroderma sinnamerense*, is a fungus found in the wetter evergreen forests of South-east Asia. Like many mycorrhizal fungi, it facilitates the growth of its host, in this case trees of the dipterocarp family.

BELOW Herb of the forest floor, this striking ginger, *Etlingera megalocheilos*, is often seen in the evergreen forests of Thailand. It is commonly known as the earth ginger because its inflorescence opens close to the ground.

BELOW The *Ganoderma* fungus grows on fallen wood in evergreen forests all over Thailand. It is sometimes used to make an infusion that is prescribed as a herbal tonic.

ABOVE A female Barking Deer (*Muntiacus muntjak*). This species is just one of Khao Yai's famous herbivore populations, so-called because of its dog-like bark. Such deer are common around the park's headquarters, and some have become unusually tame, allowing visitors to approach quite close.

ABOVE RIGHT A male Sambar Deer (*Cervus unicolor*) displays its impressive antlers which it sheds every year.

RIGHT A wild boar (*Sus scrofa*) with her variegated brood of piglets. Boar as well as deer have been heavily hunted in the past, so the protection afforded by Khao Yai, especially the grasslands near headquarters which these herbivores frequent, is vital.

ABOVE Khao Yai is the best place to spot an elephant in the wild. The Asian Elephant (*Elephas maximus*) is threatened with extinction, being hunted for its ivory. The destruction of much of its forest habitat has also contributed to its decline. Khao Yai protects some 200 to 300 wild elephants most of which hide far away deep in the forest. They live in small family herds of 20 to 30, led usually by the oldest female, and emerge at dusk into the grasslands. They browse on some 150 kilograms (330 pounds) of grass daily. Unlike the African Elephant, both sexes of which develop tusks, only the male Asian Elephant grows significant tusks (and not all the males).

LEFT Plants of the *Clerodendrum* genus are commonly found amidst the undergrowth of Thailand's evergreen forest, where their brightly coloured flowers and fruiting heads stand out against the dark foliage.

A large male tiger (*Panthera tigris*) is regularly seen around the park headquarters, where the nearby grasslands must provide him with ample prey. Few visitors, even Thais, realize that Thailand still has tigers. They are more likely to know that tigers are heavily hunted for sale to traditional Chinese pharmacists who incorporate dried tiger parts into a variety of remedies. This trade is largely responsible for the near extinction of tigers in the wild all over Asia. In recent years, as mainland China has become wealthier, the demand has increased, despite the lack of scientific evidence that tiger parts have any medicinal properties whatsoever. Now only a few thousand tigers survive in Asia, about 500 of them in Thailand, and only the best conservation areas, like Khao Yai, are secure and big enough to maintain viable tiger populations. On a positive note, however, the Royal Forest Department initiated its Tiger Project in 1995 with the Seub Nakhasathien Foundation. The aim of the project is to prevent the total demise of this noble animal in Thailand.

RIGHT A Pig-tailed Macaque (*Macaca nemestrina*) indulges in some grooming with its companion. The short curved tail explains their name. They are one of the most common monkeys in Thailand. Although they often climb trees to feed, generally they travel at ground level, which means from time to time they fall victim to vehicles travelling through Khao Yai. This species is also killed for food, and the babies are taken to be trained to climb coconut trees and harvest the coconut.

OPPOSITE PAGE The tail-less, slender body, long arms and pale hands identify this ape as the White-handed Gibbon (*Hylobates lar*). Here one performs typical branch-to-branch acrobatics. A gibbon's call is one of the most evocative sounds of Thailand's evergreen forests. Every morning, soon after dawn, the male sings a series of short crescendos which are soon taken up and elaborated upon by the female in what is known as the 'great call'. For about an hour they perform an exquisite duet, presenting a united front against would-be aggressors. Gibbons very rarely fight directly, either with their neighbours or among themselves; instead they engage in ritualized threats through song.

BELOW AND BELOW LEFT The two faces portray the dark and pale morphs of the White-handed Gibbon. This species pairs irrespective of colour and may produce dark or fair offspring, or both. Gibbons are the only truly monogamous apes and they are also the smallest.

Focus on
SOUTH-EAST THAILAND

By far the smallest region of Thailand, the 22,400-square-kilometre (8,648-square-mile) wedge that makes up the south-east takes up less than 7 per cent of the country. It has mountains to the north and east, the low-lying Prachinburi floodplain below the mountains, and hundreds of kilometres of sandy coastline to the south and west running into the Gulf of Thailand. The region supports many endemic species, including some highly coveted rare birds and one enchanting primate.

To the north lies an extension of the Phanon Dongrak Range, actually part of Esarn, but its southern slopes help water the Prachinburi floodplain. The Cardomom Range borders the east. The coastline takes a sharp zig-zag after the Bight of Bangkok and at the headland of Sattahip, a naval port from which patrol boats intercept pirates, smugglers and refugees who enter the Gulf. The land tapers to a 70-kilometre (43-mile) tail barely a kilometre wide at the Cambodian border.

The highest mountain in the region is the southern peak of Khao Soi Dao at 1,670 metres (5,479 feet) but the northern peak rises almost as high to 1,555 metres (5,100 feet). This saddle-back mountain is the stem of a small upland chain which curves round the heart of the region like a shepherd's crook: its base set into Khao Kitchakut, its tip attached to Khao Chamao and its head nuzzling Khao Ang Ru Nai. And, like a shepherd's crook, it keeps several national parks and wildlife sanctuaries from harm.

These mountains are vital to the region because their slopes deliver water year round to the orchards and coastal industries that have made the region rich. The forests on these slopes forestall the deluge that might occur were rain to cascade unchecked down the steep granite mountains. This region receives 3,000–4,000 millimetres (118–160 inches) of rain a year which is higher than anywhere else in continental Thailand. As a result, both the south-east's upland and lowland forests are naturally evergreen and, although the climate is still seasonal, the dry season is not as long or as harsh as in other parts of continental Thailand. The forests are therefore much wetter than those of the north, west and north-east and are semi-evergreen formations like those of the peninsula. But in detail they are different because the region is directly linked to southern Indo-China and its flora and fauna reflect this link.

Although it has some notable southern species, such as Sun Bears (also called Honey Bears because they like to eat bees' nests), Binturongs, Buffy Fish Owls and Moustached Hawk Cuckoos, as well as Indo-Burman animals including Gaur, elephants and Spot-bellied Eagle Owls, the south-east also has exclusively Indo-Chinese species. In the uplands, these include the Silver Leaf-monkey and birds such as the Blue-rumped Pitta, Coral-billed Ground Cuckoo and Mountain Fulvetta, while lowland forests have Siamese Firebacks and Bar-bellied Pittas among their bird species, together with Cambodian Kukri Snakes and Indo-Chinese Water Lizards. All these animals are threatened because their range is so restricted and their habitats so particular.

The Cardomom Range has helped to create a remarkable level of endemic plants and animals. Local plant varieties include cardomom and clove while amphibians not found elsewhere in Thailand are the Siamese Warty Frog and Spiny-breasted Frog. Rare birds such as the Chestnut-headed Partridge, Eastern Green Magpie and a dark form of Silver Pheasant dwell in this region. But the real wildlife gem here is the Pileated Gibbon. This is one of three gibbon species in Thailand. These South-east Asian apes are among the most attractive primates, with soft silken fur, large limpid eyes and a very touching manner. The Khao Soi Dao Wildlife Sanctuary and adjoining conservation areas are helping to save the Pileated Gibbon in this region from the entrapment of the pet trade – a loathsome business that may drive them to extinction.

In the low-lying Prachinburi floodplain, less than 10 metres (30 feet) above sea level, another significant wildlife sanctuary, Khao Ang Ru Nai, is all that remains of once-extensive forest. Hardly a tree stump survives elsewhere in the area today. It has all turned over to rice, orchards and cassava. The lowland evergreen forests of Ang Ru Nai still harbour very rare lowland forest birds, including the Black-and-red Broadbill, the endangered Bar-bellied Pitta and Woolly-necked Stork; another resident is the Temple Terrapin, now almost exclusive to Thailand.

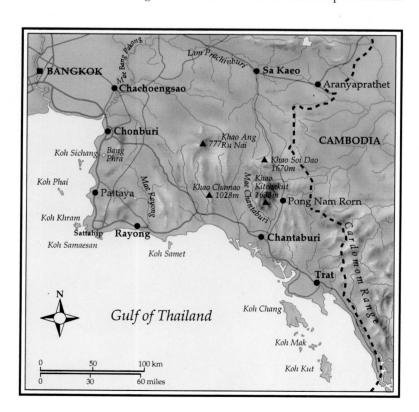

OPPOSITE PAGE Supremely agile among the branches and tree-trunks where it dwells, the Pileated Gibbon (*Hylobates pileatus*) is also considered by many to be the most beautiful of its genus. This adult male shows the black cap and bib that distinguishes him from other gibbon species.

Koh Chang is the largest island off the south-east coast and the nucleus and namesake of a marine national park. Here the forest survives inland and few people foul the sea, so the seashore is still as alluring as ever. However, some of the south-east coastline beaches and adjacent waters have been badly polluted.

An even rarer lowland inhabitant, the highly localized Siamese Crocodile, was recently rediscovered in the backwater streams of Ang Ru Nai. Common in farms, where its skin is sold to make up-market accessories, this prehistoric reptile was assumed extinct in the wild as most of its natural habitat has been settled. Crocodiles were also hunted with a vengeance, out of fear and hatred as much as economic incentive. Its survival in this sanctuary is astonishing, for Ang Ru Nai was also occupied by settlers until a few years ago. The survival of such an unloved animal is a stroke of great good fortune, but its subsequent protection is a tribute to Thailand's conservation authorities.

The saltwater crocodile has not been so lucky. It once inhabited estuaries and mangrove forests all along the Thai coastline, including that of the south-east. This part of the coast extends for about 500 kilometres (300 miles) from the mudflats around the mouth of the Mae Bang Pakong, north of Chonburi, to the sandy beaches and inlets of Trat. Apart from the rivers of the Prachinburi floodplain, which combine to become the Mae Bang Pakong, most other rivers in this region are short and steep because they rise in mountains close to the coast. After rain, these rivers carry a lot of gravel and silt, with the result that the beaches of this coastline are either mud or sand depending on their distance from a river mouth. Where there is mud, there would once have been mangrove forest, too, but this has been badly depleted in the last two decades.

The most extensive mangrove forest, formerly and now, edges the many inlets of the Khlung Spit which runs from the mouth of the Mae Chantaburi to the mouth of the Mae Wale. As the crow flies, this muddy spit covers 150 kilometres (93 miles) of the coast but the waterline itself is longer. More mangrove grows north and south of the spit in the estuary of Tha Mai (the peppercorn centre of Thailand) and the Bay of Trat respectively. This network of tidal waterways and mangroves gives refuge to the Great-billed Heron and the Masked Finfoot, two of Thailand's most reclusive waterbirds, as well as to two of its rarest pigeons, the Green and Pied Imperials.

The mangrove also sometimes harbours schools of Irrawaddy River Dolphins, but these friendly snub-nosed mammals have been so depleted by pollution and getting caught in nets that no one really knows how many survive in Thai waters today. They used to be common all round the Gulf in the brackish waters of the estuaries, but now that shrimp and oyster farms have ousted so much mangrove forest, there is a lot less for dolphins to eat. They feed on small crustaceans that crawl around the mangrove mud. However, the Irrawaddy River Dolphin, along with other intertidal species, may be rescued by a pioneering royal project in the Khlung estuaries which aims to integrate shrimp farming with mangrove regeneration.

Where south-eastern beaches have sand instead of mud they are a glistening white because the sand is derived from granite, gneiss and quartz. At close quarters they may not be as beautiful as they seem from afar because the seas of this region suffer badly from pollution. One culprit is an unbridled tourist industry with the coastal town of Pattaya being the worst offender. However, just north of Pattaya and a little inland, the municipal reservoir of Bang Phra has become an effective waterfowl resort near the open zoo of Khao Khieo and a wildlife sanctuary plus nature centre of the same name. This zoo is an improvement on its counterpart in Bangkok.

Off the south-east coast of Thailand there are around 145 islands. Most are edged with fringing reefs because the seabed, part of the Sunda Shelf, is shallow enough for coral to get sunlight. However, pollution is beginning to kill the coral and underwater visibility is sometimes obscured by the silt that comes off the land, accelerated by waterside construction and deforestation. The best-known island at present is Koh Samet, a national park that is named after its most abundant tree (apart from coconut palms), the *samet* or paper-bark tree, which is used for firewood and boat-building. Despite its national park status, the island has suffered from over-building of bungalows and tourist encroachments. It is the classic dilemma of wild Thailand yet again.

Two of this region's most lucrative resources are ruby mining and durian fruit harvesting. The rubies are embedded in a line of basalt bedrock on either side of the Thai-Khmer border from the line that links Pong Nam Ron and Pailin (both ruby frontier towns) to the open ponds of Bo Rai. The fertile, well-drained soils of the south-east are ideal for cultivating the durian, a South-east Asian forest tree which produces armour-plated pods the size of rugby balls with huge seeds inside encased in a rich yellow flesh. Various epithets have been applied to the smell of the fruit but the soft and sticky flesh has an exquisite flavour and is also highly nutritious. Thailand grows the best durian of all, a cultivar known as *morn thong* or 'golden pillow'.

Khao Ang Ru Nai

Just two hours east of Bangkok, the Khao Ang Ru Nai Wildlife Sanctuary preserves a small, 1,030-square-kilometre (398-square-mile), but vital part of the Prachinburi floodplain. *Khao* means 'mountain' in central Thai, and beneath the mountains that constitute its name lies the largest surviving tract of lowland evergreen forest in Thailand. Moreover, it is semi-evergreen rainforest that is only 250 metres (820 feet) above sea level and is exclusive to this region. Within the sanctuary is a muggy, secluded world of dark sodden soils, spiky rattan palms, tall enshrouded trees and noises made in the shadows by some of Thailand's rarest creatures. With 3,000-4,000 millimetres (118–160 inches) of rain a year, it is as lush as the evergreen forests of Peninsular Thailand. Special residents include the huge Indo-Chinese Water Lizard, and the Woolly-necked Stork which has no other home in Thailand. This extremely rare bird picks its way with care along the sanctuary's marshy streams. It has reason

to be careful. Not long ago an unsuspecting ranger stumbled over the equally rare Siamese Crocodile that snoozed in one of those streams, its knobbly back looking just like a log. It was a startling discovery, as wild crocodiles were long presumed extinct and this one's survival, with its mate, is something of a miracle. It seems to symbolize the precarious status, as well as the resilience and potential, of Khao Ang Ru Nai.

Sunset over the man-made grasslands of Khao Ang Ru Nai. They are in the centre of the sanctuary and were cleared by itinerant farmers who have since settled elsewhere. These areas are ideal for researching the natural process of forest succession and regeneration.

Sunlight filters through this evergreen formation at Ang Ru Nai Wildlife Sanctuary. The sanctuary, barely two hours from Bangkok, has the single largest tract of lowland evergreen forest left in Thailand, including the peninsula. Most lowland areas have since been settled or converted for agriculture. More significant still, this evergreen formation is exclusive to the south-east because the region has an exceptionally high rainfall for continental Thailand. As a result, the forest is a hybrid between seasonal (or dry) evergreen forests of continental Thailand and the very wet rainforests of the south. It harbours many plants and animals which are shared with southern Indo-China, making its communities of species unique. In addition to its particular conservation value, the wildlife sanctuary also has immense economic value, because it touches five of the region's seven provinces, and the bulk of their prosperity depends on the water it provides for their orchards, industry and tourism. Ang Ru Nai is a natural reservoir of water, wildlife and wealth, more effective and more efficient than any made by man. But now it is threatened by plans to build a four-lane highway that will cut the 240-kilometre (150-mile) journey from Bangkok by a mere 15 kilometres (9 miles) and save less than 25 minutes.

This blunt-fingered *Licuala* fan palm is one of several species found in the evergreen forests of South-east Asia. Its presence in Ang Ru Nai is indicative of the sanctuary's high moisture levels.

ABOVE A work of art and a lethal trap, this spectacular web belongs to the small spiny-backed orb weaver of the *Gasterocantha* genus. This spider has the disconcerting habit of weaving its intricate webs at human head height, so that unwary intruders will often find their faces enmeshed in one, but happily this is one spider that does not bite. Once its prey – mostly small flying insects – is trapped by these sticky threads, it will inject a paralysing venom, which also starts to dissolve its victim, before sucking out the contents of its body.

RIGHT Beware the funereal splendour of this black lily, *Tacca chantrieri*, for although it is graceful its tubers are poisonous and it emits a foul smell to attract the carrion flies which pollinate it. It occurs throughout the evergreen areas of Thailand, but is adapted to dense primary forest and is therefore threatened by forest degradation. Each region has its own variant of this species, this south-eastern specimen being exceptionally dark.

LEFT A male Siamese Fireback Pheasant (*Lophura diardi*) with a female of the same species (BELOW LEFT). Considered by many the most beautiful native pheasant, the Siamese Fireback is Thailand's national bird. However, these days it is a rare, probably endangered, resident of the lower evergreen slopes of eastern Thailand's mountain ranges. Ang Ru Nai protects the largest population in the country. Like all pheasants it spends most of the day on the ground, where it feeds on seeds, small fruits and insects, and roosts in trees at night. Compared to the flamboyant male, with its glossy dark blue underparts, the female pheasant has invariably much duller plumage – presumably because, being large ground-nesting birds, they need to be well camouflaged. The Siamese Fireback also used to occur in similar habitats of western Cambodia, although its present status there is unknown. All 49 pheasant species originate in Asia; 10 of them are found in Thailand.

RIGHT Unlike many lowland birds, the Spotted Owlet (*Athene brama*) is remarkably adaptable and has taken up residence in cultivated areas and villages. The fact that it is tiny, being under 20 centimetres (8 inches) tall, as well as nocturnal, undoubtedly helps. As a result it is very rarely seen, although, like all owls, it betrays its presence by its call, a distinctive assortment of high-pitched screeches and chuckles.

BELOW LEFT A large pink-orange bill and yellow face markings identify this Hill Myna (*Gracula religiosa*). Like all starlings, the Hill Myna has a large repertoire of calls and is an accomplished mimic of the human voice. For this reason it is a popular cage bird and its once huge numbers in Thailand have been greatly reduced by the captive bird trade. Although it ranges throughout Thailand it is commonest in lowland forests such as those in Ang Ru Nai.

BELOW RIGHT The Coral-billed Ground Cuckoo (*Carpococcyx renauldi*), as its name suggests, has a handsome, striking red bill, as well as a red eye-patch and legs which contrast with its black and grey plumage. It has a distinctive running gait and a hoarse deep rolling whistle. These large forest birds are very shy, difficult to see and quite rare, being confined to pockets of evergreen forest in eastern mountain ranges of Thailand.

ABOVE A mixed flock of *Graphium* and *Catopsilia* butterflies mud-puddling in a dry stream bed. Mud-puddling is a way of extracting salts from waterlogged sand where water has evaporated leaving behind the distillate. In many instances butterflies settle at the site where an animal has urinated. Such behaviour is commonly seen in the tropics but is only ever done by male butterflies, for reasons that are still not understood.

BELOW LEFT The eye-spots of this moth, *Spirama retorta*, are unusual in being on the upper rather than the lower wings. They are a twin-distance defence. From afar they help to camouflage the moth, but closer up they deter attackers by flashing alternately with the body's bright red underside as the moth flies off at high speed to settle elsewhere in the shade.

BELOW RIGHT After it pupates, this conspicuous caterpillar will turn into a Nymphalid butterfly, a relative of the admirals and tortoiseshells. Its spines are not poisonous but they do provide some physical deterrent as they would make it hard for a predator to swallow its prey. The caterpillar's colour suggests it might be poisonous to eat, however, or else it might be mimicking a poisonous species.

ABOVE The Fishing Cat (*Felis viverrina*) is one of only two wild cat species that are at all common in Thailand, the other being the smaller Leopard Cat (*Felis bengalensis*). It frequents the waterways of lowland forest areas, such as at Ang Ru Nai, crouching over a stream to catch small fish that come by with a swift scoop of its paw, flicking its prey on to the bank. Although the Fishing Cat lives by the water it is apparently reluctant to enter it. It also feeds on crabs and freshwater molluscs and, in spite of its name, the cat's diet includes rodents and birds.

RIGHT A Temple Terrapin (*Hieremys annandalii*) ambles over the sand. This species is fairly rare, being restricted to undisturbed streams and swamps of the lower Chao Phraya Basin, south-east Thailand, and adjacent parts of Cambodia, as well as some areas of the peninsula. Therefore it is effectively endemic to Thailand. This terrapin's common name may reflect the fact that turtles are often released into temple ponds by those who want to 'make merit': the Thai Buddhist notion of improving one's lot in a future life. Thai people believe that turtles are auspicious. Unfortunately, few urban Thais can distinguish between turtles and tortoises (the Thai word *tao* applies to both), with the result that many tortoises drown in the ponds.

Khao Soi Dao

This saddle-back mountain and its neighbour, Khao Kitchakut, are the highest in the south-east region. Khao Soi Dao is managed as a wildlife sanctuary while Khao Kitchakut is an adjacent national park. The aromatic name of the Cardomom mountain range is appropriate, for the region is famous for the local type of cardomom (*Amomun krevanh*) and clove (*A. testaceum*) which grow wild in the leaf-litter layer of the mountains' evergreen forest. Another endemic plant, the eaglewood tree *Aquilaria crassna*, locally known as *mai hom* or 'fragrant tree', provides the main shade. Its sap is used to make incense.

This sweetly scented forest is home to a very beautiful primate, the Pileated Gibbon. Distinguished by its black bib and tucker, this highly attractive tree-dwelling mammal is restricted to the moist mountain forests of the Cardomom and Phanom Dongrak Ranges and is now very rare. Khao Soi Dao protects this gibbon's largest population, thought to be about 1,000 pairs. Khao Soi Dao is also the only safe sanctuary for several other animals which occur only in this region, such as the Spiny-breasted Giant Frog, as well as several bird species including the Blue-rumped Pitta, the Mountain Fulvetta and a dark form of the Silver Pheasant (*Lophura nycthemera lewisi*) restricted to this area.

BELOW The upland forests of Khao Soi Dao and Khao Ang Ru Nai protect this strikingly attractive gibbon, *Hylobates pileatus* (OPPOSITE PAGE). Like all gibbons it uses its long, strong arms to swing far from branch to branch. In the wild these apes never normally descend to the ground.

ABOVE Even when moulting, the male Asian Fairy-bluebird (*Irena puella*) cuts a striking figure with its brilliant blue upper parts and bright red eyes. Once one of Thailand's commonest forest birds, it has become much more scarce in the last ten years.

ABOVE The Spotted Cat Snake (*Boiga multomaculata*) occurs all over Thailand but is commonest in the forests of the south-east, where it slithers through the trees in search of birds, mice and lizards. It often enters houses in pursuit of geckos but, although venomous, it is not aggressive.

BELOW The Green Pit Viper (*Trimeresurus popeorum*) is quick to strike and is highly venomous. Although its bite is rarely fatal to humans its venom is haemotoxic and therefore causes bleeding and intense pain. Like the Spotted Cat Snake, it is a nocturnal forest hunter which can grow to a metre (3 feet) in length, but it is confined to the higher elevations. When disturbed it vibrates its tail before inflicting its painful bite.

Cut off by mountains to the north and plains to the east and west, this little region has evolved an extraordinary number of endemics including the three birds on this page, all of which are confined to upland evergreen forest. ABOVE The delicate etching of the male Silver Pheasant's (*Lophura nycthemera lewisi*) silver and black plumage is reminiscent of the beautiful enamelled silverware that has been perfected in Thailand under royal patronage. *Lewisi* signifies the south-east's own dark race endemic to the Cardomom Range.

BELOW LEFT The Eastern Green Magpie (*Cissa hypoleuca*) is an uncommon resident of this region's evergreen forests. It is also known as the Short-tailed Magpie. Other parts of continental Thailand are occupied by its longer-tailed cousin, the Green Magpie. BELOW RIGHT This dowdy little bird is a juvenile Chestnut-headed Partridge, *Arborophila cambodiana*, of which the Thai race (*A. c. diversa*) may be a distinct species.

Koh Chang

Koh Chang, or 'Elephant Island', is the second largest island in Thailand after Phuket. Its beaches are beautiful and not, as yet, spoiled by tourist development. Though Koh Chang is closer to Bangkok than Phuket, it takes a day to get there and that has been its protection (as has a vicious breed of sand fly which island fruit farmers and fishermen must either endure or ignore). Koh Chang is the nucleus of a marine national park which incorporates 47 islands, many encircled by fringing reefs, and 450 square kilometres (174 square miles) of sea. The reefs are not as extensive or diverse as those of the Andaman Sea and Gulf of Thailand but they are still varied and underexplored. They are also some of the last coral gardens to survive the insidious pollution of Thailand's east coast.

Inland the islands vary from steep granite peaks, like Koh Chang and Koh Kut, to those that are virtually flat like Koh Mak and Koh Kradat. The latter, which means 'Paper Island', used to have the largest known herd of wild Hog Deer in Thailand but they were netted in 1986 and sent to captive breeding centres. Some have since been released in the Phu Khieo Wildlife Sanctuary in Esarn. Apart from Silver Leaf-monkeys and a few Wreathed Hornbills, animal life on the islands is limited to small species which inhabit the inland evergreen and coastal mangrove forests. Such inhabitants are the Koh Chang Frog and Pied Imperial Pigeon. Elephants adorn only the name of this national park.

The serenity of Koh Chang has been preserved by its far-flung location and its notoriety as a haven for smugglers.

Lying 5 kilometres (3 miles) off-shore, Koh Chang punctuates the southern tip of Thailand's border with Cambodia and remains an out-of-the-way island, once a pirate hideaway. Although the island is best known for its lovely white beaches with a lush green backdrop, and its underwater attractions, the vibrant colours shown here advertise the less well-known natural delights to be found within Koh Chang's inland forests. The yellow pendulous clusters of the Golden Shower Tree, *Cassia fistula* (RIGHT), alleviate the drab colouring of the long dry season. Further into the evergreen forest, the crusty red pods of a *Sterculia* (BELOW) and the orange flowers of an *Ixora* shrub (BELOW RIGHT) are a rare treat because both species are uncommon inhabitants of eastern Thailand.

FOLLOWING PAGE The lovely Than Mayom waterfall is one of Koh Chang's most striking inland features yet lies only a short walk from the sea.

Although much of Thailand's south-east coast is heavily polluted, the further reaches and islands of the Koh Chang Marine National Park offer snorkellers and divers much to enjoy. ABOVE A healthy head of mixed stony corals, in which lettuce coral (*Montipora* sp.) predominates. ABOVE RIGHT Oriental Sweetlips (*Plectorhinchus orientalis*) hovering in V formation. Primarily nocturnal, they gather in small shoals during the day, dispersing at night to feed on invertebrates on the sea bed. CENTRE RIGHT The ornate Mantis Shrimp (*Odontodactylus scyllarus*) has powerful claws for crushing molluscs. Normally carried folded beneath the front of the body, these appendages can be extended rapidly with enough force to break glass. BELOW RIGHT A Greenhead (Troschel's) Parrotfish (*Scarus troschelli*). Parrotfish tuck themselves into caves and crevices at night, encased in a mucous cocoon that is thought to prevent predators detecting their scent.

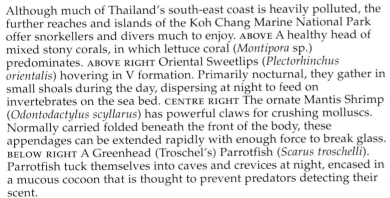

Focus on
WEST THAILAND

The west is the least disturbed region of Thailand because, until the 1980s, it had less to offer economically. It retains a unique mix of wildlife and about 40 per cent of the land has forest cover, most of which is protected by parks or sanctuaries. There are 15 conservation areas here, made up of six wildlife sanctuaries and nine national parks. Yet the region is still instantly identified by a monument to human endeavour and cruelty – the infamous bridge across the River Kwai (locally called the river Khwae Yai) built from 1943–44 by Japanese prisoners-of-war and conscripted Thai labour.

The long, thin rectangular western region is the cross-roads of Thailand. The principal highway is the Dawna-Tenasserim mountain range and the forest foothills that fringe it. This range of many ridges shields the whole western edge of Thailand like the ceremonial head-plate of an elephant on parade. This extra-long extension from the eastern Himalayas has only two main ridges in west Thailand: north of the river Khwae Noi lies the Dawna itself and the lower Thanon Thongchai, while south of that river there is the Tenasserim. Both the Khwae Yai and the Khwae Noi are tributaries of the Mae Khlong, and the valleys of these three big rivers were formed by faults in the earth's crust. These faults are still active so this region is an earthquake zone. Tremors happen all the time but few have registered more than 4.0 on the Richter Scale.

Major wildlife thoroughfares are also provided by the rivers and valleys that filtrate the Dawna-Tenasserim Range. Along all these natural byways many northern species reach the southern limit of their range, southern species meet them here but travel no further north and some species from Indo-China mingle with those that are Indo-Burmese. The result is a rich diversity of bird species such as Crested and Blue-banded Kingfishers (northern and southern species respectively) as well as Rufous-necked and White-crowned Hornbills, Bay-breasted and Streak-breasted Wood-peckers, and, among the mammals, Assamese and Long-tailed Macaques.

Macaque monkeys epitomise the richness and rarity of the region's wildlife community. All five South-east Asian species occur here; the Assamese and Rhesus Macaques of Sino-Himalayan origin go no further south or east, the Long-tailed and Pig-tailed Macaques originating from Malaysia and Indonesia go no further north. Only the Pig-tailed Macaque ranges all over Indo-China. Though all five species may be found in the region and sometimes in one area (Huai Kha Khaeng has all of them), they occupy different ecological niches.

Habitat diversity, as well as a central throughway location, allows this region to support an extraordinarily diverse flora and fauna. The western half is well watered by the south-west monsoon and has mostly evergreen forest except on steep porous slopes and land altered by man. The eastern half lies in its rainshadow and so is drier and more deciduous; but moist gulleys and dips foster evergreen forest, thus creating a mosaic of habitats with an array of wetlands. In this wonderworld of niches there are some

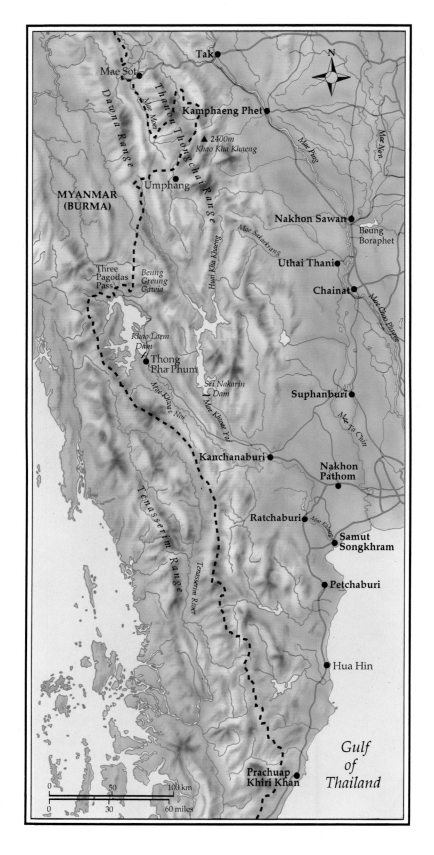

Western Thailand contains the single largest tract of protected forest surviving in mainland South-east Asia, covering over 12,000 square kilometres (4,500 square miles). This may also include the largest block of seasonal tropical forest left in Asia. Because the region is divided by the Dawna mountain range, the windward side supports evergreen formations (BELOW) watered by the south-west monsoon, whereas on the drier eastern side deciduous forest (RIGHT) predominates.

unique animal communities in which the number and composition of species speak volumes about the area's ecological wealth: 7 hornbills, 23 woodpeckers, 10 primates, 28 carnivores (8 of them cats), 3 bovids, over 65 bats and the only endemic Thai turtle – the Giant Softshell which is anything up to 1.2 metres (4 feet) long and weighs as much as 150 kilograms (330 pounds). Few areas in Asia can match this level of diversity, even around the equator.

The region's wealth of wildlife is matched by its varied habitats. These include the rich coastal mudflats and mangrove forests which rim the mouth of the Mae Khlong, as well as an abundance of mineral-licks, sink-holes and caves. Mineral-licks contain a variety of compounds (having several salts) which attract elephants, monkeys, deer, wild cattle, parakeets, pigeons and Green Peafowl. The elephants in Huai Kha Khaeng Wildlife Sanctuary, for example, appear to follow a cyclical route around the sanctuary travelling from lick to lick. Sink-holes occur where caves have collapsed. The west is full of them. Some have become ponds and lakes; others remain holes in the ground but are lined with organic debris and vegetation. Most are small being 5–50 metres (16–165 feet) across and 5–15 metres (16–50 feet) deep; but some feature on large-scale maps as 1–2 kilometres (½–1 mile) long, half a kilometre wide and up to 100 metres (330 feet) deep with steep sides. None has been studied in detail, so perhaps unknown species quite different from the world above still wait to be discovered.

Some of the country's largest caves are also in this region. One famous example is the temple cave at Khao Chong Pran in Ratchaburi province which accommodates around two million Free-tailed Bats. Every evening, at sunset, they form a long black cloud that lasts over 20 minutes as they stream from the cave to feed on insects in the fields around. Every fortnight, local monks

sell sacks of their nutrient-rich guano, collected from the cave floor, and use the income to support the temple. Bat guano is the best, and most expensive, fertilizer in Thailand, and is used on high-value crops such as pepper.

In Kanchanaburi, the Chalerm Rattanakosin National Park was specially created to protect a network of grottoes and caves over 300 metres (1,000 feet) long that undermines a hillside 59 kilometres

ABOVE Thailand supports the world's smallest as well as the largest bats. Kitti's Hog-nosed Bat (*Craseonycteris thonglongyai*) is the smallest mammal in the world, weighing only 2 grams. Its tiny eyes, large ears and compressed snout identify it as an insect-eater which finds its food by sonar, or echo-location. It is extremely rare, being confined to certain caves in the Khwae Noi region of west Thailand.

LEFT The Flying Fox (*Pteropus vampyrus*) is the world's largest bat with a wing-span of over 60 centimetres (2 feet). It eats fruit and plays a major role in forest regeneration by pollinating trees and dispersing their seeds. Its roosting habit during the day, in colonies of several thousand bats, makes it vulnerable to hunters.

(22 miles) square. The park is better known by its original local name, *Tham Than Lot* or 'water passing through the cave'. Here might once have been housed one of nature's greatest rarities. Named after the Thai naturalist who discovered it in 1973, Kitti's Hog-nosed Bat is the smallest mammal in the world (it weighs only 2 grams) and the sole representative of its family. It roosts in caves that have conical chambers with domed roofs at low altitudes in the middle part of west Thailand. It has a squashed snout (hence its name) and a wing-span of less than 8 centimetres (3 inches). It is more kindly called the 'bumblebee bat', a good description of its shape and size, but not of its status. Its main threats are damage to feeding grounds, cave disturbance and the curio trade. Tourists with strange tastes buy them stuffed as mementoes. Fortunately, others protect them by supporting the Sai Yok National Park, now their only safe stronghold. It lies beside the Myanmar border at the southern end of the Khwae Noi valley and is, at present, encircled by forest. But that forest is unprotected and may disappear, leaving Sai Yok isolated.

Forest clearance in the region is quite recent. Since the 1980s, when the Khao Laem and Sri Nakarin hydro-dams were constructed across the Khwae Noi and Khwae Yai, thousands of labourers and their families have moved in. Logging, mining, water-hungry crops such as pineapple, sugarcane and mango trees and, perhaps most intrusive of all, golf courses, have encroached on the region. For all that, the west still has fewer people and less land given over to development, and subsequent deforestation,

than other parts of the country. Retaining a healthy percentage of forest cover makes ecological sense, for these forests (with those of eastern Myanmar) are largely responsible for precipitating the south-west monsoon – the source of almost all Thailand's annual rainfall. Moisture-laden winds blow in from the Andaman Sea and start converting their load to rain as they meet the mountain forests of the Dawna-Tenasserim. Like all forests, these then store the water for slow release year round. That being so, Thailand can ill afford to lose any more forest from the region.

This may explain partly why so much of the region has been set aside for nature conservation. The largest tract of uninterrupted forest in Thailand stretches from Umphang to Kanchanaburi, covers around 14,000 square kilometres (5,400 square miles), not counting adjacent forests in Myanmar which stretch the length of the border, and incorporates 8½ conservation areas, totalling 12,966 square kilometres (5,000 square miles). Thus it is one of the largest protected forests in all South-east Asia. For a country that is widely known, and often criticised, for its deforestion, this is astonishing. It would take a gruelling hike for about a month to get from north to south of just this vast tract.

The half-protected area that is part of this conservation complex is the northern segment of the Khao Laem National Park (near Thong Pha Phum). This area is split from the rest of the park by a hydro-electric reservoir of the same name and the road to Three Pagodas Pass, deep in the mountains skirting the Myanmar border. This 512-square-kilometre (197-square-mile) wedge of park is known as *Greung Gawia* and was protected only against hunting, not logging, until recently. It was saved in the nick of time by the national logging ban of 1989. It is a densely wooded, low-lying enclave that nestles into the tail of the Dawna Range on the westward side. Its forest is a luxuriant evergreen formation that brims with colour and sound, its centre is adorned by a small natural lake and it runs next to Thung Yai, the largest single conservation area in the country.

Umphang

The Umphang Wildlife Sanctuary resembles an extracted tooth in shape, encompassing two ridges of the Dawna Range but excluding the uppermost valley of the river Mae Khlong which lies between the two. The reasons for this demarcation are clear. The ridges are primary sources of the upper Mae Khlong and Mae Chan rivers, whereas the valley is a rural settlement of mostly Karen farmers with its hub at the old enclave of Umphang town.

The Umphang sanctuary has a motley mix of forests on its mountain slopes and many small animals, but it is best known for a pair of remote forest lakes, the tallest waterfall in Thailand and a river with two-tone banks. The lakes, known as *La-Er-Or*, are most easily seen from the air. Getting there is an arduous hike. They are small, marshy and shaded, with masses of tiny leeches that wriggle around the reeds beneath moorhens, rails and Lesser Whistling Ducks. The waterfall is called *Thi Law Su* in Karen and is fed from the highest mountain in the west, Khao Kha Khaeng at 2,400 metres (7,874 feet). From there, the two-tone river is a hard day's walk. The river is a tributary of the upper Mae Khlong and flows from west to east along a line which separates black soil from red. The colours appear to delineate the southern range of teak forests. Teak trees grow on the northern bank but do not cross the river.

Picturesque Thi Law Su waterfall cascades down a classic limestone staircase from the 'strong-legged mountain', Khao Kha Khaeng, the highest in west Thailand.

ABOVE Striking black-and-white plumage identifies the Pied Kingfisher (*Ceryle rudis*). It resides by larger rivers, lakes and canals where steep banks provide suitable nesting sites. It is one of 15 kingfisher species in Thailand and still relatively common, whereas its cousin the Crested Kingfisher (*Megaceryle lugubris*) is confined to large, low-lying waterways of the north-west and is now rarely seen outside the Umphang and Thung Yai Wildlife Sanctuaries.

BELOW The male Grey Peacock Pheasant (*Polyplectron bicalcaratum*) has a short, bushy crest and iridescent violet 'eye'-spots, but it is perhaps best known for its excited *waak-waak-waak* call – a distinctive sound of the western evergreen forests, and happily still a relatively common one. This species is found in such conservation areas as Umphang up to about 1,800 metres (6,000 feet).

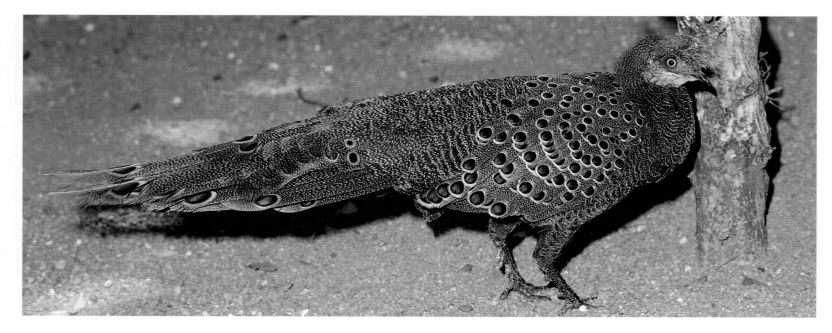

The open canopies of mixed deciduous forest let in enough sunlight to produce dense ground cover and varying leaf colour. These characteristics readily distinguish such formations from evergreen forests.

Suffocation of a tree by a strangler fig is extremely slow, taking many years before the host (whose bark is still just visible here) is fully enveloped by the constricting limbs of the fig tree. Not all figs are stranglers, though many Thai species are.

Many tropical figs are caulicolous, meaning that their fruits emerge directly from the trunk or stems, as with this fig tree (*Ficus oligodon*), which is common throughout the evergreen forests of continental Thailand.

The familiar red fruit of wild raspberries is a startling sight for western visitors to Asia, who see them only as cultivated fruits. This species (*Rubus alexifolius*) is found in upland evergreen forests of continental Thailand.

The Elephant-foot Yam, *Amorphophallus campanulatus*, is a giant herb of north and north-west Thailand's deciduous forests. It can grow to 2 metres (6 feet) high from a huge edible tuber.

Mae Wong

This lovely national park is an elegant half-circle of evergreen hills inset with lowland deciduous forest that is threaded by the Mae Wong river itself and its many tributaries. Ever since it was established in 1987, this park has been overshadowed by the Thung Yai and Huai Kha Khaeng sanctuaries which it adjoins in the south and south-west. Its western and northern boundaries run alongside the Umphang and Khlong Lan conservation areas. But, with 894 square kilometres (345 square miles) of forest that is buffered on three sides and encircles an unspoilt lowland river, Mae Wong is a highly significant park. This is because so few conservation sites in Thailand, or indeed Asia, protect lowland rivers or riverine forests intact. Lowland valleys are usually appropriated by people, as land around the Mae Wong was for a while, but the settlers moved when a national park was created there.

The river meanders through thick clumps of grass and shrub and in the dry season it shrinks into the sand leaving narrow channels above ground from which the animals drink. All around it, the forest is recovering. With its deciduous teak forest and pristine riverine habitats, it offers refuge to rare lowland mammals including tiger, elephant, Banteng, wild dogs, Golden Cats and otters. It also provides a home for some extremely rare deciduous forest birds such as the Yellow-footed Pigeon, Alexandrine Parakeet and Yellow-crowned Woodpecker. But that home is under siege from a proposed irrigation dam that threatens to drain the lifeforce of the park.

Mae Wong National Park protects some of the best mixed deciduous forest in Thailand and marks the southern limit of naturally growing teak. It adds significant value to Huai Kha Khaeng, the country's World Heritage Site, next door and is an important conservation area in its own right.

RIGHT The lovely lowland forests of the Mae Wong National Park lie inside a crescent of mountains. Much of Mae Wong was once graced by teak trees and the mixed deciduous forest that teak typifies. However, some 20 years ago settlers moved in and their yearly fires encouraged the spread of poorer, more ordinary formations, since teak forest is not resistant to fire whereas dry dipterocarp forest is, and so is bamboo. Although these settlers were relocated, to let the park recover its former glory, the core of the park is threatened again, this time by an irrigation dam. For those who enjoy the outdoor life and nature in the raw Mae Wong is ideal. It is as yet unspoiled by ugly or unnecessary modern development. No Thai national parks have yet perfected proper nature tourism, but it could still be done in this under-appreciated conservation area.

BELOW LEFT The seed pods of *Sterculia hypochra* are a striking feature of deciduous forests in the dry season, when they stand out in stark contrast to the parched colouring of the foliage, much of which may have been burned by the ubiquitous annual fires. When the pods are ripe they turn red and split open along the underside seam, exposing two rows of shiny black seeds, one on either side. Many pods then fall from the stems and ornament the ground as works of art.

BELOW RIGHT The succulent vine *Dischidia nummularia* is characteristic of the driest deciduous forests, for which its water-retaining leaves are well adapted. Like other members of the milkweed family (so-called because they contain a white latex sap), it has a symbiotic relationship with ants. In the case of this species, the ants lay their eggs in the leaves and in return probably protect the plant against leaf predators.

ABOVE The large eyes surrounded by striking rings belong to a Slow Loris (*Nycticebus coucang*), caught in flashlight glare, as it grips a branch with its broad fingertips and well-adapted thumb and great toe. As the name suggests, this little primate is normally slow moving, though it can move fast if need be. It is the only nocturnal species of Thailand's 13 primates, but its night-time activities in search of insects, fruit, flowers and eggs do not mean it is overlooked by hunters. Because of its gentle, attractive appearance it is illegally trapped for the pet trade, and it is also killed for meat.

LEFT The Banteng (*Bos javanicus*), or red ox, is one of Asia's four wild cattle species and is thought to be an ancestor of domestic cattle. Because so little of its natural habitat survives and because it is so heavily hunted it is now extremely rare. The contiguous Mae Wong and Huai Kha Khaeng conservation areas protect the largest surviving population of perhaps only 200 individuals.

BELOW LEFT The White-throated Kingfisher (*Halcyon smyrnensis*) is still a common sight at Mae Wong, with its beautiful turquoise mantle, wings and tail and its dusky-red bill. The white throat is clearly evident here.

BELOW RIGHT Another fairly common sight in the park, the populations of Spotted Dove (*Streptopelia chinensis*) would be severely disrupted by the proposed dam. The white spots on a black background around the collar and the vinous-coloured belly and breast help identify this dove.

RIGHT The Red-breasted Parakeet (*Psittacula alexandri*) is identified as much by its broad black moustache and black bar across the forehead as by its colourful breast. It favours deciduous woodlands with secondary forest and scrub, so Mae Wong is ideal. Like the other four parakeets located in Thailand, it is severely threatened by the wild bird trade.

FAR RIGHT The mixed deciduous forests of Mae Wong and Huai Kha Khaeng protect the only sizeable population of Thailand's rarest parakeet, the Alexandrine Parakeet (*Psittacula eupatria*). Its huge red bill makes short work of fruits, nuts and seeds and it uses its feet to manipulate its food.

BELOW LEFT Large-tailed Nightjars (*Caprimulgus macrurus*) are common inhabitants of open woodland but are rarely seen because they are nocturnal and when at roost by day they are well camouflaged. The tiny bill belies a huge gape into which fall insects as the birds feed on the wing. Their distinctive resonant *chonk-chonk* call is a regular night-time feature.

BELOW RIGHT Belonging to the crow, jay and magpie family, the Rufous Treepie (*Dendrocitta vagabunda*) is an inveterate thief like its cousins, with a penchant for other birds' eggs. Like all the other birds on this page, it prefers dry dipterocarp and mixed deciduous woodlands.

Thung Yai

Thung Yai is not only the largest single conservation area in Thailand, it is also the birthplace of nature conservation in Thailand. It therefore has a value that is historic as well as ecological. In the early 1980s, it was threatened by a huge hydro-dam that would have done immense harm had it gone ahead. Fortunately it was halted, but the area's ecological value is being compromised by mining that has gouged out its western side and by settlement at its centre.

Its name means 'big field' and at its centre lies a 100-square-kilometre (38-square-mile) 'field' of savanna grassland with gently rolling hills, dotted with tufty palms, multi-headed cycads and stunted deciduous trees. But Thung Yai encompasses much more than that. Its 3,622 square kilometres (1,398 square miles) include mountains, valleys and upland plains. It is bounded on three sides by protected forest and its western border adjoins a forested part of Myanmar. It also contains two rivers: the Mae Khlong is swift, steep and rocky, while the Mae Chan is open and meandering. In the middle of the sanctuary they merge to form the Upper Khae Yai, a big brown river that forges through a tall, precipitous valley edged with evergreen forest. The Crested Kingfisher – largest and rarest of its kind – is found there, as is the rare Lesser Fish Eagle; and in quiet parts of the Mae Chan elegant Oriental Darters perch above the river waiting to spear unwary fish below.

A small herd of Gaur, or Asian Bison (*Bos gaurus*) browse in the relative safety of a conservation area. The Gaur is the largest of Asia's four wild cattle species, standing just under 2 metres (6 feet) at the shoulder. The range of the animal more or less coincides with that of its near relative the Banteng, except that, because it is primarily a browsing species of evergreen forests (as opposed to a grazing species of deciduous forests and grassland), it never crossed the Sunda Shelf to Borneo during the last ice ages. Today it mostly occurs in upland areas because that is where evergreen forest survives.

RIGHT This charming orchid, *Dendrobium cariniferum*, is found only in the deciduous forests of northern and north-western Thailand. The moisture-retaining pseudo-bulbs on its stems indicate that it is well adapted to the long dry season of continental Thailand.

BELOW LEFT The Mae Chan river flows through the heart of Thung Yai to join the upper Khwae Yai. At its lower reaches it is the only stretch of this river system where it is safe to cross from one side of the sanctuary to the other. It is therefore a strategic thoroughfare for wildlife.

BELOW RIGHT Using its sharp-pointed horns and the hard frontal ridge of its forehead, an adult Gaur can kill an assailant with one blow. Even leopards and tigers will rarely tackle one of these enormous beasts. Generally, however, Gaur will choose to avoid conflict rather than engage.

ABOVE The White-winged Duck (*Cairina scutulata*) was long presumed extinct in the wild in Thailand. In the late 1980s, not long after the discovery of three birds held by a farmer in Esarn, several were seen at dusk on a quiet forest lake in the far interior of Thung Yai.

ABOVE The Kalij Pheasant (*Lophura leucomelana*) is an Indo-Burman bird which does not extend east of the Dawna Range. This is an immature female, whose plumage will darken with maturity. The red-legged race (*L. l. crawfurdii*) shown here is found in south-west Thailand.

FAR LEFT The double-legged segments of this arthropod identify it as a millipede (Polydesmidae). In contrast centipedes have only one leg per segment and are carnivorous, whereas most millipedes are herbivores.

LEFT The transparent wings of a Green Dragontail (*Meges virescens*) may be a form of camouflage as it is hard to see this butterfly in flight.

BELOW These roosting Roundleaf Bats (*Hipposideros larvatus*) at Thung Yai are among 60 known species found there, making it one of Thailand's most important bat sanctuaries.

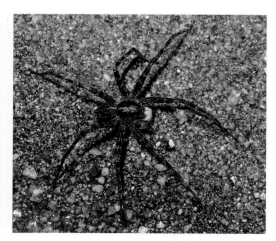

ABOVE A female fishing spider (*Thalassius* sp.) scurries along a gravelly stream bed, carrying her egg sac.

ABOVE LEFT Ground gingers (*Curcuma aeruginosa*) smother the central savanna grasslands of Thung Yai in the dry season and are especially noticeable after the annual fires, when their colourful blooms stand out against the blackened soil. This bright pink variety is thought to be endemic to Thung Yai.

BELOW LEFT The savanna grasslands of Thung Yai are famous for their tall multi-branched cycads, many of which have three or four heads and look like tree ferns. Like all cycads they are dioecious, that is plants which are either male or female. The female plants (seen here) have clusters of round woody fruits while the males have erect central cones. Cycads were thriving in the days of the dinosaurs and beyond, some 120 to 155 million years ago. Therefore those that survive today are evolutionarily important as living fossils.

ABOVE RIGHT This rare member of the rose family, *Raphiolepis indica*, is found only in the uplands of north and north-western Thailand.

RIGHT The distinctive shape and colouring of *Gmelina arborea* blossoms, with their yellow landing-pads and inviting interiors, suggest that they are pollinated by heavy-bodied insects such as beetles or bees. This common inhabitant of Thai deciduous forests is a fast-growing native tree species and is widely grown in South-east Asia as an alternative to eucalyptus for paper and pulp.

BELOW RIGHT The hood-like spathe of this arum lily, *Remusatia vivipara*, is sheltering several Chrysomelid lily-beetles, which are probably species-specific pollinators of this plant. Plant-insect relationships such as this are very common among the aroid plants.

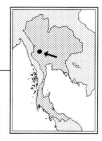

Huai Kha Khaeng

This sanctuary has a legendary status in Thailand as the finest conservation area in the country, and as the spiritual home of one of its most dedicated conservationists. Seub Nakhasathien helped to propose Huai Kha Khaeng as a UNESCO World Heritage Site but did not live to see this proposal accepted. With 2,780 kilometres (1,073 square miles), the sanctuary is smaller than adjoining Thung Yai but better because it has no settlers within its boundaries. As a result it is more intact than any other conservation area in Thailand.

Huai Kha Khaeng retains the best tracts of deciduous forest in the country and protects the largest Thai populations of the rare Red Dog and Banteng and the only population of Red-headed Vultures. It also has an incredible 22 woodpecker species including the White-bellied and Great Slaty, two of the largest and rarest Old World woodpeckers. However, none of these is as rare as the sanctuary's wild Water Buffaloes. These huge beasts hide away in a lower valley whose stream rises in the north of the sanctuary and runs right through its centre. The banks of this untroubled stream are stippled with the imprints of other wild animals: elephant and tiger, fishing cats and otters, civets and deer. Though wary and shy, Green Peafowl are the most evident animals in the valley. At dawn and dusk their triumphant calls proclaim what they themselves do not know, that they are the last survivors of their kind in Thailand.

Huai Kha Khaeng is Thailand's premier conservation zone for many reasons, including its status as a World Heritage Site. Together with adjoining Thung Yai it forms the core of a conservation area encompassing every forest type of continental Thailand.

The tiger is the largest of the Asian cats, of which at least eight species are found in this sanctuary alone. More tigers may prowl about the riverine forests of Huai Kha Khaeng than in any other areas of Thailand. This is because there is abundant water and prey and, at present, better protection than in most other conservation areas in the country. Tiger pug marks are often evident in the soft sand and mud lining the Huai Kha Khaeng river. After a kill a tiger frequently drags its prey close to water so that it can drink while also eating. Sambar Deer, Banteng and wild pig are its preferred prey. Tigers tend to hunt at twilight or at night, covering perhaps 20 kilometres (12 miles), using sight and hearing rather than sense of smell. It is estimated that

in the wild they may live for about 15 years, but their survival is gravely threatened even in Huai Kha Khaeng by hunters leaving poisoned bait.

FOLLOWING PAGES To look across the mixed deciduous forests of eastern Huai Kha Khaeng, at the end of the rainy season, is to sense why this sanctuary was named a World Heritage Site. Under its extensive canopies lie some of the rarest large mammals in Thailand: elephants, Banteng, Red Dogs and Golden Cats to name a few. It is hard to imagine that, but for the logging ban of 1989, this view would now be a landscape of stumps and desecration.

ABOVE LEFT *Peristrophe lanceolata* is a common flower all over continental Thailand, growing in deciduous and evergreen forest.

ABOVE RIGHT Early in the morning at the height of the dry season, an elephant and her calf amble across Huai Kha Khaeng. A calf will be nursed by its mother until it is three to five years old. It suckles with its mouth and will take several years to grasp the skilful use of its trunk. With plenty of fodder and no human settlements, Huai Kha Khaeng is an exceptional sanctuary for elephants. However, its herds were heavily preyed upon for ivory, and infants were taken into captivity, until protection was improved in 1990.

LEFT Elsewhere in Asia *Cassia alata* commonly colonizes wastelands but in Thailand it has been found only in natural clearings of the western forests.

BELOW LEFT This *Pseuderanthemum* sp. is a quite rare plant of north and west deciduous forest.

BELOW RIGHT Huai Kha Khaeng supports what is possibly the last truly wild population of Asia's Water Buffaloes (*Bubalus bubalis*). Bigger, faster and shyer than the docile domestic breed, the wild buffalo is rarely seen, and perhaps only 100 individuals are left. Its footprints are its most distinctive sign because they are so much larger – 20 centimetres (8 inches) – and rounder than those of Gaur or Banteng. The buffaloes live in the alluvial lowlands of southern Huai Kha Khaeng.

Treetops catch the sunlight, forming just part of a rich mix of habitats with myriad flora and fauna following the Huai Kha Khaeng river (in the foreground). This gentle, sand-bottomed waterway meanders for 100 kilometres (60 miles) through a broad valley, and is exceptional in being the central feature of the sanctuary and not a mere boundary marker. It is also unique in having all its headwaters and catchment forests within the same protected area.

LEFT The Small-clawed Otter (*Aonyx cinerea*) ranges along the riverine habitats of the Huai Kha Khaeng valley where it eats small fish, crabs and molluscs. This sanctuary also boasts two other otter species: the Smooth-coated Otter (*Lutra perspicillata*) is the largest species and occupies the slower, lower reaches of the river, while the Eurasian Otter (*L. lutra*), common in Europe but rare in Asia, inhabits the evergreen upper reaches where the waterways are rockier and the fish smaller. Few areas in Asia still support these three species together because otters are so susceptible to riverine pollution and persecution by people and dogs.

BELOW LEFT Another rare resident of this river valley is the Green Peafowl (*Pavo muticus*) of South-east Asia. It is the largest pheasant of all and is not as quiet as its scientific name suggests. At dawn and dusk in the breeding season its trumpet calls ring out across the valley. The bird seen here is a sub-adult male which has not yet grown the characteristic breeding plumage of some 200 elongated tail-coverts, the green feathers above the dark brown tail.

OPPOSITE PAGE The flora and fauna diversity of Huai Kha Khaeng is greatly increased by its mix of habitats. Here a sharp contrast between savanna grassland (the driest of the deciduous dipterocarp formations) and the adjacent evergreen forest is indicative of changes in soil types.

BELOW The Red-headed Vulture (*Sarcogyps calvus*) survives in Thailand only in the river valley of Huai Kha Khaeng where it scavenges on the bodies of dead animals. The near total demise of Thailand's four vulture species is a mystery as they are neither hunted for food nor kept as pets. They appear to have fallen victim to superstition, poisoning from baited carcasses meant for tigers, and a reduction in natural carrion. This is a worrying trend as there are probably no more than two dozen left in this sanctuary.

BELOW Beware the furry charm of these vine pods, *Mucuna pruriens*, for they are covered with stiff stinging hairs which if touched will cause intense skin irritation. This plant is characteristic of open areas, including forest trails, where its dangling pods and sinister purple-black flowers often hang in the path of passing pedestrians. The leaves in this picture belong to another vine.

Huai Kha Khaeng harbours seven of Thailand's twelve hornbill species (the other five are confined to the south) including the Great Hornbill, *Buceros bicornis* (LEFT), with its gold-coloured head and neck. This large bird has a massive 2-metre (6-foot) wing-span. The white eye identifies this one as female. The male's eye is red. The male Wreathed Hornbill, *Rhyticeros undulatus* (TOP), is distinguished from the female (ABOVE) by his white neck and yellow throat pouch.

Huai Kha Khaeng has an especially rare hornbill species, the Rufous-necked (*Aceros nipalensis*) seen here (FAR LEFT) with the bright orange-red neck of the male. This species has been all but eliminated from the rest of its range in northern Thailand (along with most other hornbills) by excessive hunting. LEFT The Brown Hornbill (*Ptilolaemus tickelli*) occurs in Huai Kha Khaeng as a western sub-species (*P. t. tickelli*). Unlike most hornbills, it practises co-operative breeding whereby offspring (usually males) help their parents feed sibling chicks.

OPPOSITE PAGE The sanctuary's forest canopy protects hornbills as they nest only in tall living trees and are primarily fruit eaters. Thus large tracts of primary forest, again supplied by Huai Kha Khaeng, are needed for different species to survive together in viable numbers.

Kaeng Krachan

This is the largest, and one of the most dramatic, national parks in Thailand. It occupies 2,915 square kilometres (1,125 miles) of mostly pristine evergreen forest beside the Myanmar border and is barely three hours from Bangkok. Yet, surprisingly, it remains largely unexplored. Virtually nothing is known about its flora and small fauna and very little about its large animals.

The interior is reached by an old logging road (wisely kept only one-lane wide) which winds up and around the ridge that leads to the heart of the park. In the early morning this drive is magical. The road is hugged on either side by forest that reverberates with the *toi-oi-oik* of Green Broadbills, the *waak-waak-waak* of a Grey Peacock Pheasant and the whooping duets of gibbons claiming their territorial rights. At intervals there are super-spectacular views where the forest drops into valleys that are spread with a coating of cloud so thick you feel you could touch it. You may also see a distant bevy

of hornbills flying silently across this billowy 'sea'. Kaeng Krachan has many birds, some northern, some southern, some peculiarly out-of-place, like the Ratchet-tailed Treepie that hails from Indo-China. It is an exciting, wild and rugged place to hike through. The forest trails can be followed for hours, or even weeks, with a guide; but the hiker must carry all essentials and expect to meet large mammals, including, perhaps, a Sumatran Rhinoceros – reputed to still be lurking in its depths.

The tranquil beauty of this sunset scene belies the fact that this irrigation reservoir has flooded the central lowlands of Kaeng Krachan's eastern edge. The mountains in the background are mostly limestone but have a granite core.

RIGHT Beyond the drying scrublands of this park's eastern edge there is a vast area of evergreen forest with a wealth of wildlife as yet unsurveyed. Kaeng Krachan deserves more attention from researchers because it is the most significant conservation area in the Thai Tenasserim and because it adjoins even better forests in Myanmar. According to local lore, the Sumatran Rhinoceros survives in the park's remote interior. Sceptics demur, but no one doubts that Kaeng Krachan would reward more research investment. It also lends itself to limited long-distance hiking for hardy naturalists with, ideally, domestic elephants to transport food and gear around the hilly forest trails.

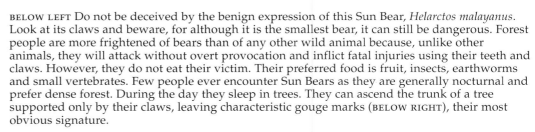

BELOW LEFT Do not be deceived by the benign expression of this Sun Bear, *Helarctos malayanus*. Look at its claws and beware, for although it is the smallest bear, it can still be dangerous. Forest people are more frightened of bears than of any other wild animal because, unlike other animals, they will attack without overt provocation and inflict fatal injuries using their teeth and claws. However, they do not eat their victim. Their preferred food is fruit, insects, earthworms and small vertebrates. Few people ever encounter Sun Bears as they are generally nocturnal and prefer dense forest. During the day they sleep in trees. They can ascend the trunk of a tree supported only by their claws, leaving characteristic gouge marks (BELOW RIGHT), their most obvious signature.

Thailand's four leaf-monkeys (or langurs) can be hard to distinguish because three of them have white eye-rings and pale mouth-patches. But only two, including this young Banded Langur (*Trachypithecus melalophos*), and the Dusky Langur, are ever seen in Kaeng Krachan. Although both co-inhabit the Thai–Malay peninsula, the banded species tends to occur at lower elevations and is therefore the rarer.

Typically slumped in a tree during daylight hours, this Binturong (*Arctictis binturong*) rests in the shade of tall evergreen forest. Also known as the Bear Cat, it is in fact the largest civet. It can climb a tree with ease but does so rather slowly using its long prehensile tail to keep its balance. Binturongs eat insects, small birds, rodents and fruit.

The protruding tube entrance made of wax by *Trigona* sweat bees leads to their nest in this hollow tree. As their name implies, sweat bees are attracted to the salt in sweat, but luckily they are stingless, unlike their relatives, the honey bees.

RIGHT Exceptionally alert, and needing to be with tigers stalking the undergrowth, this Fea's Barking Deer (*Muntiacus feae*) is a rare species and little is known of its behaviour. It is confined to the semi-evergreen forests of the Tenasserim mountain range where it browses at dusk on the leaves of seedlings and herbs. It is smaller and darker than its co-resident cousin, *Muntiacus muntjak*, but its voice is much the same. It was named after an Italian priest, Monsignor Fea.

BELOW LEFT The two-tone colouring of the Asian Tapir (*Tapirus indicus*) obscures its outline so that night-prowling tigers are less likely to recognize it as prey. When lying down in evergreen forest during the day, it resembles a large rock. This disguise, together with the thick hard skin around its neck, protects it from predators. It can also avoid predators by escaping through dense spiky undergrowth which would deter a thinner-skinned animal. Young tapirs are born with camouflage stripes which they lose in their first year. Although it is known as the Asian Tapir to distinguish it from its South American cousins, it is restricted to evergreen forests between Sumatra and the West Thailand–East Myanmar border.

BELOW RIGHT This pretty shrub is one of two dozen *Ixora* species found in Thailand, a few of which are introduced ornamentals. The genus is named after an Indian deity and some plants are known as 'Flame of the Woods' because their bright red flowers contrast so dramatically with the dark green of the forest.

Khao Sam Roi Yot

This remarkable little park, the first coastal park in Thailand, occupies the 'knee' above the narrow part of the peninsula and faces into the Gulf of Thailand. It covers officially only 98 square kilometres (38 square miles) but is probably the only place in Thailand where visitors could see almost 300 species of birds in one weekend just a few easy hours from Bangkok. Sand, sea, marsh, mountain, mangrove, mudflats and caves, and their associated fauna – this park has them all.

The name *Khao Sam Roi Yot* means 'mountain of three hundred peaks' and that is the feature that dominates its landscape. The mountain is limestone, with a jagged crest and spectacular caves. Its forest is dry and open but this makes it easier to see its animal inhabitants such as Peregrine Falcons, White-bellied Sea Eagles, Mangrove Whistlers, Forest Wagtails and Dusky Leaf-monkeys. The inland side of the mountain has the park's most important habitat, its marshland. It is the largest protected freshwater marsh in Thailand and supports a wealth of wetland birds such as pelicans, Purple Herons, Painted Storks, Pygmy Geese, Marsh Harriers, Streaked Weavers, Garganey and Whistling Ducks. Between the mountain and the sea there are mangroves, mudflats and sandy beaches lined with pines. At any one time there may also be 48 species of shorebirds probing for food in the soft mud and sand including stints, stilts, sandpipers, sanderlings, knots, plovers and greenshanks. No wonder this is named as one of Asia's most important places for migrant waterbirds.

The freshwater marsh of Khao Sam Roi Yot lies sheltered under the jagged outline of the mountain ridge which gives the park its name 'Three Hundred Peaks'. This national park is one of the best wildlife wetlands in Thailand.

The spectacular limestone peaks at the centre of Khao Sam Roi Yot are covered by scrubby forest which is characteristic of such dry precipitous crags. In spite of its apparent sparsity, this vegetation harbours many birds such as Laced Woodpeckers, Puff-throated Babblers and the finely marked Forest Wagtail, as well as a surprising number of large mammals including leopard, Serow and crab-eating macaques. Although these limestone crags are the most dramatic feature of the national park, they are not the most important from a conservation point of view. That distinction goes to the mangroves and marshlands east and west of them. Both habitats have been encroached by prawn farms (seen on the right of the picture below), but now many of these have been abandoned because a fatal waterborne virus has infected captive prawn populations in Thailand. Over a century ago another water-dependent disease, this time malaria, claimed the life of Rama IV, one of Thailand's most distinguished monarchs who is better known in the west as King Mongkut. He was bitten by a malarial mosquito while in these marshes watching an eclipse of the sun which he had predicted, and died two months later.

Khao Sam Roi Yot's freshwater marsh is a haven for wetland birds and one of the best places in Thailand to see over-wintering visitors. Its occupants include the Black-crowned Night Heron (*Nycticorax nycticorax*) (TOP LEFT); the Pacific Reef Egret (*Egretta sacra*), including this dark morph (TOP MIDDLE); the Streaked Weaver (*Ploceus manyar*) (TOP RIGHT); the Garganey (*Anas querquedula*) (FAR LEFT); and the Northern Pintail (*Anas acuta*) (LEFT).

BELOW LEFT The Greater Adjutant (*Leptoptilos dubius*) is Thailand's largest, and one of its rarest, overwintering storks. Like most large waterbirds it has suffered from hunting and habitat destruction, and its case is made worse by the fact that Thais think it hideous and therefore do not sympathize with its plight.

Unlike other storks it flies with its neck retracted. BELOW RIGHT The Painted Stork (*Mycteria leucocephala*) was once common and widespread but is now a rare breeding visitor and passage migrant. Its pale pink facial skin will turn red in the breeding season.

OPPOSITE PAGE, BELOW LEFT This sapling *Rhizophora* is one of several mangrove trees which have been replanted in a heroic effort to regenerate the mangrove forests that have been badly degraded by the prawn farmers. As they mature they will be recolonized by a rewarding variety of avian species, such as those which probe in soft or liquid mud to find their food, as well as mudskippers and crimson one-armed crabs. In spite of its tiny size, Khao Sam Roi Yot could be a paradise for bird enthusiasts because it supports so many species in such a variety of habitats, all within easy reach of the park headquarters. This in turn would help the local economy as well as conservation.

ABOVE The Whimbrel (*Numenius phaeopus*) is a common winter wader visitor to the coastal mudflats and sandy beaches of western and southern Thailand. Apart from its characteristic beak it has a very distinctive call, a clear whinnying *ti* trill of seven notes.

RIGHT The Black-faced Spoonbill (*Platalea minor*) is occasionally seen in Thailand as an overwintering visitor on a few coastal mudflats. In recent years it has not been seen at Khao Sam Roi Yot except in flight on its way to safer sites south of Thailand.

BELOW RIGHT Khao Sam Roi Yot contains one of only two protected breeding sites for Purple Herons (*Ardea purpurea*) in Thailand, and only 10 to 15 pairs remain here. This big wading bird, with its serpentine neck and dagger-like bill, will breed only in large reed swamps, few of which survive. Consequently, it is now an uncommon resident but remains a fairly common migrant. Other breeding waterbirds at Khao Sam Roi Yot include the Cotton Pigmy Goose, Cinnamon Bittern and Purple Swamphen. More splendid still, this marsh is the only known wintering area in the world for the rare Manchurian race of the Paddyfield Warbler.

Focus on
SOUTH THAILAND

Thailand's south is a long 1,000-kilometre (620-mile) stretch of land that is divided between the Andaman Sea and the Gulf of Thailand, extending from southern Myanmar to Malaysia. This region also includes hundreds of islands with spectacular coastlines and marine wildlife.

Because it is so long, people often assume that the south must be Thailand's largest region but, in fact, in land area it is only 70,000 square kilometres (27,000 square miles), which is quite a lot less than the north, west and north-east. The region is also one of the most independently minded in Thailand, with one-quarter of the population Muslims of Malay stock. In fact the further south you go, the more Malay the region becomes ethnically and in outlook. From Phuket and Phattalung, the proportion of Thai Malays rises sharply until, south of Satun, they make up three-quarters of the population. Most speak Thai, but many in the far south do not. They speak Yawi (a northern Malay dialect) and have stronger ties across the southern border.

As for the northern border, few can agree where the south of Thailand actually begins. Some say the south starts from the long thin leg of Prachuap Khiri Khan, where the boundary with Myanmar bulges into Thailand. Here, the country narrows to a strip of less than 15 kilometres (9 miles) wide with room for little more than a coastal road, a railway line, some cultivated slopes and seaside settlements. But in other opinions the south starts where the Myanmar border runs into the sea leaving a narrow Thai peninsula of only 40 kilometres (25 miles) between the east and west coasts. This area is known as the Isthmus of Kra after the penetrative estuary that stretches from Kraburi to Ranong and takes over border duties from the ridge of the Tenasserim mountain range.

There are three mountain ranges in the peninsula, all offshoots of the Tenasserim, all running close together roughly north-south. They divide the peninsula into west and east. Where the main Tenasserim Range ends at the Isthmus of Kra, the Phuket Range takes over for the next 400 kilometres (250 miles) before it dives into the Andaman Sea and ends with its namesake archipelago. This range is not high – few peaks exceed 1,000 metres (3,280 feet) – but it rises steeply and hugs the western coast leaving little room for a coastal plain. This mountain-to-sea proximity prompts the highest rainfall in Thailand on the windward side (the south-west monsoon comes from the Andaman Sea). In fact, the west coast region of Ranong has the highest rainfall in Thailand with around 5,000 millimetres (197 inches) a year.

The transition from continental Thailand, with its strongly seasonal vegetation, to the shorter, less severe dry season and higher rainfalls of the peninsula, is marked by the Isthmus of Kra. From here, deciduous and dry evergreen forests give way to semi-evergreen formations, sometimes referred to as seasonal, or Thai-type, rainforest (as opposed to aseasonal evergreen rainforest of the Thai-Malay border). Trees of the dipterocarp family still predominate although the species differ from zone to zone.

It remains easier to distinguish the southern rainforests from forests further north because they are generally taller, darker and more humid. They also have a damper leaf-layer and more palms, lianas and epiphytic plants. One interesting area, Thaleban National Park, straddles the transition zone between the two forest types. Within this small park, close to the Thai-Malay border, forested slopes with towering trees surround a deep upland lake. The park is a haven for birds such as the rare Narcissus Flycatcher and the more common Dusky Crag Martin.

In southernmost Thailand, across the toe of Pattani, Yala and Narathiwat, there is another transition zone between the Thai-type, semi-evergreen rainforest and the Malay-type everwet rainforest which is equatorial and therefore largely aseasonal. To the lay onlooker both types of forests look fairly indistinguishable, but the change of rainforest type is significant. The change is brought about by the year-round rainfall distribution (rather than amount of rainfall) and more constant levels of humidity. The far south, along with the eastern seaboard south of Suratthani, receives rain from both the north-east and south-west monsoons because its mountains are not high enough or wide enough to create a significant rainshadow. Thus rain falls most months and the short dry season of February and March does not sear the land (as six to eight dry months invariably do). The wetter nature of the far south also influences the distribution of particular bird species such as the Garnet Pitta, the Rhinoceros Hornbill and the Grey-chested Flycatcher as well as myriad different plants. As with the human population, most of Peninsular Thailand's animals and plants share closer affinities with Peninsular Malaysia and with the islands of Sumatra, Java and Borneo, than with the rest of Thailand.

The bird community in the south as a whole differs from the rest of Thailand. About 150 bird species belong to the Sundaic zoogeographic region and are largely confined to the semi-evergreen forests of the south although some, such as Crested Wood Partridges, Malaysian Honeyguides and Red-bearded Bee-eaters, do extend to the south-west. Others, including the Moustached Hawk Cuckoo and Scaly-crowned Babbler, have not yet been seen in the south-west but are found in the south-east where the seasonal evergreen forests are unusually wet. However, most Sundaic birds do not travel beyond the Isthmus of Kra, although they may range further north on the Myanmar side of the Tenasserim Range where there is more lowland forest.

There are some mammals as well that are restricted to this region, but on the whole they do range also into south-west Thailand. They include the Dusky and Banded Leaf-monkeys, Flying Lemurs, Mouse Deer, Hairy-nosed Otters and Flat-headed Cats as well as several squirrels, rats and bats.

OPPOSITE PAGE Water Buffalo browse near rice fields flanked by steeply forested mountains. Almost all of south Thailand's narrow coastal plains have been cleared and converted to rice cultivation as well as rubber or oil palm plantations.

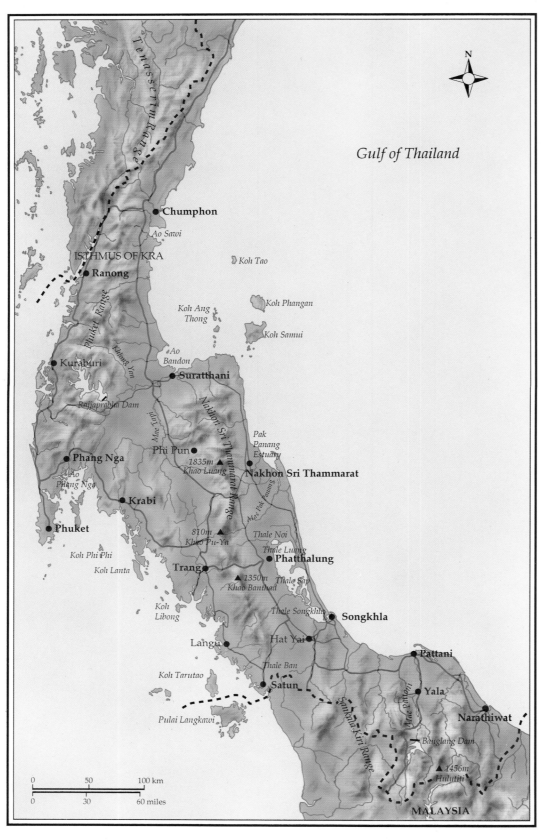

Gulf of Thailand

OPPOSITE PAGE The southern coast of Thailand is spectacular, as this scene of soft white sands, azure seas and fringing coastal forest of coconut palms and casuarina pine at Karon beach attests. However, to the top of the picture lies the downside of this natural beauty – the high-rise buildings and tourist impact of Phuket. This west-coast resort has long been famous as one of the world's most beautiful islands, and Karon beach was among the most lauded, but concrete blocks and a towering condominium are compromising its elysian magic. Under Thai law, coastal buildings should not exceed the height of a coconut palm. The most pleasing hotels and beach bungalows have respected this regulation and are invariably more popular than opportunistic eyesores nearby. Technically Phuket is almost a peninsula rather than an island, but its isthmus is under water and a causeway now connects it to the mainland of Phang Nga. So, at 543 square kilometres (210 square miles), it is the largest Thai island with valleys in the interior criss-crossed with rubber, coconut and pineapple plantations. Thailand's two south coasts have quite different characters as a result of great tectonic movements 50–60 million years ago, when the Indian plate hit mainland Asia causing the mountain chains in south Thailand to tilt so that the western slopes fell sharply into the sea as the east slopes rose. Over subsequent millennia a steady build-up of sediment carried by waterways created an ever-broadening coastal plain to the east, while fast-flowing western streams carved a crenellated coastline with a very narrow plain. The result is also that the west coast has many more islands (the peaks of flooded hills) than the east coast and more of its beaches are bays with separating headlands. Its seas are rougher than in the east in the rainy season but also tend to be clearer because short rivers carry less sediment. Finally, and certainly not least, its coral reefs are bigger and better.

The lowlands of the interior are worth distinguishing from the coastal plains, even though coastal plains are lowlands, too, and may include sizeable inland areas. But the original rainforest cover of the lowland plains is very different from the casuarina, mangrove and marsh formations normally associated with coastal vegetation. The south's lowlands are also further divided into those which cover lower hill-slopes, or foothills, up to about 600 metres (2,000 feet) above sea level (and therefore not part of the coastal plain), and those referred to as level, or extreme, lowlands which are under 200 metres (650 feet).

Such distinctions may seem hair-splitting but, from a conservation point of view, they are important. Lowland forests have a more diverse flora and fauna than other terrestrial habitats and many species are confined to them because the soils associated with such lowlands encourage forests that are taller and richer than those of neighbouring uplands. This is especially so in the south where mountain slopes are steep, rainfall run-off is rapid and moisture levels are high.

Most southern lowlands are on the Gulf of Thailand side and in the cross-peninsula corridor that is formed by the Tapi river.

The Tapi runs from Krabi to Suratthani and is the longest river in the south, running for 230 kilometres (143 miles). Shorter rivers have lowland valleys, too, notably those of the Khlong Saeng which was deluged by a dam, the Khlong Yan which is similarly threatened, and the Trang, which, like the Tapi valley, is mostly settled and farmed.

Lowland forests of the peninsula are an endangered habitat because most of them have been converted to rubber and oil-palm plantations and, encouraged by government subsidies, rubber is also being planted in the hills by small-scale farmers. As a result, less than 5 per cent of the level lowlands retain any forest cover, over half the hill-slopes have been cleared and the rest are partially logged. This has had some devastating consequences, one of which has been that the function of watershed slopes has been seriously impaired.

The effect of this was dramatically demonstrated in November 1988. That month it rained unusually hard in Nakhon Sri Thammarat and, unlike most downpours, continued unabated for days. When it stopped, some 2,000 square kilometres (770 square miles) of farmland in Phipun were buried under two metres of silt and logs, hundreds of lives were lost, tens of thousands were made homeless, the local infrastructure was smashed and a nation was shocked by media coverage of the catastrophe which left no one in Thailand unaware anymore of what can happen when hillside forests are over-logged. Southern slopes have always been subject to erosion but never on this scale. Slopes that had been shielded from rain by the spreading crowns of well-rooted forest trees and layers of understorey shrubs were now at the mercy of the elements. Well-spaced ranks of rubber trees, or any single crop, do not dissipate the force of falling rain as forests do, nor can they stabilize the soil. Their roots are too shallow and too uniform. So when torrential rain hit the steep unguarded slopes of Phipun, their coating slipped and came cascading down, taking with it every tree, log and boulder in its way as well as the humus and soil of an estimated 1,000 years. The valley was buried, its hillsides left bare.

In the outcry that followed these landslides, concessionary logging was banned nationwide, and still is banned. This logging was supposed to be selective but, in practice, Thai concessionaries had never logged according to plan. Every valuable tree was felled in and around the concession. Plots which should have been restored to log again in 30 years were taken over by settlers, many of whom were hired by the logging company. Such encroachments exacerbated erosion, landslides, flooding and drought. But they alone are not to blame. Small-scale loggers, swidden farmers and agri-businesses do as much damage over time and their activities did not stop with the logging ban, though the rate of forest clearance certainly slowed.

Of course, when such habitats vanish, so does their wildlife. The lowland forests of Thailand are home to many species which live only at low elevations. This dilemma is clearly seen among birds. Every year, some 160 species migrate to, or through, the peninsula; about a third of those seek refuge in original lowland forest and of these one-sixth depends on lowland forest exclusively.

However, that one-third of species comprises nearly three-quarters of the total number of individual migrant birds and the species entirely dependent on lowland forest make up almost half of the total. So, from a conservation point of view the surviving lowland forests are disproportionally important. Such species are primarily peninsula birds but 60 of those inhabit mainly lowland forest while 48 do so exclusively. Thus if the peninsula loses what little is left of its lowland forest, it will lose up to one-third of its forest birds and much of its avian splendour.

This is equally true of the 150 species of resident forest birds. These include the big, dark nocturnal Bat Hawk which is a rare resident, as is the Crested Fireback Pheasant, and also the stocky Blue-rumped Parrot, the long-tailed Chestnut-bellied Malkoha, the Reddish Scops Owl with its hollow *whooo*, the Scarlet-rumped Trogon with its bright plumage, the Red-crowned Barbet with its large brightly coloured head, the equally brightly plumaged Fiery Minivet and the Long-billed Spiderhunter with its staggeringly long curved beak. Their names alone tell us something of the amazing diversity of birds these forests protect.

Perhaps the saddest loss of all would be Gurney's Pitta, a secretive but strikingly marked terrestrial bird that is restricted to the Thai-type rainforest in the peninsula. For 30 years it was feared extinct, its demise brought about by the near total destruction of its lowland forest habitat. But in 1986 it was re-discovered after a four-year search by two sleuthing ornithologists, Philip Round and Uthai Treesucon of Mahidol University.

Year after year they had scoured patches of forest they knew to have been the bird's home, but to no avail. These lowland forests can accommodate up to seven pitta species (Giant, Blue-winged, Blue, Banded, Garnet, Mangrove and Gurney's), all of which make similar sounds, are secretive and scarce, and neither Round nor Treesucon was familiar with the species they sought, except in captivity. However, they were able to obtain a tape-recording of a captive bird's call, including the short explosive *lilip* that is the male's territorial call.

In the forest they then used this to challenge resident males, hoping for a response they could then locate. For days they searched, scouring the ground for a pitta's bounding gait and upright stance, for the tell-tale flash of yellow, black and blue, for the whirring wings of the elusive bird in flight or the tremulous *skyeew* of Gurney communication. On the eve of day five they made contact and *Pitta gurneyi* appeared, bouncing along the trail. Since then 25 pairs have been found in this residual patch of lowland forest in Krabi, and the Royal Forest Department has made it a wildlife sanctuary, Khao Pra Bang Kram.

With luck and effective protection, Gurney's Pitta will survive. The same cannot be said of a discovery made in the lowlands of Suratthani. A nesting pair of Storm's Storks was spotted in the Khlong Saeng valley, less than 150 kilometres (90 miles) away. Besides being the first and (as yet) only record of this stork in Thailand, it was the first ever breeding record. But, within weeks of this discovery, the chicks were taken, the adults disappeared and the valley was subsequently dammed (see page 160). All ten Thai storks are endangered by hunting and habitat destruction. Such big birds are slow and easy to see, and all of them live in the lowlands where too little land is set aside for wildlife conservation.

It is not on land, but rather under the sea, that the south truly comes into its own. The long coastline facing both the Gulf of Thailand and the Andaman Sea has a very rich marine fauna. Thailand is at an underwater crossroads with the Andaman Sea forming part of the Indian Ocean and the Gulf of Thailand, via the South China Sea, forming part of the Pacific Ocean.

The semi-seasonal climate of the south, with its prolonged rains and short dry season, allows fruit trees to proliferate. Among the fruits piled on this market stall in Suratthani are several kinds which derive from forest species: jackfruit, pomelo, salak, sataw, mangosteen and rose apple. The orange salak (*Salacca edulis*) is also known as snake-fruit because of its scaly skin. Sataw trees (*Parkia speciosa*) produce the long green pods (hanging to the right) and are native to southern Thai forests. They are pollinated exclusively by bats. Their bitter seeds are eaten as a vegetable. The huge knobbly jackfruit (*Artocarpus heterophylla*) is related to breadfruit and durian. It too is eaten as a vegetable, sliced and fried, or as a fruit when ripe. Pomeloes (*Citrus grandis*) are similar to grapefruits but sweeter, while the dark purple mangosteen (*Garcinia mangostana*) is known as the 'queen of fruits' because its opaque white segments are so delicious. The bright red rose apples (*Eugenia aquea*) are delightfully refreshing. Pineapples (the only non-native species here) are a recent crop, responsible for a fair bit of forest encroachment.

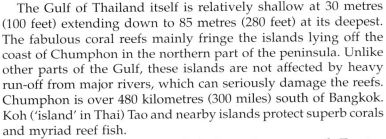

A chained and trained Pig-tailed Macaque harvests coconuts. An efficient monkey can identify a ripe fruit, twist it until the stalk snaps and throw it down to the trainer below. Hard-working monkeys can harvest 1,000 nuts a day.

Tell-tale signs of a rubber tree (*Hevea braziliensis*) being tapped for its sap. Thailand has become a major rubber producer, outstripped only by Indonesia and Malaysia, supplying one-fifth of the world's total. Consequently rubber trees have largely replaced lowland forests of the peninsula, thereby threatening many native species.

The Gulf of Thailand itself is relatively shallow at 30 metres (100 feet) extending down to 85 metres (280 feet) at its deepest. The fabulous coral reefs mainly fringe the islands lying off the coast of Chumphon in the northern part of the peninsula. Unlike other parts of the Gulf, these islands are not affected by heavy run-off from major rivers, which can seriously damage the reefs. Chumphon is over 480 kilometres (300 miles) south of Bangkok. Koh ('island' in Thai) Tao and nearby islands protect superb corals and myriad reef fish.

Thailand's Andaman coast includes at its very south Tarutao National Park. This was Thailand's first marine national park (established in 1974) and it is set among 51 mountainous islands covering 1,490 square kilometres (575 square miles) of sea near the Straits of Malacca. The west Thai coast extends for 870 kilometres (540 miles) to the northern border with Myanmar. Along the way lie the Surin and Similan Islands which are granite-based outcrops with a rich diversity of marine life. The west coastline is also famous for its sheer limestone cliffs, formed many millions of years ago by the calcium carbonate skeletons of marine organisms.

While there are many marine species found on both sides of Thailand, there are also several found only off one coast but not the other. Over a hundred species of reef-dwelling fish alone have been recorded just in the Andaman Sea ranging in size from minute gobies 20 millimetres (¾ inch) long to the occasional visiting Whale Shark up to 18 metres (60 feet) in length. Other rare species include the Trumpet Shell and the Green Turban Snail while only a few specimens of Anenome Coral have ever been found in Thai waters.

The brochure images of long sandy beaches, coconut groves and sparkling blue water inhabited by striking sea fans and butterflyfish are very much fact, not fancy. However, while Thailand can proudly boast naturally crystal-clear waters there are now significant threats from tin-mining, coastal shrimp farming, untreated waste disposal, deforestation and unchecked tourism. Conservation efforts are trying to contain these threats, with mixed results. They include the Phuket Marine Biology Centre, the Thai Coastal Resources Management Unit and the Yadfon Foundation. Together, they and others may help to preserve the riches of Thailand's southern coasts.

Khlong Saeng and Khlong Yan

Khlong is the southern Thai word for a tributary or canal, and both the Khlong Saeng and Khlong Yan feed into the Mae Tapi. However, in 1986, the Saeng was all but obliterated by the Rajjaprabha, or Chiew Larn Reservoir. Both of these rivers' catchment slopes form much of their namesake wildlife sanctuaries. Lying side-by-side, these sanctuaries also link four other conservation areas – Khao Sok, Sri Phangnga and Kaeng Krung national parks with Khlong Nakha wildlife sanctuary – a total of 3,605 square kilometres (1,391 square miles). Khlong Saeng is the largest at 1,154 square kilometres (445 square miles).

Khlong Yan is just under half that size but more complete because it retains its riverine habitat. Khlong Saeng would have been an even more significant wilderness area but the best lowland areas now lie under water because of the dam. Nevertheless, the dam was instrumental in providing the first breeding record of Storm's Stork.

This big, black-bodied bird with its bright red bill was not known in Thailand until two were seen nesting in a tree beside the rising waters of the reservoir. A month later they had two chicks but, within weeks, these were stolen. A search was mounted at once and within 24 hours the chicks were brought back but they could not return to the wild because the parent birds had abandoned the vandalized nest, and one chick had a broken beak which was repaired with a fibreglass frame. Instead they were taken to a local wildlife centre where they still live.

A typical forest view of the semi-evergreen formation which characterizes most of southern Thailand. Because of the short dry season, it is wetter and more luxuriant than the seasonal evergreen forest of continental Thailand.

RIGHT Tall, dense, humid and dark forest appears impenetrable to the human eye. Within the slatted shadows of these forest floors, a thousand creatures slink about unseen: regal Clouded Leopards, tiny delicate Mouse Deer, hulking three-toed Tapir and scaly-coated Pangolins, all of them searching, listening, sniffing the air for food or foe. Meanwhile over 70 species of amphibians and reptiles lumber, slither and leap. Nineteen toads, frogs and froglets vie for space with seven turtles and tortoises, four monitor lizards (including the rare red-headed), the huge Blood Python and seven pit vipers, some of the deadliest snakes in Asia. Snakes usually choose to stay out of sight, as indeed do most animals, which is why these forests look so empty even though they are filled with the sounds of life. Such sounds might include the squeaky *tiririt* of the Olive-backed Woodpecker, the rapid *took took took* of the Red-crowned Barbet and, from overhead, the shrill *yik-yee* of Wallace's Hawk Eagle as it scans the ground for prey. The forests of the south tend to be darker than their continental counterparts because the thicker canopy screens more light the lower down the light tries to reach.

BELOW LEFT Southern forests are the source of many cultivated fruits, including the jackfruit (*Artocarpus heterophylla*).

BELOW CENTRE A Dawn Bat (*Eonycteris spelaea*) extracts nectar from the flower of a wild banana and simultaneously collects pollen around its snout which it will then transfer to another plant. Fruit bats are such important pollinators of forest trees that many species would die out without their services. BELOW RIGHT Bananas (*Musa* sp.) occur naturally in forests as well as being grown commercially.

LEFT The King Cobra (*Ophiophagus hannah*) is the largest poisonous snake in the world, reaching lengths of 5–8 metres (16–26 feet), and is exclusively terrestrial. It is also the only snake known to build a nest, out of soil and leaves, which the female guards until the eggs hatch. It eats cold-blooded animals, especially lizards, as well as other snakes including pythons and cobras, and is immune to other snake venom. It inhabits forests and plantations nationwide and flees from people unless provoked. Once threatened, it is a dangerous adversary, being fearless, agile and lethal. Its venom is an effective neurotoxin causing paralysis and death from respiratory failure or cardiac arrest in less than an hour. Even elephants and buffalo avoid it because an adult King Cobra can inject enough poison in one bite to kill the largest animal.

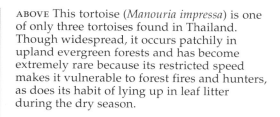

ABOVE This tortoise (*Manouria impressa*) is one of only three tortoises found in Thailand. Though widespread, it occurs patchily in upland evergreen forests and has become extremely rare because its restricted speed makes it vulnerable to forest fires and hunters, as does its habit of lying up in leaf litter during the dry season.

Denizens of the forest floor are well camouflaged: the Dwarf Toad (*Bufo parvus*, FAR LEFT ABOVE) is Thailand's smallest toad and is found only in the wettest evergreen forests of the south, south-east and west. Males change their colour to reddish-brown in the breeding season. The tiny Torrent Frog (*Amolops* sp., LEFT ABOVE) inhabits the fast-flowing rocky streams of evergreen forest, where its mottled body colour blends well with its lithic green background. The millipede (FAR LEFT BELOW) is equally well coloured for its habitat of leaf-strewn forest floor. This arthropod is one of many detritivores which convert leaf litter into humus, thereby enriching the soil. The giant forest scorpion (*Heterometrus* sp., LEFT BELOW) is nothing like as dangerous as it is assumed to be. It may sting if unduly alarmed but the poison is not fatal, though the swelling will hurt for a few hours. Some people keep these scorpions as pets. They are about the size of a man's hand.

This dramatic red fungus (probably *Hygrocyba firma*) is known among mycologists as the 'jewel of the forest'. It is probably one of many similar species, but Thai forest fungi have not yet been studied or identified in detail.

This fungus is *Psathyrella splendidus*, a litter-rotter which was recently described from Malaysian rainforests, but here it is found in the semi-evergreen forest of peninsular Thailand.

Wood-rotting fungi such as this (*Fomitopsis* sp.) are major decomposers of fallen trees, including the largest trunks. Fire, logging and wood collection pose significant threats to the multifarious organisms at this level on the forest floor.

This red fruiting ginger (*Kaempferia rotunda*) is widespread in Thailand and commonly associated with open or secondary forest. Its presence in Khlong Saeng indicates that parts of this wildlife sanctuary have been logged. Like many gingers, its rootstock is used in Thai folk medicine.

RIGHT Gingers are among the most ubiquitous understorey plants, but little is known about how their seeds are dispersed. Researchers at Chulalongkorn University are exploring the link between forest tortoises and gingers since there is reason to believe that forest tortoises eat fungi and geophytic plants, and are major seed-dispersers of ground gingers. If this is so, then the demise of forest tortoises through hunting and fire will devastate the floral character of the forest floor.

FAR RIGHT The emerging flower of this ginger (*Etlingera littoralis*) is much yellower than its northern counterpart (see page 98). As it matures it will open into a flat refulgent star and defy the darkness of the evergreen forest floor.

Khao Sok

There are two ways to enter the Khao Sok National Park, on foot or by boat. The first route is via a winding rural road which follows the park's southern edge beneath a jagged green escarpment. Headquarters occupies an inlet in this natural barricade. From there a network of animal trails weaves around great buttressed trees, through rocky streams and bamboo groves, past patches of blue-green iridescent ferns, hanging lianas and spindly palms that anchor in the mulch of many seasons. The lianas may be *Tetrastigmas,* known as 'drinking lianas' because their corky stems contain water that is potable. Their roots may also contain the filaments of *Rafflesia kerrii,* a parasitic plant that bursts out of its host to open into the largest flower in Thailand, with a 70-centimetre (28-inch) diameter. The huge reddish bloom smells of rotting meat, attracting the carrion flies that are its pollinators. It features in southern Tenasserim forests and is a Khao Sok speciality, but it is now extremely rare.

Access to the park by boat is along the Rajjaprabha reservoir. This offers a fast and noisy alternative to the stealthy forest approach, but the view across the water is dramatic. The reservoir extends for 50 kilometres (30 miles) but is rarely more than 2 kilometres (1 mile) wide with tributary arms on either side and mountains all around.

The craggy skyline etched by the limestone face of the Phuket mountain range forms a haunting backdrop to the Rajjaprabha reservoir at Khao Sok National Park. It is hard to believe that this tranquil beauty was formed by a hydro-dam.

The jagged limestone ridges of Khao Sok and neighbouring Khlong Saeng are home to bats, monkeys and Serow, but their dry, tenacious forests are too precipitous to support many large mammals. That is why the Rajjaprabha reservoir was so damaging to the ecology of these wildlife reserves: it obliterated the central valley and therefore the bulk of the area's lowland forest. Patches of lowland forest do still dot the area, but those of significant size lie beyond the conservation boundary and are now secondary forest and scrub (RIGHT). Most of the streams outside the inundation area are rocky and rapid like this one (BELOW RIGHT), with similarly enclosing forest. This hillstream habitat suits some stream fauna but not those of open riverine habitats or slower-moving lowland streams. Animals which are associated with this habitat include the Soft-shell Turtle, the Torrent Frog (see page 162), and the Chestnut-naped Forktail (*Enicurus ruficapillus*) whose shrill whistle can be heard beside rocky streams up to 900 metres (2,950 feet). In Khao Sok there is also a notable tree palm, *Borassodendron machadonis*, a rare wild relative of the commonly cultivated palmyra palm, and a variety of towering bamboos (BELOW LEFT), in addition to the tall distinctive dipterocarps which characterize southern evergreen forests.

ABOVE AND LEFT Animal camouflage has evolved to perfection in the Clouded Leopard (*Neofelis nebulosa*), but sadly has not protected it from the captive pet and fur-coat trades. This nocturnal cat is more adapted to arboreal life than other Asian felines, hence its short legs, large paws and long, muscular tail. It also has much longer canine teeth and an exceptionally powerful jaw, enabling it to kill with a single puncturing bite. Unlike other cats, it uses its rasp-like tongue to strip its prey of fur or feathers before eating the meat.

BELOW LEFT The tiny Mouse Deer (*Tragulus javanicus*) stands only about 20 centimetres (8 inches) at the shoulder. It is the smaller of two mouse deer, both of which are Sundaic species and co-habit in Khao Sok. They too are nocturnal and secretive and may not be as rare as they seem.

BELOW RIGHT This Serow (*Capricornis sumatraensis*) is a youngster, but it is the larger of Thailand's two goat-antelopes and more widespread than the Goral. Serow prefer the limestone mountains and cliffs which are thickly clad with forest, as they can take refuge and feed in the most inaccessible areas, using well-worn trails to descend to the plains for water or to find a mate. Because they are agile and sure-footed, and mainly nocturnal, they are hard to hunt on home territory. This has not prevented their being ambushed beside their exit trails. They are killed mainly for the scent gland (which can be seen in the photograph) below the animal's eye.

When the Rajjaprabha dam was built, it flooded the Khlong Saeng valley and created 50 islands. Terrestrial mammals were stranded and myriad other residents were displaced. Gibbons and monkeys, such as this Pig-tailed Macaque (*Macaca nemestrina*, RIGHT), suffered more than most because they cannot swim and soon ran out of food on their island prisons. Primates and squirrels, including the Red-cheeked Flying Squirrel (*Hylopetes spadiceus*, ABOVE), were stranded in trees cut off by rising water. A thousand animals were rescued, however, by a project which tried to mitigate the impact of the dam. It was a valiant effort but could not succeed when 164 square kilometres (63 square miles) of riverine habitat were lost. It would even have been difficult for Hard-shell Turtles (*Heosemys grandis*, TOP) to adapt as they like slow-moving streams and rivers, not rocky upland tributaries or large still water-bodies. It is a common misconception that aquatic and amphibious species of river valleys can adapt to reservoir life. In fact, rivers and reservoirs are totally different habitats. Rivers are shallow, forward-flowing and aerobic, with herbaceous banks, whereas reservoirs have deep, somewhat stagnant anoxic water and a fluctuating shoreline which is either too dry for aquatic plants or too wet for bankside vegetation.

RIGHT Typical plants of this national park include these striking and contrasting seedpods of *Sterculia lanceolata*, a widespread tree of evergreen forests, and the haughty flowerhead of *Globa pendula* (FAR RIGHT), a rare ginger of southern forests.

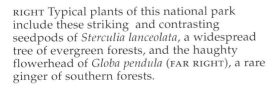

Koh Samui and Koh Ang Thong

Koh Samui in the Gulf of Thailand is the picture-book tropical island with white beaches that have coconut palms behind them and an azure sea in front. It is located 650 kilometres (400 miles) south of Bangkok and 35 kilometres (21 miles) off the Kra Peninsula. Some 30 kilometres (20 miles) further north-west lies Koh Ang Thong, a marine national park with 50 islands and 84 square kilometres (32 square miles) of superb limestone formations, lagoons, caves, coral reefs and sea. A mere 15 years ago Koh Samui was not well known except to its inhabitants whose fishermen forebears settled there some 1,500 years ago. Tourism is now a major part of island life. Lying off the east coast of the peninsula, Koh Samui and the neighbouring marine national park have two sources of rain, the south-west and north-east monsoons. The reefs are sometimes obscured by silt from the Tapi river, but when the water is clear they offer some superb sub-marine scenery.

The Koh Ang Thong islands are the spawning grounds of Thailand's beloved *pla thu*, the short-bodied mackerel that was once common food but has now become quite rare. In the middle of 'mother island' (*Koh Mae Koh*) there is an emerald sink-hole lake that formed when a cave fell in and filled with semi-salty water. These islands have many caves housing bats and beetles and Edible-nest Swiftlets whose labours provide the key ingredient for birds' nest soup.

Coconut trees appear to cover most of Koh Samui's land away from its beautiful beaches. In fact 2,000,000 coconuts are shipped to Bangkok every month, leaving little room for other vegetation except mango and cashew trees which are also grown commercially.

RIGHT Thailand's offshore national parks protect not only submarine flora and fauna but also coastal birds, some of which are now rare on the mainland, such as this young White-bellied Sea Eagle (*Haliaeetus leucogaster*). This bird flies close to the water to search for prey and will use its long talons to pick up fish just below the surface. The survival of this species is now largely dependent on the rugged inaccessible nature of its island retreats.

BELOW LEFT The Pied Imperial Pigeon (*Ducula bicolor*) is chiefly restricted to the coastal forests of steep offshore islands where it stays in the trees, usually high in the canopy. It feeds on fruit. Its creamy-white plumage is an immediate aid to identification, but you are more likely only to hear its deep booming call.

BELOW RIGHT This well-camouflaged lizard (*Calotes emma emma*) is widespread in the island forests of Koh Samui and its neighbours.

ABOVE RIGHT The 80-island archipelago of Koh Samui and Koh Ang Thong is the only one of any significance off the Gulf Coast of the peninsula. The islands are the northern peaks of the Nakhon Si Thammarat Range which runs south to Trang and Tarutao. Unlike islands off the Andaman coast, those in the Gulf are affected by the silt dispersed by all Thailand's major rivers. The longest river in the south, the Tapi, deposits its load right alongside this archipelago.

ABOVE LEFT Most of the islands in this archipelago are uninhabited, although native fishermen have harvested these waters for over 1,000 years. Here a classic view of the Ang Thong archipelago also illustrates the hardy scrub vegetation (in foreground) that is typical of these limestone outcrops.

LEFT An intriguing feature of Ang Thong National Park is the crater lake in the centre of Mae Koh island. Known as Thale Nai, this lake is encircled by vertical cliffs, a typical characteristic of limestone sink-holes. Its colour changes from emerald to aquamarine according to the cloud cover.

RIGHT The Green Turtle (*Chelonia mydas*) is the only herbivorous sea turtle, feeding on algae and sea grass and weighing up to 180 kilograms (400 pounds). Primarily nocturnal, it tends to doze on the sea bed during the day. Like all marine turtles, it is threatened by egg-harvesting, fishing nets, beach disturbance and hunting. Thai seas once supported five marine turtles but only four survive, the Leatherback, the Hawksbill, the Olive and the Green. The Loggerhead has disappeared. They are killed for their meat (a South-east Asian delicacy) and for their shells. The Leatherback is the largest, weighing up to 900 kilograms (2,000 pounds) and feeds almost exclusively on jellyfish. It lays its eggs in warm tropical sands but otherwise lives in temperate and polar seas, diving to depths of 1,000 metres (3,300 feet). Olive turtles are the smallest, up to 50 kilograms (110 pounds), and live on shrimps and crabs.

The coral reefs of the Ang Thong National Park harbour an enormous variety of extraordinary and decorative inhabitants. BELOW RIGHT Two stunning white nudibranchs (*Kentrodoris funebris*) on a blue sponge (*Adocia* sp.). These shell-less marine molluscs carry external gills, extending from their bodies in feathery fronds.
BOTTOM Gorgonian corals are a common feature of the reefs. When seen in groups, their plant-like polyps are well-named 'underwater gardens'. This one appears to have a pink and white brittlestar entwined in it. BELOW LEFT A Pink Anemonefish (*Amphiprion perideraion*) nestles in the tentacles of its host anemone *Heteractis magnifica*, the species with which it most commonly has a symbiotic relationship.

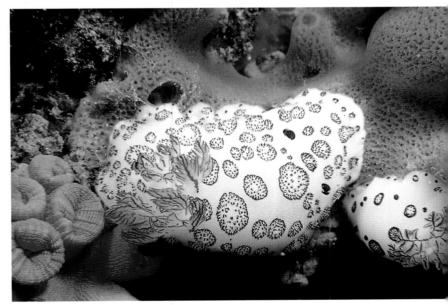

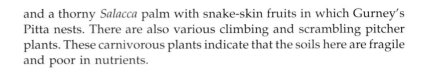

Khao Pra Bang Kram

An hour away from the fabulous coast of Krabi is an equally fabulous, but more exclusive, forest preserve, the Khao Pra Bang Kram Wildlife Sanctuary. Better known as Khao Nor Chuchi, this site is famous the world over as the only place that protects Gurney's Pitta, a bird that was long thought to be extinct. Much of the Gurney's Pitta habitat has disappeared because the lowland forests of the south have been replaced by oil palm, rice and rubber trees. Khao Pra Bang Kram is virtually all that remains with its 183-square-kilometre (70-square-mile) area, but it does support about 25 pairs of these rare birds as well as another 310 bird species, more than any other area in the south. Many of these other birds are also lowland specialists and therefore rare, including the Blue-rumped Parrot, Giant Pitta, Long-billed Spiderhunter and Rufous-collared Kingfisher. Their forest is dominated by tall, hardwood dipterocarps under which there are many types of palms including rattans, pandanus (in swampy areas)

and a thorny *Salacca* palm with snake-skin fruits in which Gurney's Pitta nests. There are also various climbing and scrambling pitcher plants. These carnivorous plants indicate that the soils here are fragile and poor in nutrients.

OPPOSITE PAGE The swamp-strewn lowland forests of Khao Pra Bang Kram are the lifeline of many specialist lowland species such as the birds shown on this page. This relict patch is almost all that remains of the forests that once filled the plain between the parallel ranges of Phuket and Nakhon Si Thammarat.

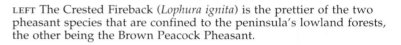

LEFT The Crested Fireback (*Lophura ignita*) is the prettier of the two pheasant species that are confined to the peninsula's lowland forests, the other being the Brown Peacock Pheasant.

BELOW LEFT This female Crested Wood Partridge (*Rollulus rouloul*) is as colourful as her mate but lacks his maroon crest and red eye-patch.

BELOW RIGHT A male Gurney's Pitta (*Pitta gurneyi*) – the rarest of all these birds – at the nest with two chicks, their gaping beaks just discernible.

Thale Sap Lagoons

Thale means 'lake' in southern Thai but in fact here four linked lakes or lagoons (Noi, Luang, Sap and Songkhla) extend for 80 kilometres (50 miles) along the coastal lowlands of Phattalung and Songkhla covering over 1,500 square kilometres (580 square miles). Together the lakes form a vast inland sea that is one of the natural wonders of Thailand. They began to form 150 years ago when the sediment flow from the river of Talung (now Phattalung) finally engulfed the large offshore island of Koh Yai (or Tantalem), leaving only one opening in the south which is now protected by a spit. Thus Thale Songkhla is salty, Thale Noi has fresh water and the lakes in between are brackish. But the character of each changes slightly with the season. When rain comes down from the mountains via a multitude of streams, the salt water is diluted; but during the ensuing dry season, the sea intrudes again. It is a sophisticated ecosystem that mixes mangroves, Irrawaddy Dolphins, sea fish and molluscs with woodlands, lotus lilies, river terrapins and waterfowl.

Splendid concentrations of birds occur in Thale Noi, a small, pretty circular lake ringed with sedge beds, marshes and spindly melaleuca, 'paper-bark' trees. The most attractive route there is through a canal from the adjacent lake, Luang. Beyond this narrow waterway is a riot of jacanas, swamphens, herons and terns with hoards of egrets, Lesser Whistling Ducks, Garganey and Cotton Pygmy Geese. In amongst them all you may even see Black-winged Stilts and Painted Storks as this is the only place these two are known to breed.

The Purple Swamphen (*Porphyrio porphyrio*) is surprisingly common given that it is a large and colourful resident of open wetlands. Its long-toed feet allow it to walk on the floating vegetation of this lagoon habitat. Here the female is alert to the grunting demands of her hungry chick.

RIGHT The pronounced kink of its long snaky neck, black dagger-like bill, blue eye-line and feathered tail of its breeding plumage identify this graceful Great Egret (*Egretta alba*). It feeds on small fish and water insects which it stabs with its bill. It is both a common resident and a winter visitor.

BELOW This heronry beside Thale Noi accommodates a number of species, of which three are present in this picture: Cattle Egrets (*Bubulcus ibis*) in their buff breeding plumage; Little Egrets (*Egretta garzetta*) with their elegant white plume and blue eye-line; and, silhouetted on its nest, a Little Cormorant, (*Phalacrocorax niger*).

ABOVE A rare Spot-billed Pelican (*Pelecanus philippensis*) comes into land among its fellow birds. This species is the only one of its kind to occur in Thailand. It comes as a winter visitor but does not appear to breed here as it once did. The lagoons favoured by such aquatic birds are one of South-east Asia's most important wetlands and a vital staging-post on the Asia–Pacific flyway of migratory waterfowl.

ABOVE The marshlands north of Thale Noi are covered with melaleuca ('paper-bark') formations which serve as an ecological sponge, regulating the flow of fresh water into the lagoons and the Phanang river of Nakhon Si Thammarat. However, in recent years this crucial service has been compromised by drainage and over-grazing, much of it by domestic water buffalo.

ABOVE The toe-spread of the Bronze-winged Jacana (*Metopidius indicus*) is almost as long as its body (though this is obscured by the lagoon water). This bird is a common resident of Thailand's lakes and marshes, as yet unaffected by habitat destruction, hunting or pollution.

ABOVE The dark brown streaks on the underparts of a Yellow Bittern (*Ixobrychus sinensis*) identify it as a juvenile. As with other bitterns this species is shy and difficult to observe although it is a fairly common resident and winter visitor.

LEFT A Purple Heron (*Ardea purpurea*) stands sentinel on Thale Noi lake, one of the four Thale Sap lagoons. These are, in effect, an enormous inland sea barely 2 metres (6 feet) deep which sustains a wealth of wetland birds and coastal dolphins.

The waterscapes of Thale Noi are at once spectacular and serene, with a floating cover of water lilies concealing the busyness of underwater life while providing a platform for aquatic birds and amphibians. Other species inhabit the reed-beds and marshlands beyond.

BELOW LEFT This beautiful lotus (*Nelumbo nucifera*) is a native water lily, but it is also cultivated for its edible seed pods and stems.

BELOW RIGHT The pink lilies (*Nymphaea lotus*) are also native and widespread but they are propagated for ornamental more than culinary purposes. They also occur with white flowers.

Ton Nga Chang and Khao Banthad

Like most of Thailand's inland conservation areas, these two wildlife sanctuaries are mountainous and, like most mountains, they serve as watershed slopes. Here, this is essential for there are no other such slopes in this part of the peninsula except for Khao Pu-Khao Ya which is north of them. Together they maintain the ecological phenomenon that evolved at their feet – the semi-saline lakes of Thale Sap. Ton Nga Chang is named after a double-runnel waterfall which plunges down a flat stone face like two enormous elephant tusks and then becomes the turbulent stream that enlivens the visitor centre.

The centre's most rewarding feature is a beautifully plotted forest trail which lets you move silently to listen for the sound of wildlife hidden in the undergrowth. Bird life is abundant with many of the peninsula's most exclusive species, among them six hornbills, five malkohas, four trogons, three spiderhunters, two hawk cuckoos and the Narcissus Flycatcher. Amphibians and reptiles are plentiful, including Slender Toads, Wrinkled Frogs, Dwarf Geckos and a Blind Snake. But the rarest, and most threatened, residents of all are the Sakai, Thailand's last true forest people. The Sakai are hunter-gatherers who travel round the forest in family groups, building temporary shelters from leaves and bamboo and hunting game with blow-pipes.

These two torrents give Ton Nga Chang its name: 'elephant tusk waterfall'. The mountain forests of this wildlife sanctuary, together with those of Khao Banthad (OPPOSITE PAGE), channel rainwater into the Thale Sap lagoons – their vital ecological lifeline.

LEFT Camouflaged to perfection, a flying lizard (*Draco blanfordi*) belies its name because it does not actually fly, but rather glides like other flying lizards by stretching a flap of abdominal skin between its fore and hind legs.

BELOW LEFT The Tokkae (*Gecko gecko*) is well known because of its distinctive call (its name is onomatopoeic). Geckos are the only lizards with a voice. It is also familiar because it occupies houses as readily as forest, coming out at night to feed on moths. It is often seen walking up smooth vertical walls and across ceilings with the aid of its fleshy toe-pads.

BELOW CENTRE The defence mechanism of this Zygaenid moth (*Chalcosia auxo*) is to mimic the coloration and behaviour of a deadly poisonous butterfly which stores cyanide compounds in the cuticles of its wings – the part that predatory birds and lizards touch first when they mean to bite.

BELOW RIGHT Looking like a ball of fluffy white string, an immature bug of the Flatidae family extracts juices from the leaves and stems of plants with its sucking mouthparts. It will replace its waxy wig-like filaments several times until its final metamorphosis. The adults look like butterflies and are sometimes known as butterfly bugs. Flatid bugs live on trees and shrubs and tend to be host specific.

BELOW LEFT This well camouflaged forest snail is feeding on a small papery tree fungus.
BELOW CENTRE A bush cricket protects itself by looking like the leaves it lives on, in this case a creeper that is attached to the bark of a tree.
BELOW RIGHT The glow worm larvae of Lampyrid beetles are about 8 centimetres (3 inches) long. This one is a female and the night-piercing glow of her chestnut tail segments will attract a male, a flying beetle.

The Great Argus (*Argusianus argus*), unlike other pheasant species of the south, is not dependent on lowland forest, preferring to inhabit hill slopes up to 900 metres (3,000 feet). Both sexes emit loud resonant calls which are readily traced to an approximate location, but the male can be located exactly by the *kwow-wow* calls it gives to advertise its presence during the breeding season. The bird uses its beak and wings to clear a circular dancing ground from which it endeavours to attract a mate by fanning its wings in a peacock-like display. The bird above is female. Her mate looks much larger because his super-long secondary wing feathers and elongated tail more than double his length.

This cluster of bright red berries belongs to a *Piper* vine, a wild member of the family which produces peppercorns, the mainstay of the multi-million-dollar spice trade.

This is the seed-encrusted spadix of *Epipremnum giganteum*, a member of the Arum family and common in the evergreen forests throughout Thailand.

These flame-coloured cones belong to *Zingiber spectabile*, another widespread species of evergreen forests. Seeds will develop in the hinges of the overlapping bracts.

Chalerm Pa Kiet Swamp Forest

This unique habitat in the toe of Thailand was rescued by royal patronage in 1991 and became a wildlife sanctuary with a superb research station. Known locally as *Pa Phru* ('swamp forest'), it is more precisely a peat swamp forest which is why its water and many plants are rusty red. It formed thousands of years ago when sand banks created a coastal depression which filled with silt (mostly impermeable clay) and vegetative debris which slowly turned to peat. Swamp forests are almost impossible to negotiate on foot, but in this one a magnificent wooden walkway has been constructed above the clear dark water, tangled roots and vicious thorns, winding round the aerobic trees and vines and flop-mopped palms. The forest feels primeval as it is so humid and still and peculiar. Water flows imperceptibly past the flickering shadows of myriad fish, including a 'walking' catfish, and the roots that emerge like elbows to breathe the lightly peat-scented air.

Though small, this forest has a remarkable flora and fauna. Fifty plants are first Thai records, many are exclusive; the 'duck's foot tree' provides wood as light as balsa; Narathiwat baskets made from *lipao* vine are intricate, robust and exceptionally beautiful. The bird community is also unique. Out of 140 species, 27 are rarely seen elsewhere in Thailand. These include the large Green Pigeon, Blue-crowned Hanging Parrot, Reddish Scops Owl, Rufous-tailed Shama, Sooty-capped Babbler and Malaysian Blue Flycatcher. The swamp is also home to the semi-aquatic Flat-headed Cat.

The swampland of Chalerm Pa Kiet is now a protected area, so the secondary vegetation in the foreground should revert to the tall swamp forest beyond. Beneath the vivid green of this distinctive flora there are several metres of saturated peat overlain with knee-deep water.

RIGHT The swamp waters of *Pa Phru* appear to be still but are in fact flowing all the time. They are the forest's security. If water is drained and the peat dries out, swamp forest is vulnerable to fires above and below ground, the latter being hardest to extinguish. Once the peaty substrate is destroyed, this swamp forest cannot regenerate, for although the water level may drop naturally by a metre (3 feet), the physical and chemical properties of the peat do not change as they do if artificially drained and burned.

BELOW LEFT *Wrightea dubia* is a threatened little tree that once grew in lowland evergreen forest all over Thailand.

BELOW CENTRE This discreetly coloured frog is probably the rare *Rana doriae*. It is only ever seen in southern rainforest during the rainy season.

BELOW RIGHT The deceptive rear-wing rudders of *Pachlioptacoon doubledavi* are a feature of all swallowtail butterflies.

BELOW Because it is confined to lowland forest waterways and marshes, the Grey-headed Fish Eagle (*Ichthyophaga ichthyaetus*) is one of Thailand's most endangered raptors. The swamp forest of Chalerm Pa Kiet protects the only breeding pairs in the country and their presence there attests to the singular value of the place and the status of its fish.

BELOW This gawky bird is a Lesser Adjutant (*Leptoptilos javanicus*). It is a very rare resident but a small population lives here. The visible white triangle at the base of the wing, and the generally dark underwings, help tell this species apart from the noticeably larger Greater Adjutant (*Leptoptilos dubius*) which has mottled brown underwings.

Budo and Hala-Bala

As their lyrical Yawi names indicate, these two areas belong to the 'Malay' tip of Thailand where they conserve small tracts of equatorial rainforest that occur only south of Pattani and Satun. Both are relatively new protected areas because they were controlled by Muslim separatists and, even now, are not always safe. However, that has not stopped Dr Pilai Poonswad from starting a new hornbill project in Budo National Park. Her attachment to these large broad-winged forest birds with their huge, distinctive bills is undiminished after 18 years of studying their behaviour and ecology, first in Khao Yai then Huai Kha Khaeng, and she now supports a team of committed young researchers whose aim is to forestall the demise of these spectacular birds through research and education. Hornbills are supremely effective flagships for forest conservation because they, and their calls, are so distinctive and because they nest exclusively in the tall trees of primary forest, preferably dipterocarp.

Budo and Hala-Bala sustain nine hornbill species, including the Wrinkled Hornbill which verges on extinction, especially as local hunters claim 'ownership' rights over the hornbill nests they find. Dr Pilai has hired as many of these locals as funds will allow to join her research team and turn protectors, data-gatherers and educators. This resourceful strategy will help not only hornbills but also the less conspicuous rarities of this rainforest habitat including the Agile Gibbon, Dayak Fruit Bats, Bronze Cuckoos, Malaysian Eared Nightjars and Grey-chested Flycatchers.

The newly gazetted areas of Budo and Hala-Bala protect the best of southernmost Thailand's equatorial rainforest. From above this formation looks much like semi-evergreen rainforest, but it is slightly taller and wetter with some different constituent species.

RIGHT A male Rhinoceros Hornbill (*Buceros rhinoceros*) waits outside the nest in this tree cavity, ready to attend the female inside. Hornbills favour emergent dipterocarp trees for their nests. When the male has found a good cavity, he invites the female to inspect it and, if she approves, she will mate. She then seals herself inside with a mix of mud, faeces and regurgitated fruit. That done, she discards her major feathers and stays imprisoned for 3 to 4 months while raising her young. During that time she depends on her mate for food. If he is killed she dies of malnutrition because, although she can break out of her nest, she cannot fly or feed without feathers. The Rhinoceros Hornbills have the most conspicuous horn on the top bill, called the casque. Although they look heavy, most hornbill casques are filled with a light sponge tissue.

BELOW LEFT The tail of a Helmeted Hornbill (*Rhinoplax vigil*) is longer than that of other family members. This species is also the only one to have a solid casque. Known as hornbill ivory, it was much in demand by Chinese craftsmen who carved it into elaborate trinkets. The function of the casque is not known, but it may help regulate body heat or resonate the calls.

BELOW RIGHT An aptly named White-crowned Hornbill (*Berenicornis comatus*) perches beside the nest. His mate is just visible through her prison window. This species is quite rare.

Had Chao Mai and Koh Libong

In 1993 this small coastal park and island wildlife sanctuary gained public prominence when a young Dugong appeared in the seagrass beds that distinguish their shallow waters and stayed until the day he died a year later. It was a timely arrival, for the animal dubbed *Tone* (meaning 'Alone') was seen to symbolize the success of local fishermen in safeguarding the seagrass habitat that Dugongs, or Sea Cows, depend on from the rapacious fishing methods of commercial trawlers. *Tone* repaid the love and pride that villagers felt by allowing himself to be handled and photographed by visitors. His media appeal helped villagers keep the trawlers at bay, and advance their seagrass restoration project with the help of the admirable Yadfon ('Raindrop') Foundation, which fosters local community conservation.

Tone drowned in a trawler net and became another victim of the fishing fleet that is desecrating Thai seas, so his death is as much a symbol of coastal conservation as his life. In this coastal stretch there is much to conserve. At low tide, the sandy beaches and mudflats sometimes shimmer with thousands of jostling shorebirds: curlews, plovers, sandpipers and sanderlings along with the rare Nordmann's Greenshank, huge aggregations of Bar-tailed Godwits and at least ten types of tern. The mangrove swamps around Had Chao Mai and Koh Libong are also enriched by the Brown-winged Kingfisher, Mangrove Pitta and Masked Finfoot, while their inland marshes and woods support a few Black-necked Storks.

These cows are leaving Had Chao Mai having spent the day feeding on the scrubby remains of its natural vegetation. The 94-square-kilometre (36-square-mile) park is battling to protect its mangrove swamps. This attractive scene was, in fact, photographed from the new road which has blocked the beach from the mangrove belt behind, and the mangrove is visibly sick.

These apparently quite different plants are, in fact, the male and female forms of *Cycas rumphii*, a coastal cycad. The plump male cone (ABOVE RIGHT) bears sporophylls, or pollen-sacs, within its bracts. Dispersed by the wind, the pollen is carried to the nearby female (ABOVE LEFT) to fertilize the naked ova, visible here in the leaflike inflorescence.

RIGHT The Dugong (*Dugong dugon*) is a large but gentle marine mammal which feeds almost entirely on underwater plants, especially seagrasses. The square muzzle is an adaptation to underwater grazing. Dugongs must come to the surface to breath every 10–15 minutes and this has led to many accidentally drowning in nets. They have been decimated also by hunting and the silting or pollution of coastal feeding grounds. They are no longer seen in huge herds but local conservation projects are trying to reverse the trend.

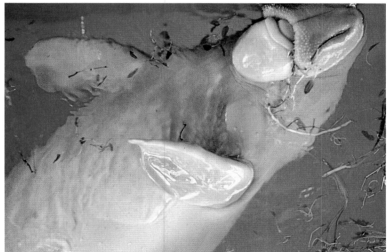

RIGHT Taken at the end of a terrifying climb to the top of Had Chao Mai's headland, this view looks over dugong habitat which includes the seagrass beds seen here as purple shadows. The protected waters of Had Chao Mai and Koh Libong offer the best chance of survival to Thailand's endangered dugongs. This is thanks to local fishing communities as well to the conservation authorities. Dugongs and traditional fishermen share a devastating adversary: the commercial trawler fleet.

ABOVE The life of a marine turtle is a heroic saga of survival. A female Green Turtle (ABOVE LEFT) crawls ashore at night to dry sand and with her flippers laboriously digs a hole in which she lays 80 to 150 eggs. After concealing the nest, she returns to the sea. If she avoids being killed for her meat, she will lay 3 to 4 times in one year at two week intervals, but not in consecutive years. Turtle sex is determined by temperature. Warm nests produce females, cooler or deeper ones males. The eggs will hatch 50-60 days later, at night (provided they have not been taken by poachers). The babies tear open their soft-skinned eggs, scramble to the surface and scurry towards the shining moonlit sea, like these infant Green (ABOVE CENTRE) and Leatherback Turtles (ABOVE RIGHT). If the beach-front is brighter than the sea, the hatchlings will head inland to almost certain death. Even at sea their chance of survival is slim because they take 20 to 50 years to mature (a long time to avoid modern fishing nets) and the females must then run the risk of coming ashore to breed. Not long ago, sea turtles came by the score to Thailand's beaches to lay their eggs, but this habitat is generally now too noisy and bright and too many turtles have died. However, there are now a number of turtle conservation projects in Thailand where volunteers watch nesting beaches to safeguard laying females and to take the eggs to a protected incubation site elsewhere. It is a positive step, with thousands of hatchlings released each year into conservation waters.

LEFT Life and death on the beach: a Ghost Crab (*Ocypode ceratophthalma*) captures a cicada. Its camouflage, from which it gets its name, blends in perfectly against the sand.

BELOW LEFT At low tide, Thai beaches are embossed with these exquisite geometric patterns. They are made by sand-bubbling crabs (*Scopimera* sp.) which dig burrows in the sand and then emerge to feed. As a crab moves sideways, it scoops an outward trench, sieving sand through its jaws to extract food particles and depositing the remaining sand in pellets behind it.

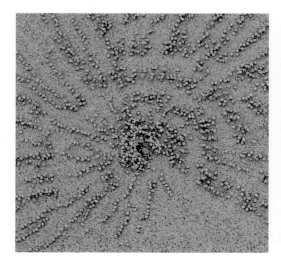

RIGHT There are good stands of protected mangrove forest around Koh Libong. The characteristic aerial roots of a mangrove tree are prominent in the foreground of this picture. Mangrove forests are breeding grounds for much marine life as well as being intertidal zones of unexpected biodiversity and a vital buffer between the land and sea. They used to fringe a third of southern Thailand but over half has been destroyed by charcoal manufacturers and intensive prawn farmers.

BELOW LEFT With its glossy black head and slender neck extended and its red legs trailing, a graceful Black-necked Stork (*Ephippiorhynchus asiaticus*) flies over possibly its last remaining sanctuary in Thailand. The sandy swards of Had Chao Mai and the woods of Koh Libong are the only two places in Thailand where this rare stork can be found. Observers have reported that it no longer appears to be breeding, in which case it must be close to extinction.

BELOW RIGHT No danger of extinction for this very common resident, the Red-wattled Lapwing (*Vanellus indicus*). This bird inhabits dry bush country, marshes and river valleys all over Thailand except those of the north-east.

OPPOSITE PAGE, BELOW RIGHT The mudskipper (*Buliothalmis* sp.) is a characteristic inhabitant of mangrove forests. This fish can remain out of water (when the tide is out) for long periods, breathing through an aqualung. It can 'skip' across the mudflats in pursuit of insect prey by using its pectoral fins as 'arms'. It keeps its eyes moist by rolling them round in their sockets.

Phang Nga Bay

Viewed from a boat on a calm, turquoise Andaman Sea too sheltered and too shallow to be troubled by monsoon storms, Phang Nga Bay offers a location of metaphysical scenery. Some 40 islands rise in chiselled shapes like molars, capped with forest scrub, or as gigantic humps with pitted cliffs and caves. This is a drowned karstland; in fact, it is the tail-end of the Tenasserim mountain range with all but its peaks now inundated and embedded in silt. Behind the outer wall of many islands is a hollow interior, worn away by water, hidden for millennia from the modifying hand of man. These astonishing chambers can be reached by canoe through arches that appear at low tide. Inside is a dark, echoing crypt where stalactites are barnacle-clad and lapped by the changing tides. Some caverns open into spectacular sky-lit conservatories in which miniature tropical gardens are maintained by a random assortment of animals.

Phang Nga Bay depends on mangrove forest for its wildlife diversity, water clarity and ecological equilibrium. However, most mangrove, in fact some of the best stands in Thailand, is beyond park boundaries, set aside for charcoal. If you take a knowing guide to lead you round the wooded canals, it soon becomes obvious why mangroves are known as the nurseries of marine life. Around the aerial roots of the many mangrove trees, both mud and water teem with fish, frogs and coloured crabs which otters and cats pursue. Higher up, bats, lizards and monkeys share the evergreen branches with myriad birds, among them the elegant Oriental Darter.

The most famous landmark of Phang Nga Bay is this sculptured limestone protrusion called Koh Khao Pingkan. Many might recognize it as the eye-catching setting for the James Bond film, *The Man with the Golden Gun.*

ABOVE, RIGHT and BELOW Sensational limestone outcrops punctuate the skyline of Phang Nga Bay. These islands are, in fact, the southern peaks of the Phuket mountain range, their foothills now under water. The bay is shallow and sheltered but its substrate is too soft and its water too turbid to allow the establishment of coral. Though there are no reefs, there are some spectacular caves which are the hollow interiors of islands. The best way to explore the bay is by small boat or canoe, which will take you right into the hollows and tiny concealed beaches.

ABOVE Years and years of wave action have undercut the base of the jagged limestone stacks, leaving overhanging cliffs and small hidden bays.

LEFT Many caves and tunnels emerge at low tide to lead you under an island and sometimes into caverns which have hollowed out inside.

OPPOSITE PAGE Some limestone cliffs are so sheer that no plant can find a foothold, but the fact that any plants grow on scraggy faces such as this is something of a miracle. These cliffs are at the southern edge of Phang Nga Bay. As a landscape, this bay is unparalleled for the views and adventures and impressions it offers. As a conservation area, however, it is inadequately protected against the demands of tourism.

BELOW A stalactite formation like a petrified waterfall in one of the dark, echoing chambers beneath the islands of Phang Nga.

Phuket Island Area

Phuket Island says everything good and bad about wild Thailand. It was once known as the 'Pearl of the Andaman Sea' and even ten years ago it certainly was a gem, for its natural habitats were second to none: silica white sand in a chain of crescent bays, translucent turquoise seas with a diadem of islands, coral reefs which dazzled with colour, crustacea and fish, a luxurious crown of rainforest and a mangrove fringe that enriched the rocky eastern shore harbouring such rarities as the Copper-throated Sunbird. But today Phuket is more famous, or infamous, as a fashionable seaside resort. Plane-loads of people arrive by the hour to savour this tropical retreat, though the attributes that draw them are being overwhelmed. To cite just one example, only a few turtles now dare to come ashore to lay their eggs in the soft white sand. Previously five turtle species (Leatherback, Loggerhead, Hawksbill, Olive and Green Turtles) all came here, but now the beaches are too busy and their lights too bright. Those resilient turtles return to the Had Nai Yang National Park which also protects a strip of casuarina coastal forest and the island's largest living reef.

On the north-east corner of the island, one patch of primary forest survives in the Khao Phra Tieo National Park. Long overlooked as a site of little significance, this tiny park is the only place known to have Thailand's rarest palm, *Kerriodoxa elegans*. It is also the site for a commendable conservation project to rehabilitate the White-handed Gibbon.

The coastlines of Phuket and its offshore islands are naturally endowed with superb beaches, though it is rare to find one undisturbed by modern-day encroachments.

ABOVE The famous beaches of Phuket get their fine white sand from granite intrusions on the western side of the mountain chain. This is the well-known Karon beach.

RIGHT The seaside Morning Glory (*Ipomoea pes-caprae*) is an important colonizer of many tropical beaches because its long creeping and rooting stems form dense patches which help stabilize the sand. *Pes-caprae* means 'goat's foot' which the shape of its leaves is meant to resemble. Unfurled, the pink flowers are the size of an adult human hand. It has been known for the leaves to be used as a poultice and the juice for fish stings.

LEFT Little natural vegetation survives in the interior of Phuket. The proud red trumpets of the convolvulus *Ipomoea hederifola*, most commonly seen in degraded forest areas, help to compensate for this lack. However, the tiny Khao Phra Taeo Wildlife Reserve protects the last of Phuket's primary rainforest. It also accommodates the country's only comprehensive rehabilitation project for gibbons.

BELOW Mating bugs of the family Pyrrhocoridae. The male is the smaller one; if the female moves off, he must follow.

BELOW LEFT The dark metallic green plumage helps identify the Nicobar Pigeon (*Caloenas nicobarica*). Now very rare, this large pigeon survives in evergreen forest on a few undisturbed islands off the Andaman coast. Its disappearance is mostly due to persecution.

BELOW RIGHT This handsome lizard is *Calotes mystaceus*, a shade-loving species which inhabits cultivated areas all over the country. In the breeding season, this male will assume a bright blue coloration with reddish patches along both sides.

OPPOSITE PAGE Phi-Phi island epitomizes the idyll of this Andaman archipelago with its silken beaches and caerulean sea. It lies some 40 kilometres (25 miles) east of the southern tip of Phuket.

Surin and Similan Islands

Lying some 50 kilometres (30 miles) off the coast, the Surin Islands Marine National Park has five islands, while further south the Similan Islands National Park consists of nine and lies about 90 kilometres (55 miles) east of Phuket. The real natural treasure of these celebrated island clusters lies under the Andaman Sea which shelters striking and diverse coral formations as well as a wealth of marine life including giant Manta Rays and Whale Sharks. With park protection since the early 1980s, the reef, as well as the leeside sands and island forests, remains as pristine as any in Thailand. The western side of the Kra Peninsula, from Tavoy to Tarutao, is a submerged coastline, tilted down when tectonic movements warped the land and left foothills under water with only the peaks to show for the upheaval there had been. Also under water between the land and the deep sea trench there is a shelf which creates conditions that corals like best: shallow water, little sediment, firm substrate,

constant salinity and temperatures above 18°C (65°F). As a result, the sheltered side of these islands supports over 200 hard corals, more soft corals and thousands of other marine fauna. Turtles surface from these waters to lay their eggs on the fine white sandy beaches. Further inland the island forests of Similan harbour some rare off-shore species such as the Nicobar Pigeon and Ruddy Kingfisher, and marine birds of prey including the Peregrine Falcon.

The islands of the Similan National Park support the finest coral reefs in Thailand. Here a reef is clearly visible through the crystal sea.

ABOVE This magnificent lionfish may attract the attention of divers with its exotic looks, but it should be approached with extreme caution and certainly not touched. Among its feather-like dorsal fins are venomous spines which can inflict painful injuries. There are several species of lionfish and this one is the Common Lionfish or Turkeyfish (*Pterois volitans*), seen against a background of colourful gorgonian sea fans.

RIGHT Mating cuttlefish (*Sepia pharonis*). These creatures can constantly change their colour and pattern to match their surroundings or confuse predators. The black, long-spined sea-urchin (*Diadema setosum*) in the foreground is one of the most common sea-urchin species in the Indo-Pacific region. It often hides in the coral during the day, emerging at night to feed.

ABOVE This Tasselled Scorpionfish (*Scorpaenopsis oxycephala*) can change its colour to become almost indistinguishable from its background. It carries a dangerous venom in its dorsal spines.
BELOW Like all pufferfish, this Star Pufferfish (*Arothron stellatus*) can inflate its body with water to make it difficult for predators to swallow. The attendant remora or suckerfish (*Echeneis naucrates*) is one of several species that swim with or attach themselves to large fish and turtles.

ABOVE A Golden Damselfish (*Amblyglyphidodon aureus*) in night-time coloration. Behind it, a soft tree coral (*Dendronephthya hemprichi*) extends its polyps.
BELOW The Leopard Shark (*Stegastoma fasciatum*), sometimes called the Zebra Shark because the juveniles have stripes, is a harmless bottom-dweller. It is usually found resting on sand during the day, and feeds at night on molluscs and small fish.

BELOW LEFT Moray eels (*Gymno-thorax* sp.) are not as fearsome as they look, as the gaping jaws are merely to aid breathing. They usually retire into crevices during the day and emerge at night to feed on fish and octopuses. BELOW RIGHT The common name of the Hinge-beak Shrimp (*Rhynchocinetes hiatti*) derives from the hinged extension to the carapace which can be directed upwards at right angles. Although brightly coloured, these shrimps blend well with their habitat, and at

night are almost invisible to their predators. OPPOSITE PAGE Vividly banded Clark's Anemonefish (*Amphiprion clarkii*) with a large anemone, *Entacmaea quadricolor*, which is securely wedged within a crevice, its base safe from predators. The surrounding colour is provided by *Goniastrea* sp. stony corals, red soft tree coral (*Dendronephthya hemprichi*), Zoanthid soft coral and various encrusting corals.

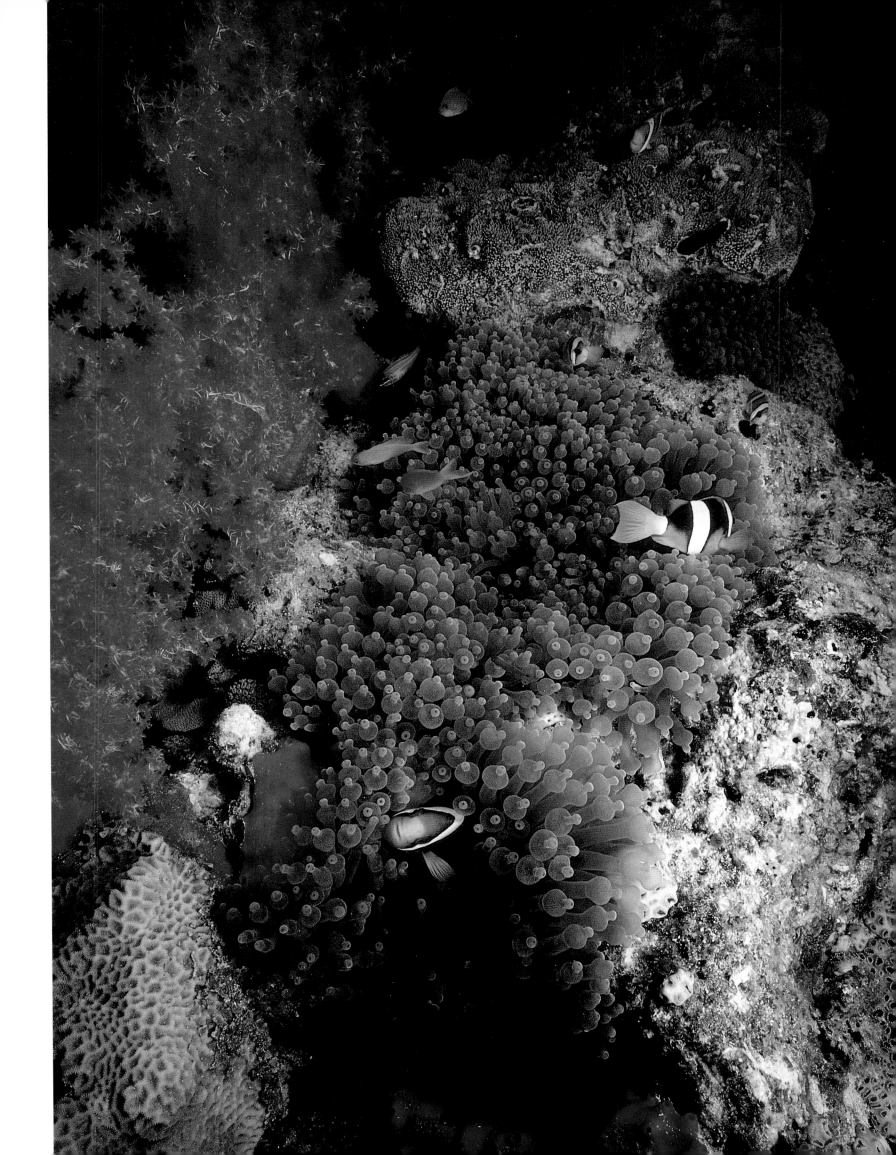

Summary of Major National Parks

Of Thailand's different types of protected area, only the 77 national parks are intended to combine conservation with tourism. The wildlife sanctuaries do not, as a rule, cater for tourists as they are meant for biodiversity conservation and research. This summary identifies the most important national parks, some of which are given more in-depth treatment in this book (see Contents).

THE NORTH

Doi Inthanon encompasses Thailand's highest mountain, a granite massif. It contains some scenic waterfalls such as Mae Ya and a range of habitats from a small sphagnum bog at the top to dry dipterocarp forest at the bottom and evergreen forests in between. Its wildlife suffers from forest clearance and hunting by tribal people but it is still an excellent birdwatching area, with many montane species not found elsewhere in Thailand, and it harbours a rich assemblage of insects and flowering plants.

Doi Luang, established in 1990, is one of Thailand's most recent parks. It lies in the Phi Phan Nam mountain range near Nan and has a mix of forest types with a rich range of wildlife. It also has spectacular views looking over to Laos, several impressive waterfalls and a great many caves.

Doi Suthep–Doi Pui comprises a twin-peaked mountain with deciduous forest on the lower slopes and evergreen forest higher up. In spite of being small and somewhat disturbed, the park supports an astonishing variety of trees and flowering plants, including many orchids. Doi Suthep has long been revered by the people of Chiang Mai because it accommodates the Phuping Royal Palace and the Wat Phra That temple, with its famous Buddha relic.

Mae Yom contains the largest surviving stand of teak forest in Thailand and the only undammed river of any size (the Mae Yom), though that too is threatened. It is also one of few parks in the country which can offer river rafting, besides having some attractive natural scenery including river valley habitat and a large mountain pond, each of which draws different animal species.

THE NORTH-EAST

Khao Yai is the premier national park because it was the first to be created and because it is within easy reach of Bangkok. It is a hilly area of seasonal evergreen and deciduous forest with grasslands and mineral licks where deer, elephant and tiger are quite often seen. The Pileated and White-handed Gibbons overlap in the park and some hybrid individuals occur. It is an excellent area for seeing birds, including hornbills.

Nam Nao has an attractive rolling landscape of mixed and dry deciduous forest dotted with patches of pine and several mountain peaks. It supports a rich array of wildlife, including elephant, gibbons and Gaur, which it shares with the contiguous Phu Khieo Wildlife Sanctuary, but it has been detrimentally affected by Highway 12, which cuts through it, and by the Chulabhorn Dam.

Phu Chong Nayoi adjoins forest reserves in Laos and Cambodia and is therefore important as a transfrontier reserve (along with the adjacent Yot Dom Wildlife Sanctuary) for many species of wildlife. Because the civil war in Cambodia has put it out of bounds for years, its wildlife is under-studied, although it is known to support the rare Pileated Gibbon and the White-winged Duck.

Phu Hin Rong Kla was a stronghold of the Communist Party of Thailand until the early 1980s and its fauna has suffered as a result, but it has some dramatic sandstone formations (created by years of weathering), splendid views and an interesting flora with many species which are confined to sandstone soils.

Phu Kradeung is a spectacular steep-sided sandstone mountain topped by a broad, flat plateau which offers stunning views of the region around, including other table-top mountains. The slopes support deciduous forest with evergreen in dips and gulleys but much the most interesting part of the park is the plateau. This resembles an oriental pleasure garden, with delicate flowering plants such as orchids and gentians growing amidst stunted heathers, rhododendrons and lichen-covered rocks.

Thap Lan and Pang Sida are contiguous and would be one of the largest and most important conservation areas in the country were Thap Lan not so degraded. Years of official neglect and unofficial exploitation have left some areas with no forest but, with better protection, they would regenerate and the parks would then attract more interest. They have some attractive scenery and could support more elephants and wild cattle than most other areas.

Thung Salaeng Luang is a low undulating area with pine–oak and mixed deciduous forests interspersed with semi-natural grasslands which blaze with colour when the flowering plants bloom. The park has several salt-licks and freshwater ponds which attract various herbivores and predators including deer and wild dogs. There are spectacular waterfalls and some 200 bird species, one of which (the Short-tailed Parrotbill) is rarely seen elsewhere.

THE SOUTH-EAST

Khao Kitchakut adjoins the larger Khao Soi Dao Wildlife Sanctuary. They occupy the northern tip of the Cardomom mountain range of Cambodia and, along with the Khao Ang Ru Nai Wildlife Sanctuary, protect the largest remaining block of evergreen forest in south-east Thailand. They also protect some unique animals including Pileated Gibbons, Blue-rumped Pittas, dark Silver Pheasants and Spiny-breasted Frogs. Indentations at the top of Phrabat mountain are believed to be footprints of Lord Buddha.

Koh Chang is a marine park which covers some 50 islands and is named after the largest. Much of Koh Chang itself is forested. The surrounding sea supports a colourful range of corals and fish which are not yet suffering from pollution, unlike other south-eastern waters. Being far from Bangkok and close to Cambodia, Koh Chang has so far been spared the worst effects of mass tourism.

THE WEST

Chalerm Rattanakosin, better known as Tham Than Lot, lies in the limestone hills due north-west of Kanchanaburi. It is a popular weekend site because of its many caves and waterfalls. It is historically interesting because the Burmese army based itself there in the eighteenth century to attack the former Thai capital, Ayutthaya, leaving many artefacts. It is too small to be of much value to animals, except to bats and other creatures of limestone habitats, but it is an attractive park.

Erawan is Thailand's most visited national park because it features a spectacular staircase waterfall with water that is aquamarine from limestone. The park lies on the leeside of the Dawna Range and is dominated by dry deciduous forest which supports some large mammals, although poaching is a problem.

Kaeng Krachan is the country's largest park. It lies in the Tenasserim Range alongside Myanmar, and is characterized by lush evergreen ridges, ethereal morning mists and calling gibbons. It has a very rich fauna, with several rare species such as Fea's Barking Deer and the Ratchet-tailed Treepie, a bird that is otherwise only known in Vietnam, Laos and Hainan Island.

Khao Laem is divided by the reservoir that covers the Khwae Noi river. Half the park lies between the reservoir and Myanmar, but does not connect to forest over the border, while the other half tucks into Thung Yai on the northern side of the Khwae Noi valley. This used to be the Greung Gawia Non-hunting Area, a block of dense seasonal evergreen forest that supports an exceptionally rich avifauna. At its centre, there is a natural lake.

Khao Sam Roi Yot, a small, somewhat threatened park, is a paradise for birdwatchers because its freshwater marshes, craggy limestone cliffs and mudflats are within easy reach of one another and teem with different species. The park itself is only a short drive from the seaside resort of Hua Hin and from Kaeng Krachan.

Mae Wong is an attractive park that is ringed by a crescent of mountains. It is contiguous with the Huai Kha Khaeng Wildlife Sanctuary and shares much of its wildlife, including the largest population of Banteng in Thailand. Like Huai Kha Khaeng, it also protects an intact lowland waterway which gives refuge to many deciduous riverine animals but, unlike its neighbour, its mixed deciduous formation includes teak trees.

Sai Yok National Park lies between the Khwae Noi river and Myanmar. It is a mix of deciduous and seasonal evergreen forest with many limestone caves, some of which accommodate Kitti's 'Bumblebee' Bat, the smallest mammal in the world. In fact this is the most important conservation area for Kitti's Bat, and it is also an attractive and popular holiday park. Most visitors choose to sit by the river and waterfalls rather than go looking for wildlife.

Sri Nakharin touches Huai Kha Khaeng Wildlife Sanctuary to the north and Erawan National Park to the south. It curves around the reservoir that hides the Khwae Yai river. It is an important watershed but is badly degraded by poaching and encroachment. The park is drier than it was, with deciduous forest covering most of its limestone slopes. Its wildlife is depleted, but used to include large herds of elephant and Banteng as well as many birds.

THE SOUTH

Ao Phang Nga offers spectacular panoramas of about 40 limestone islands, set like statues in a shallow bay, most of them covered in forest scrub and weathered crags. Mangrove lines the bay, though little of it is protected or exhibited. By contrast, island caverns and interior canals are often visited by boats and canoes, especially at low tide when cave mouths open. The flora and fauna inside these islands is especially interesting.

Budo protects the last of southern Thailand's Malay-type rainforest. Until recently it was controlled by separatist insurgents and has therefore not been well surveyed but it is known to support some of the bird species that are confined to this forest zone, including Rhinoceros Hornbills.

Had Nai Yang is an increasingly popular venue for tourists wishing to escape the busy, sprawling conurbations of Phuket. The park contains the last stretch of casuarina coastal forest on the island and its beaches are an important nesting site for four species of marine turtle. Offshore, it protects some of the best coral reefs around Phuket.

Khao Luang encompasses the highest mountain in the south. Rainforest covers most slopes but low-statured forest takes over at higher elevations. It is biologically interesting because, as well as supporting rainforest species like the Argus Pheasant, it is the only mountain in the peninsula high enough to support montane birds. Some of those species, including the Green-tailed Sunbird, are endemic southern races.

Khao Pu–Khao Ya covers a crested ridge of evergreen forest with several limestone outcrops standing beyond the main boundary of the park in fields of lowland agriculture. The park protects the watershed of the Thale Noi and Thale Sap Non-hunting Areas to the east and south-east and, together with the Khao Banthad Wildlife Sanctuary (from which it is separated by a road), is one of the largest protected areas in the peninsula.

Khao Sok adjoins the Khlong Nakha and Khlong Saeng Wildlife Sanctuaries and has some very dramatic landscapes with sheer cliffs overlooking lush evergreen forest, lofty limestone outcrops and tumbling streams. It also encompasses the Rajjaprabha reservoir. It was once fabulously rich in wildlife with tapir, elephants and tigers as well as *Rafflesia kerrii*, the largest flowering plant in the world but, sadly, poaching is prolific and some species are now scarce.

Koh Similan and Koh Surin are the best marine parks in Thailand. Their islands are rimmed with fine white sand, although the Similans are also stacked with sand-smoothed granite boulders. Inland, the evergreen island forests are home to the last Nicobar Pigeons. The fringing reefs are more diverse, more colourful and more visible than any other reefs in Thailand.

Tarutao is primarily a marine park, but its main island also protects a large block of island rainforest. The park includes around 50 islands and rocky outcrops near the Thai-Malay border in the Andaman Sea. Few large animals occur although Dugongs, dolphins and whales are sometimes seen. Some marine turtles nest on isolated beaches but, unfortunately, many of the reefs have been dynamited by fishermen, killing many corals and diminishing fish diversity.

Thale Ban is a rich tract of mountain rainforest which adjoins the Ton Nga Chang Wildlife Sanctuary and the Malay border. The park's most notable feature is a small upland pond which attracts many birds, including the rare Masked Finfoot. This pond is also the habitat of tree-dwelling flying frogs which can be seen leaping into the water. The forest supports Helmeted Hornbills and limestone outcrops are home to Dusky Crag Martins, Peregrine Falcons and Serow goat-antelopes.

Thale Noi Non-hunting Area consists of a large circular freshwater lake surrounded on three sides by *melaleuca* marshland and reedbeds and on the fourth, to the south, by the Thale Sap lagoons. This area is immensely important for waterbirds, both resident and migratory, and supports the only known breeding site of Painted Storks in Thailand. The lake is also an important local fishery.

Bibliography

Aksornkaew, S., Maxwell, G.S., Havanond, S. and Panichsuko, S. (1992) *Plants in Mangroves*. Chalongrat Company, Bangkok.

Anderson, E.F. (1993) *Plants and People of the Golden Triangle*. Dioscoroides Press, Portland, Oregon, USA.

Anon (1976-84) *Flowers in Thailand*. Nature Series. Viratham Press, Bangkok

Anon (1989) *Culture and Environment in Thailand*. A symposium of the Siam Society, Bangkok.

Arbhabirama, A., Phanthumvanit, D. and Elkington, J. (eds) (1987) *Thailand Natural Resources Profile*. Thailand Development Research Institute, Bangkok.

Bernard, H.U. (ed) (1991) *Southeast Asian Wildlife*. Apa Publications, Singapore.

Bock, C. (1986) *Temples and Elephants: Travels in Siam 1881-1882*. Oxford University Press.

Brockelman, W. (1992) A rapid assessment of forest, wildlife and river ecology in the area affected by the proposed Kaeng Sua Ten Dam (Mae Yom National Park). World Bank Publication prepared by the Conservation Biology Centre, Mahidol University, Bangkok.

Campbell, R. (1935) *Teak Wallah*. Hodder and Stoughton, London.

Charoenwongsa, P. and Bronson, B. (1988) *Prehistoric Studies: the Stone and Metal Ages in Thailand*. Thai Antiquities Association, Bangkok.

Chettamart, Kutintara, Vejaboosakorn, Praktong and Vivajsirin (1987) *Assessment of National Parks, Wildlife Sanctuaries and other Reserve Development in Thailand*. Kasetsart University, Bangkok.

Conservation Data Centre (1989) *Birds of Khao Yai National Park*. Department of Biology, Faculty of Science, Mahidol University, Bangkok.

Conservation Data Centre (1989) *Birds of Doi Inthanon National Park*. Department of Biology, Faculty of Science, Mahidol University, Bangkok.

Cox, M.J. (1991) *The Snakes of Thailand and their Husbandry*. Krieger Publishing Company, Malabar, Florida.

Davies, S. (ed) (1987) *Tree of Life: Buddhism and Protection of Nature*. World Wide Fund for Nature with Earl and Associates.

Davis, S.D., Heywood, V.H. and Hamilton, A.C. (eds) (1995) *Centres of Plant Diversity: a Guide and Strategy for their Conservation*. Volume II: Asia, Pacific and Australasia. WWF and IUCN, Gland, Switzerland.

Donner, W. (1978) *The Five Faces of Thailand: an Economic Geography*. C. Hurst and Co, London.

Du Puy, D. (1983) The wildlife sanctuary of Phu Luang, Thailand and its rich orchid flora. *The Orchid Review*, UK.

Du Puy, D. (1984) Flowers of Phu Luang Wildlife Sanctuary. *Kew Magazine*, The Royal Botanic Gardens, Kew, UK.

Felton, H. (ed) (1986) *Contributions to the Knowledge of Bats in Thailand*. Courier Forschungsinstitut Senckenberg, Frankfurt.

Graham, M. and Round, P.D. (1994) *Thailand's Vanishing Flora and Fauna*. Finance One Public Comapany Ltd, Bangkok.

Gray, D., Piprell, C. and Graham, M. (1991) *National Parks of Thailand*. Industrial Finance Corporation of Thailand, Bangkok.

Gremli, M.S. and Newman, H.E. (1993) *Marine Life in the South China Sea*. Apa Publications, Singapore.

Humphrey, S.R. and Bain, J.R. (1990) *Endangered Animals of Thailand*. Sandhill Crane Press, Gainsville, Florida, USA. This is the published version of the original manuscript (Bain and Humphrey 1980) which was not revised but, although out-of-date, is still useful.

Jacquat, C. (1990) *Plants from the Markets of Thailand*, Editions Duang Kamol, Bangkok.

Jintanugool, J. and Round, P.D. (1989) Thailand. In Scott, D.A. (ed) *A Directory of Asian Wetlands*, IUCN, Gland, Switzerland.

Kijngam, A., Higham, C.F.W. and Wiriyaromp, W. (1980) *Prehistoric Settlement Patterns in Northeast Thailand*. University of Otago Press, Dunedin, New Zealand.

King, B., Woodcock, M. and Dickinson, E.C. (1975) *A Fieldguide to the Birds of South-east Asia*. Collins, London.

Kottelat, M. (1989) Zoogeography of the fishes from the Indochinese inland waters with an annotated checklist. *Bulletin Zoologisch Museum*, Universiteit van Amsterdam 12:1.

Lekagul, B., Askins, K., Nabhitabhata, J. and Samruadkit, A. (1977) *A Field Guide to the Butterflies of Thailand*. Saha Karn Bhaet Co Ltd, Bangkok.

Lekagul, B. and McNeely, J.A. (1977) *Mammals of Thailand*. Saha Karn Bhaet Co Ltd, Bangkok.

Lekagul, B. and Round, P.D. (1991) *A Guide to the Birds of Thailand*. Saha Karn Bhaet Co Ltd

Lohmann, L. (1990) Remaking the Mekong. *The Ecologist* 20:2.

McMakin, P. (1988) *A Field Guide to the Flowering Plants of Thailand*. White Lotus Company Ltd, Bangkok.

Majchacheep, S. (1989) *Marine Animals of Thailand*. Pra Pittaya Publishers, Bangkok.

Monkolprasit, S. (1984) *The Cartilagenous Fishes (Class Elasmobranchii) found in Thai waters and Adjacent Areas*. Faculty of Fisheries, Kasetsart University, Bangkok.

Mouhot, H. (1864) *Travels in the Central Parts of Indo-China (Siam), Cambodia and Laos*. 2 Vols. John Murray, London.

Nabhitabhata, J. (1991) *Endangered Species and Habitats of Thailand*. Ecological Research Department, Thailand Institute of Science and Technology, Bangkok.

Nakhasathien, S. (1987) *The Discovery of Storm's Stork (Ciconia stormi) in Thailand*. Forktail Vol. 3 Birdlife International, Cambridge, UK.

Nakhasathien, S. (1989) Chiew Larn Dam Wildlife Rescue Operation. *Oryx* Vol 23.3. Flora and Fauna Preservation Society, Cambridge, UK.

Nakhasathien, S. and Stewart-Cox, B. (1990) *Thung Yai-Huai Kha Khaeng World Heritage Nomination*. Royal Forest Department, Bangkok.

Natural History Bulletin of the Siam Society, Bangkok. This publication dates back many years and contains a great variety of papers of interest to the specialist and lay researcher alike.

Nutaphand, W. (1979) *The Turtles of Thailand*. Siamfarm Zoological Garden, Bangkok.

Parr, J. W. K., Mahanopp, N. and Charoensiri, V. (1993) Khao Sam Roi Yot: one of the world's most threatened parks. *Oryx* Vol 27:4. Flora and Fauna Preservation Society, Cambridge, UK.

Pendleton, R.L. (1962) *Thailand: Aspects of Landscape and Life*. Duell, Sloan and Pearce, New York. Although this is now an old publication, it remains one of the best accounts of Thailand's soil.

Phengklai, C., Niyomdham, C. and Ueachirakan, W. (1991) *Flora in the Peat Swamp Areas of Narathiwat*. Phikul Thong Study Centre, Sombun Press, Bangkok.

Pinratana, A. *Butterflies of Thailand*. Vol. 1 (1974), Vol. 2 (1983), Vol.3 (1979), Vol.4 (1981), Vol.5 (1985), Vol.6 (1988). Viratham Press, Bangkok.

Pinratana, A. and Lampe, R.E.J. (1990) *Moths of Thailand*. Vol.1: Saturniidae. Bosco Offset, Bangkok.

Piprell, C. and Boyd, A. (1991) *Thailand: The Kingdom Beneath the Sea*. Artasia Press, Bangkok.

Poonswad, P. (1993) Forest Flagships. *World Birdwatch* Vol 15:3.

Poonswad, P. (1995) Nest site characteristics of four sympatric species of hornbills in Khao Yai National Park. *Ibis* 137.

Poonswad, P. and Kemp, A.C. (1993) *Manual to the Conservation of Asian Hornbills*. Sirivatana Interprint, Bangkok.

Poonswad, P. and Tsuji, A. (1994) Ranges of males of the Great Hornbill *Buceros bicornis*, Brown Hornbill *Ptilolaemus tickelli* and Wreathed Hornbill *Rhyticeros undulatus* in Khao Yai National Park, Thailand. *Ibis* 136.

Pongsabutra, P. (ed) (1991) *Illustrated Landforms of Thailand*. Chulalongkorn University, Bangkok.

Round, P.D. (1988) Resident forest birds in Thailand: their status and conservation. International Council for Bird Preservation (Monograph 2), Cambridge, UK.

Round, P.D. and Treesucon, U. (1986) The rediscovery of Gurney's Pitta (*Pitta gurneyi*). *Forktail* Vol. 2. Birdlife International, Cambridge, UK.

Round, P.D. and Treesucon, A. (1991) *Birds of Khao Sam Roi Yot*. Conservation Data Centre, Department of Biology, Faculty of Science, Mahidol University, Bangkok.

Round, P.D. and Treesucon, U. (1995) *Birds of Khao Phra Bang Khram Wildlife Sanctuary*. Conservation Data Centre, Department of Biology, Faculty of Science, Mahidol University, Bangkok.

Santisuk, T. (1988) An account of the vegetation of northern Thailand. *Geoecological Research* Vol. 5. Franz Steiner Verlag, Stuttgart.

Seidenfaden, G. Orchid genera of Thailand (1973-79) Dansk Botanisk Arkiv. (1983-88) Opera Botanica, Copenhagen.

Smith, H.M. (1945) The freshwater fishes of Siam, or Thailand. US National Museum Bulletin No. 188. Smithsonian Institution.

Smitinand, T. (1975) *Wild Flowers of Thailand*. Aksornbandit Press, Thailand.

Smitinand, T. and Larsen, K. (eds) (1970-1993) *Flora of Thailand* Vols 2-5. Vol. 6 (No. 1 only). Forest Herbarium, Royal Forest Department, Bangkok.

Smitinand, T., Santisuk, T. and Brockelman, W.Y. (eds) (1985) *Nature Conservation in Thailand in Relation to Social and Economic Development*. The Siam Society, Bangkok.

Stewart-Cox, B. (1987) Thailand's Nam Choan Dam: a disaster in the making. *The Ecologist* 17:6.

Taylor, E. H. (1962) The amphibian fauna of Thailand. *Science Bulletin* Vol. 14. University of Kansas, USA.

Taylor, E.H. (1963) The lizards of Thailand. *Science Bulletin* Vol. 14. University of Kansas, USA.

Taylor, E. H. (1965) The serpents of Thailand and adjacent waters. *Science Bulletin* Vol. 45:9. University of Kansas, USA.

Taylor, E.H. (1970) The turtles and crocodiles of Thailand and adjacent waters. *Science Bulletin* Vol. 49:3, University of Kansas , USA.

Thirakupt, K and van Dijk, P-P. (1995) *The Turtles of Western Thailand: Species Diversity, Population Studies and Conservation Implications*. Chulalongkorn University and The Siam Society, Bangkok.

Whitmore, T.C. (1975) *Tropical Forests of the Far East*. Clarendon Press, Oxford.

Wolstencroft, J., Parr, J. and Goodey, M. (1993) *Survey of Wetlands in North-east Thailand*. Asian Wetland Bureau, Kuala Lumpur.

Wongsiri, S. and Laolohakarn, S. (eds) (1990) *Biodiversity in Thailand*. The Science Society of Thailand, Bangkok.

Index